本书由澳大利亚墨尔本
from the University of
（Asia Institute, The　　　　　　　　lbourne）资助出版

From Empire to Republic:
Thinkers and Politics in China from the Fall of the Ming Dynasty to the 20th Century

从帝制到共和：
明末至民初中国思想的变迁

◆刘　一　杜立平　姜德成　郭珍谊　高保强　著

湖南师范大学出版社

图书在版编目（CIP）数据

从帝制到共和：明末至民初中国思想的变迁 / 刘一，杜立平，姜德成
等著 . —长沙：湖南师范大学出版社，2011.12
　ISBN 978-7-5648-0683-5

　Ⅰ.①从… Ⅱ.①刘…②杜…③姜… Ⅲ.①政治思想史—研究—中
国—明代～民国—英、汉 Ⅳ.①D092

　中国版本图书馆 CIP 数据核字（2011）第 023674 号

从帝制到共和：明末至民初中国思想的变迁

刘　一　杜立平　姜德成　等著

◇策划组稿：郭振兰
◇责任编辑：郭振兰　胡亚兰
◇责任校对：欧继花
◇出版发行：湖南师范大学出版社
　　　　　　地址/长沙市岳麓区　邮编/410081
　　　　　　电话/0731-88873071　88873070
　　　　　　网址/https：//press. hunnu. edu. cn
◇经销：湖南省新华书店
◇印刷：天津画中画印刷有限公司
◇开本：710 mm×1000 mm　1/16
◇印张：13.25
◇字数：217 千字
◇版次：2011 年 12 月第 1 版
◇印次：2024 年 8 月第 2 次印刷
◇书号：ISBN 978-7-5648-0683-5
◇定价：46.00 元

前　言

　　《从帝制到共和：明末至民初中国思想的变迁》一书，旨在通过对十七世纪中叶至民国初年各阶段具有代表性文献的介绍、分析，展现该历史时期中国思想变迁的概貌，并试图勾勒出明末至民国初年间，反帝制思想萌芽以及新文化思潮发展的脉络。

　　本书采用中、英文双语形式，以英文对十七世纪中叶至二十世纪初年中国思想发展的脉络以及所选人物、作品进行介绍、分析；中文部分，则包括所选文献的原文、对原文的注解以及原文的现代汉语译文。

　　作者希望，无暇系统研究原始文献的读者，能够通过阅读本书，接触到与此时期思想发展有直接关系的文献资料，并通过这些资料，了解近代中国思想的变迁。对于广大英语爱好者来说，本书不仅为其提供了一个深化英语学习的机会，亦有助于其直接了解西方学者对这一历史时期中国思想变迁的看法。我们同时也希望，粗通汉语的外国人士，通过阅读本书，能够借助英文的介绍、分析，进一步提高其汉语水平，同时亦加深对中国近代思想变迁的了解。

　　作者还真诚希望，通过这一著书体例，本书能为读者了解中国近代思想发展的脉络以及海外学界对此问题的观察视角，提供一个简捷且有一定效果的途径。但能否实现这一初衷，还有待于广大中外读者的论定。

刘　一（Lewis Mayo，The University of Melbourne，Australia）

杜立平（Du Liping，The University of Melbourne，Australia）

姜德成（Jiang Decheng，The University of Melbourne，Australia）

郭珍谊（Guo Zhenyi，The University of Melbourne，Australia）

高保强（Gao Baoqiang，La Trobe University，Australia）

目 录

一、论明末至民国初年中国思想的变迁

Modern Chinese Political Thought and the Transition from Monarchy to Republic

In the year in which the 100th anniversary of the establishment of a Chinese republic was marked, the most significant public occasion in the United Kingdom of Great Britain was the celebration of the marriage of Prince William, son of the heir to the throne, to Catherine Middleton. The last hundred years of British political history have been characterized by the remarkable stability of the institution of monarchy, which has been exposed only to mild challenges.[1] The past hundred years of Chinese political history, on the other hand, have been characterized by the depth of public commitment to the institution of republican government, and this likewise has not been seriously challenged. Political modernity in the United Kingdom has entailed the survival of an unelected upper house made up of nobles. Modern Chinese political culture, by contrast, is characterized by the absence of any institution that resembles a formal nobility.[2]

The territory over which the British monarch is currently sovereign is dramatically smaller than was the case a century ago, when London was the capital of a worldwide empire that had been acquired over several centuries of conquest. The territory over which the Chinese state currently claims sovereignty is essentially the same as that ruled by the Qing Dynasty in 1911; the only exception is Mongolia, whose independence is formally acknowledged by the government in Beijing. The institution of dynastic monarchy in Britain has proved far more durable than has the imperial state over which that monarchy once ruled; in China, the territorial structure has proved more durable than the institution of dynastic monarchy which formerly ruled it.

A 17th-century observer might have predicted different fates for dynastic monarchy and republicanism in China and the British Isles. Charles Stuart, King of England, Scotland and Ireland and a number of colonies overseas, was executed in 1649 and a republican commonwealth was proclaimed, which lasted until 1660.[3] Although the Stuart Dynasty was restored, its attempts to recover its powers were curtailed, and it was replaced in 1714 by the Hanoverians, forerunners of the current dynasty. Also in the 18th century, the enduring power of the Anglophone republican tradition was marked by the establishment of republics in some parts of the British colonial territories in North America (even though the British monarch has continued to be head of state in other parts of the Americas, including Jamaica, Barbados, Grenada and Canada). Although the ruling dynasty in 17th-century China, the Ming, experienced a crisis in the early 17th century that roughly coincided with that of the Stuart Dynasty in the British Isles, and was replaced by another dynasty, the Qing, in 1644, the institution of dynastic monarchy in China was if anything stronger at the end of the 17th century than at any time in previous history.[4]

What, then, explains the intensity of the resistance to dynastic empire in China in the early 20th century? This anti-dynastic movement broke out at a time when dynastic empire in Britain and in many of its overseas territories was at its zenith, and was indeed so strong that both supporters and opponents of dynastic rule in China entertained the possibility that core portions of the Qing empire might come under British control; the power of the British monarchical state was symbolised most powerfully by the burning of one of the palaces of the Qing Dynasty by British forces in 1860, an event that has a powerful place in the patriotic imagination in early 21st-century China. How was dynastic monarchy able to survive in Britain while it was driven out of Qing territory? One answer might be that the British monarchy has been better at deflecting opposition to itself than was its Qing peer—indeed, its association with global conquest may have lent it a prestige in the eyes of its subjects that the Qing, which engaged in no successful new conquests after the 18th century, did not enjoy. Another explanation might be that the reduction of the British monarchy's substantive power between the 17th century and the present has been the major reason for its survival, and that it was the failure of the Qing state to accept limitations on its power that led to its downfall. A further argument might be that the overthrow of the monarchy in 1911 was the product of a much older tradition of Chinese resistance to dynastic rule which had been evolving over a long period of time.

Some modern commentators see the 17th century itself as a crucial point in the development of this tradition of questioning dynastic monarchy. As Qing rule was being established, Chinese political thinkers who had grown up in the last years of the Ming Dynasty put forward visions of the state that seemed to question not only the legitimacy of the incoming Manchu rulers (whose right to rule was questioned by some former Ming subjects on the grounds that they were ethnically and culturally outside of the Chinese cultural zone) but also the very idea of powerful monarchical rule unconstrained by any external sanction—and perhaps even the principle of dynastic monarchy itself. [5] Late 19th and early 20th-century advocates of a Chinese republic suggested that 17th-century Chinese political thinkers were not simply opponents of foreign rule (and thus progenitors of 20th-century Chinese nationalism) but opponents of monarchical rule (and thus progenitors of 20th-century Chinese republicanism) . [6] In their narratives, republicanism in modern China appears not as a foreign import but as a fulfilment of the insights of China's most enlightened thinkers from recent centuries, and beyond these, from remote antiquity. A longstanding Chinese cultural preference for celebrating the accomplishments of scholar officials—particularly those selected for their learning and wisdom and not their distinguished parentage—rather than the deeds of emperors could be understood as a reflection of an innate preference for "subjects" rather than rulers. [7]

Yet at least some of those who supported the establishment of a republic in 1911 saw it not less as an end in itself—a form of government that was morally superior to one based on hereditary authority—than as a means for strengthening China. For a good many republican revolutionaries in the early 20th century, dynastic empire had proven incapable of producing a strong and prosperous country when it was faced in with challenges from the representatives of the new industrial empires—from Europe, the Americas, Oceania and Japan—the 19th century; the only solution seemed to be to replace it with a new form of state. [8] For much of the hundred years since 1911, and even before that, discussions about politics have been concerned not only with preserving or transforming social relations in the name of producing a more just and moral society, but also with the augmentation of national strength, a strength that was (and is) to be measured in terms of the standing of the state in world terms. While the radical phases of the revolutionary process have been characterized by an intense concern with the situation of the poor and the weak, a preoccupation with whether or not the country is rich and strong has been equally significant. Those who hold state power and those who aspire to it have both, at different times, sought to mobilize people around the cause of improving the lot of the socially, economically and politically disempowered and around the cause of making the country powerful and wealthy. In some cases, both causes have been espoused at once, and often people committed to one cause have also been enrolled in the other.

The question as to whether the republic is a moral end—one that might fuse the idealism of thinkers from the Chinese tradition with those of republican idealists from other intellectual lineages, whether they be involved with the English, American or French revolutions of the 17th and 18th centuries or the Marxists and anarchists of the 19th and 20th centuries—or a means to national strengthening has been a debate that has played out through much of the last century and into the present. In fact, this debate may run much further back in the history of republican thought. The dominant tradition of political thinking in imperial China from the Han Dynasty until the end of the Qing was one that presented the state as a moral entity that existed within a web of ethical relationships which it was the job of those in the state to perfect. The idea that the state was primarily an instrument of power was a much less explicit tradition, and has probably been most often identified with the philosophy of Han Feizi. However, the republican project in 20th-century China has in many respects been forged by a combination of arguments: the argument that the republic would make the country stronger, and the argument that republicanism was a morally superior form of government—one which would constitute either a radical disruption to a system of hereditary monarchy that was thought at some level to be foreign to the essential properties of the Chinese system or be a fulfilment of ancient tendencies in Chinese thought. [9]

The establishment of the republic was tied up with the related but separate question of revolution. [10] Like the republic, revolution was understood by some as a means and by others as an end. For much of the 20th century, the idea of a revolutionary transformation of the social order dominated political thinking in China. One consequence of this concern with revolution was a critique of ideas that seemed to stand in the way of radical change. Thinkers whose concern was the consolidation of an existing order rather than its overthrow or profound transformation were often strongly condemned. What Chinese intellectuals sought in both the Chinese and non-Chinese traditions of political thought was ideas that favoured rebellion and critique. Even members of the elites, who we might suspect would generally be sceptical about revolutionary processes that would render their own social position precarious, embraced some parts of this radical critique. By the late 20th century, enthusiasm for the rhetoric and practice of revolutionary change had begun to lessen, replaced (as in many other societies in the late 20th century) by the idea of reform and the idea that social change is best measured by economic growth and not by radical transformations of power structures. While the ideal of the republic as a particular kind of moral community was retained, it was arguably conceived more and more as a means towards the goal of creating a strong and rich China. By this time, of course, the project of dismantling the structures of dynastic monarchy had been so effectively accomplished that any chance of restoration (which was still a vague possibility even in the 1930s and 1940s in the form of the Japanese puppet state of Manchukuo where the last emperor of the Qing Dynasty was on the throne) was completely eliminated. [11] At this stage, political thinkers from the past whose interest was in national strengthening acquired a new level of respectability. In particular, the idea of building up the economy and the military for the purpose of defending national culture enjoyed a new legitimacy. [12] Earlier nationalist radicals may have criticised these thinkers because of their continued loyalty to a dynasty that was seen as both conservative and non-Chinese, but as the cause of anti-Manchu nationalism which had animated the 1911 revolution ceased to be a live political issue, people who had advocated strengthening the Qing Dynasty by the adoption of western technologies emerged as the forefathers of the late 20th and early 21st-century patriotic administrators. [13]

Neither the officials who sought to defend the old order through programmes of institutional consolidation and later of systemic reform nor the revolutionaries and rebels who tried to overthrow it can be left out of an account of contemporary Chinese political thought, because the ideas of both have contributed to it. The contemporary Chinese state is an inheritor of the revolutionary movement, and celebrates the achievements of the revolution. At the same time, it presents itself as an inheritor of a longer tradition of culture and political morality, a tradition that is associated with dynastic China. In this regard, perhaps the Chinese state differs little from the contemporary United States of America, which celebrates its revolution while continuing to honour the order of monarchical culture which that revolution attempted to overthrow. A concrete example of this tendency is the pervasive enthusiasm for the plays of Shakespeare, which were originally produced in a dynastic monarchy and address its concerns (kings, queens, princes and princesses are the primary focus of Shakespeare's plays about history) . However, while few people see any contradiction between the profound US commitment to republicanism and this engagement with monarchical culture, in China the republican and monarchical traditions of political thought are often presented as being in a tense and problematic relationship to each other. [14]

The first generation of stable territorial republics in the modern era (as opposed to city-state republics such as those found in Italy or Switzerland in the European late Middle Ages and the Renaissance) all appeared in non-industrial countries which had only small middle classes. These were the republican states in the Americas founded between the 1770s and the 1820s. [15] Although a regicidal revolution occurred in France in the 1780s, monarchical rule was re-established (with some interruptions) and a relatively stable republic was created in France only in 1870 (there were twelve years of republican government in France between 1792 and 1804, and slightly more than three years of republican rule between 1848 and 1851) .

Following the anti-colonial rebellion in the Philippines in the early 1890s and the parallel revolt against Spain in Cuba (which both provoked intervention from the United States, bringing about the conversion of both these states into colonies or semi-colonies), a second wave of republican revolution began worldwide. [16] The Chinese revolution of 1911 was the second major republican revolution of the 20th century—having been preceded not quite a year earlier by the overthrow of the monarchy in Portugal—and was one of the first in a series of global displacements of ruling dynasties around the world in the early 20th century.

In this context, the history of the transition from empire to republic in modern China can be plotted both as a story of intellectual and political developments unfolding within the Chinese system and as part of a wider global story of the modern disruption of dynastic monarchy by forces hostile to it. By the early 1920s, Turkey, Germany, Russia and Austria—along with other places ruled by the Ottoman, Hohenzollern, Romanov and Habsburg imperial families—had followed China on the path to establishing national republics in the place of monarchies and empires. A number of factors were involved in these shifts, including crises in the internal governance of the imperial states, global critiques of the structures of social privilege that those states maintained (in particular the status privileges of elites) and defeats in the system of international competition (whether military, economic or diplomatic). All of these factors contributed to the loss of support for dynastic states—states which, like the Qing Dynasty, had enjoyed great power for several hundred years. [17]

Many narratives of these processes of imperial displacement present them as the ending of old orders of cultural power. [18] Structures of ritual and of tradition, along with bodies of belief that had been associated with the dynastic system, were subjected to critique and supposedly replaced, transformed or discarded. Histories of modern Chinese intellectual life frequently invoke the idea of a cultural or spiritual crisis in which either the entire edifice of traditional Chinese thought was called into question or significant parts of it were subject to critique. In these narratives, the establishment of the republic marks not simply the end of dynastic empire, but a watershed in which a traditional cultural order collapsed and was replaced either by a modern one or by no coherent order at all. From this perspective, the enhanced interest shown in recent times in those thinkers who sought to strengthen the Qing cultural order suggests that rather than constituting a radical break with the Qing, the republic was an attempt to strengthen the state which built on the foundations of the work of Qing-era reformers. This view might suggest that contemporary China is an inheritor of the agendas of those seeking to strengthen the Chinese state in the Qing period. [19]

At one level, the sense that the contemporary state in China inherits some of the agendas of the Qing Dynasty reminds us that the overthrow of dynastic monarchy and the strengthening of the state are different processes, even though they may unfold at the same time. The common assumption that republican revolution is part of a process of political modernization, or that the maintenance of monarchy involves the preservation of tradition is a questionable one. Throughout the contemporary world, states that are formally republics and states that are formally dynastic monarchies are physically adjacent to each other: Canada (monarchy) and the United States (republic); Japan (monarchy) and South Korea (republic); Denmark (monarchy) and Germany (republic); Cambodia (monarchy) and Vietnam (republic); Papua New Guinea (monarchy) and Indonesia (republic). It would be difficult to develop any kind of typology of historical progress or regress based on the contrast between monarchies and republics, and it is certainly difficult to argue that the process of modernization leads automatically to republicanism or vice versa. A claim that that Canada was more traditional or more modern than the United States, or that the United States was more modern or more traditional than Canada, would be hard to sustain. While it is certainly the case that revolutionaries justified their action against the Qing on the grounds that dynastic monarchy was an outmoded institution, we should be careful about accepting this argument at face value. State strengthening may sometimes involve the destruction of monarchy and sometimes its consolidation.

Overall, modern Chinese politics has been shaped by both revolutionary and state-strengthening impulses, and it is important to do justice to both traditions in examining the history of political thought both leading up to and following the establishment of the republic. Equally, we must acknowledge the force of political ideas from within the classical tradition as well as those from outside it. Radical, reformist and state-consolidating ideologies all drew on classical precedent. Arguments over the meaning of the classics and what message one should draw from them were intense, as were critiques of rival positions. [20] The projects of both revolution and republic could both be explained as fulfilments of ideas in the classics. Indeed, one line of interpretation of the fall of the Qing is that it came about not because of a loss of faith in the ideas in the classics, but because of an intensified desire on the part of key individuals to see long-cherished ideals of a good society finally brought to realization. The weakening of the power of the Qing state was not so much a sign of the lessening of commitment to older ideologies as an attempt to fulfil those ideologies.

It has been suggested above that the revolution against the Qing was part of a wave of revolutions against dynastic empires taking place in the late 19th and early 20th centuries. It has also been suggested above that this phase of worldwide political upheaval can be read as a successor to an earlier phase of global political disturbance in the early 17th century that brought new regimes to power in many different parts of Eurasia. One way

of reading the events of the 19th century in China is to see them as rekind-
ling calls for the rectification of the order of power which had been issued
by political thinkers two centuries earlier. According to this interpretation,
the crises of the 19th century gave a new force to ideas that had been produced by Chinese thinkers contending with the political crises of the 17th
century; these crises were affected not only by new structures of international power, but also by new 18th and 19th-century ideas about political
and economic organization and about the natural world which had been produced in significant measure by the fallout from the 17th-century crises in
other parts of the world (most notably in Western Europe).

　　Challenges to the stability of states are interpreted through the ideas a-
bout politics that are in circulation in those states. For the major literate
polities in Eurasia over the last millennium this has meant the ideas con-
tained in the corpus of classical texts that their educated elites had read, re-
flected on, reproduced and challenged. In the Islamic world this was the
corpus of texts in Arabic and the other scholarly languages of Islam; in the
places influenced by Indic traditions it was writing in Pali, Sanskrit and a
wide range of vernaculars and other languages that had been influenced by
these classical ones; in Christian countries it was the various languages in
which the Bible was rendered; for Jews it was Hebrew; and for Europeans
it was the combination of the Judaeo-Christian scriptures and the writings
of Greek and Latin antiquity, studied both in classical and vernacular languages. Even the most heretical or dissenting of writings were framed in
dialogue with these specific textual traditions. In China in the period in
question, as in most other literate societies on earth up until the end of the
19th century, the corpus of classical texts was the source of scholars'
shared culture and the object of their most intense intellectual engagement.
These works structured their experience of reality and, above all, of political events. Wars, machinations at court, budget deficits and surpluses,

progress up and down the ladder of promotions—all of these things were read about, written about and thought about with reference to the body of classical texts that were the foundation of a scholar's training.

If one attempts to examine the fall of the Qing through the frameworks of historical sociology, one would perhaps look for factors such as the capacity of the state to generate revenue, its success or failure in maintaining the allegiance of key social constituencies, economic cycles, the number of positions available in the bureaucracy versus the number of people applying for those positions and so on. However, for a great many observers, the critical question raised by the history of the movement from dynastic monarchy in the Ming and Qing era to the republican revolution is the transformations and continuities in systems of elite thought. For many Chinese people in the present, the salient feature of this period is the question of how Chinese institutions, ideas and cultural practices were affected by contact with institutions, ideas and cultural practices that were coming in from the maritime world of the east coast of the Qing state, i. e. from Japan and from the states centred on the North Atlantic rim. [21] Though questions of revolution, the strength or weakness of the state, the proper organization of economic life, and the relationship between rulers and ruled dominated political and intellectual life for much of the 20th century, by the beginning of the 21st century the problem of relationships with "the West" and its cultural, social and political systems had become a central a theme in discussions about politics and thought. The history of engagements with the West and questions of how, why and whether Chinese systems of thought should adjust themselves to Western ideas have become among the most fundamental areas of cultural discussion in contemporary China. [22]

To a great extent the current interest in the relationship between Chinese and Western thought reinvigorates an intellectual paradigm that was powerful in non-Marxist writing on modern Chinese history in the mid 20th century (most strongly associated in the Anglophone world with writers such as Tsiang Tingfu and John King Fairbank). This paradigm emphasised the problem of relationships between Chinese thinkers and Western influences that were coming into China from outside from the 19th century onwards. For this reason, the texts selected in this volume present a range of key writings in modern Chinese political thinking that is very similar to those found in anthologies of work on Chinese thought produced in the mid 20th century. The recent renewed focus on the interaction between Chinese thought and western ideas has much to do with the increased emphasis on the Confucian tradition in contemporary Chinese intellectual discussions, which very often come from people who are not trained primarily in the study of the Chinese classical corpus.

To some extent, the focus on the relationship between Chinese and Western concepts in recent discussions of the history of modern Chinese political and social thought is a mark of the displacement of dynastic monarchy as a core political problem and its replacement by the idea of a national cultural tradition whose survival or destruction becomes the central issue. From the beginnings of the dynastic era until 1911, the question of the transmission of a set of ethical teachings was connected to the question of the transmission of political power from monarch to monarch and from ruling house to ruling house; this question was connected to, but separate from, the transmission of the content of Confucian, and, arguably, of Daoist and Buddhist teachings. [23] After 1911, the question has been framed more and more in terms of the transmission of Chinese culture and the relationship of Chinese culture to other cultural traditions. Thinking about the state, society and political and social morality has been successfully uncoupled from the problem of monarchy, in much the same way as the work of political philosophers in the English monarchical tradition such as Thomas Hobbes and John Locke are studied in the contemporary USA—a republic—without their relationship to monarchy arising as an issue of major concern (a small number of academic commentators excepted) .

We may observe that the anti-monarchical tradition has successfully assimilated to itself elements from the monarchical tradition by defining them as part of a broader national culture that is the collective inheritance of patriotic people in the present. Whereas in the 1980s debates on the direction of the country tended to focus on how best to implement the programme of scientific modernization, since the middle of the 1990s such debates have often focused on how best to uphold Chinese cultural structures, and indeed, what the core features of those cultural structures are. For thinkers in the early and mid 20th century, the problem was often one of how far elements of traditional Chinese thought might or might not contribute to the nation's progress; the question in the early 21st century has for many people come to be how far the nation's progress might or might not contribute to the enhancement or preservation of traditional Chinese thought. Although the contemporary preoccupation with the relationship between Chinese and Western thought might seem to signify the continuity of a set of questions running back to the 19th century, it can be argued that this current preoccupation is a sign of the interplay between traditions of thought that call for radical reordering in the name of overcoming injustice and inequity (of which the tradition of revolutionary republicanism is the most obvious modern manifestation) and those that call for of the consolidation of the established system in the name of avoiding the violent disruptions of radical change and preserving social peace. Indeed, one way of understanding modern Chinese political history is to observe that those who hold state power, or those who aspire to hold it, have oscillated between supporting the cause of radical reordering and the cause of defending cultural and institutional continuities, be they real or imagined.

The traditions of revolution and the traditions of self-strengthening are thus equally significant constituents of the history of modern Chinese politi-cal thought, and both of them affect the way in which citizens who belong to the republican present look back on the inheritance of the dynastic past. This combination of revolutionary and state-strengthening tendencies is perhaps common to all states that have founded by a republican revolution against dynastic monarchy, where the affirmation of state strength must be combined with the emotional and intellectual appeal of ideas of the over-throw of the monarchical system. The concept of a division between Chi-nese and Western thought has enabled this tension to be successfully nego-tiated: critics of monarchy from within the Chinese intellectual tradition help to affirm that the project of republicanism is not bound up with the de-struction of Chinese cultural traditions (thus refuting, for instance, those Chinese scholars who chose to support the Japanese-sponsored monarchical state in Manchukuo in the 1930s)[24] while also demonstrating to those in the era of republics who associated all aspects of the traditional Chinese cultural inheritance with the preservation of the hierarchies of dynastic monarchy that there was within the gallery of classical thinkers a group of people who could be seen as supporting radical change and republican rule. At the same time, appreciation (albeit often qualified or critical) for the endeavours of those Qing officials affiliated with the cause of self-strengthening enabled republican revolutionaries to present the cause of state consolidation as con-nected to the revolutionary project by suggesting that the ideologies of the Qing state were not simply associated with the defence of dynastic monar-chy but could equally be seen as affiliated to the patriotic agenda of the re-publicans themselves. The contradictions between revolution and self-strengthening translated in the Qing into political struggles between sup-porters of the established order, radical reformers and revolutionaries, and in the post-dynastic era into struggles between supporters of the republic who called for radical transformation of the social order and supporters of the republic who opposed such radical transformation. This divergence in agendas could effectively be bridged by presenting the foundational opposition as one between Chinese and non-Chinese thought; China and the West could each be presented as either conservative or radical, depending on the political stance of the individual concerned. For this reason, right on the eve of the 100th anniversary of the republican revolution, on the website devoted to the subject of guoxue or national learning (which is often associated with the cause of a revived Chinese traditionalism) one can find both materials that honour the memory of scholars loyal to the Qing as well as materials that celebrate the revolution. The notion that the republic is an instrument for the displacement of Chinese culture can be dispelled as surely as the idea that traditional Chinese culture is an instrument for the perpetuation of dynastic monarchy; at the same time, the ideological differences between defenders and critics of traditional Chinese culture can be subsumed within a common identity as contributors to the history of Chinese thought.

Interpreting the modern history of Chinese political thought primarily in terms of an opposition between China and the West has thus enabled old ideological conflicts to be incorporated into a common narrative, the battles between republicans, moderate reformers and dynastic loyalists and later between leftists, centrists and rightists can be depicted as part of a shared story.[25] Republican revolution can be shown as the only project that could prevent Chinese traditional culture from being overwhelmed by cultural influences foreign to it, or as the only way to reconcile the needs of traditional culture with the demands of modernity, or as the only way of throwing off the shackles of tradition and embracing the cause of modernity. In the same way, Chinese culture could be seen as affiliated with the structures of a traditional hierarchy of deference, respect and order, with a liberal tradition of free discussion, free trade and individual liberty, or with a radical tradition of opposing the inequities of hierarchical power, private wealth and deference to privilege. At the same time, Chinese culture could be presented either as a unique structure in the family of world cultures, or as part of the common inheritance of humanity standing equal to its peers in other places, or as possessing a recipe that could redeem or liberate human-kind as a whole. [26]

Chinese intellectuals from the early 1900s to the 1940s and in the late 20th to early 21st centuries espoused different versions of these positions. Was Chinese traditional thought a peer of the conservatisms, liberalisms and radicalisms of other global cultural traditions, or an alternative to them? Was it behind, in step with, or ahead of other traditions of thought? Should it avoid, co-operate with, learn from or instruct other cultures? These arguments are not very different from those found among scholars from other contexts who define themselves as part of a cultural/intellectual totality, be it "Western", European, Islamic, South Asian, African, Oceanic, Southeast Asian, Central Asian or American (by which is meant here the cultural systems not only of the United States but also of thinkers who define themselves as belonging to the Americas as a cultural/geographic zone). It might be argued that one of the basic problems for the founders of revolutionary citizen republics ever since this form of state was pioneered as a durable type of political organization in North, Central and South America and the Caribbean in the late 18th and early 19th centuries is how to articulate a set of cultural antecedents for these regimes when there were few historical examples of territorial states in human history that were not dynastic empires or slave-holding republics (it took until the 1860s for the United States to develop a model of republican government state that did not involve slave-holding). Equally, it might be argued that in states where formal monarchy has successfully constrained the republican impulse (such as England or Australia), the problem for historians of political

thought is how to sidestep the contradiction between the continued enthusiasm for, or at least tolerance, of, dynastic rule and the rhetorical force of
the idea of general meritocracy.

Thus in contemporary monarchies haunted by the spectre of republicanism and in contemporary republics haunted by the spectre of monarchy,
accounts of political thought must find ways around the fact that the movement from monarchy to republic is neither fully achieved nor fully resisted.
How are presidents to be written about so that they do not look like kings,
queens or colonial governors reincarnated? How are monarchs or their representatives to be written about so that the question of why they are not yet
presidents or why they are already too much like presidents can be avoided?
One of the key solutions to this problem is to invoke the division between
modernity and tradition; this makes it possible to avoid addressing the fact
that many of the societies that are considered to be not yet modern in an e-
conomic or institutional sense are republics and many of the societies that
are considered to be economically or institutionally modern are monarchies.
Another solution is to stress the contrast between Western and non-West-
ern traditions of political thought. Both of these strategies for dealing with
the republican/monarchical divide in political thought are deployed in accounts of modern Chinese politics and philosophy, as they also are in much
writing about the Euro-American tradition (where the fact that Britain,
Spain and the Netherlands are monarchies and France, the USA and Germany are republics is obscured either by the idea that their traditions of political thinking are shaped by the common heritage of the West which or by
their shared participation in the culture of modernity, whether this participation be in favour of modernity or in opposition to it). Equally, narratives of modern Chinese political thinking present the story of Chinese
thought in terms of an underlying unity supplied by Chinese thought—
which is shown as struggling with, adopting, paralleling or resisting the

thought systems of the West and (to a lesser extent Japan) in the course of the last century and a half—or as a story of the continuities or discontinuities between traditional and modern thought. [27] In this regard, many histories of Chinese and Western modern political thought seem to be structured not by the enduring problems of the relationship between monarchical and republican structures but by an East-West/Tradition-Modernity contrast.

Anti-Qing republicans, like other nationalist revolutionaries, presented the ruling dynasty as unqualified to rule the majority populace because they were foreigners. Spanish and English monarchs and their colonial representatives were unqualified to rule Southern, Central and North Americans on the grounds that they were outsiders. The ruling dynasty in Great Britain changed its name from Saxe-Coburg Gotha to Windsor in July 1917 (a few months after the British monarch's cousin, the Russian tsar, had abdicated, and six years after the fall of the Qing Dynasty) on the grounds that a change of name would weaken the cause of English nationalists who might have argued that the ruling dynasty was German. The Aisin-Gioro family was much less successful than its peer, the House of Saxe-Coburg Gotha, in convincing the majority of those over whom it ruled that it was part of their own ethnic group. In China as in the USA when American revolutionaries drove out loyalists to the British crown, some who continued to feel loyalty to the fallen dynasty fled abroad; Qing loyalists, however, were much less successful than their Canadian predecessors at preserving a space for dynastic rule in the same landmass as their revolutionary republican peers. Ironically, monarchical rule continued on the former soil of the Qing Dynasty until 1997, ending when the United Kingdom finally ceded its control over Hong Kong to the republican state in Beijing, leaving no one in the former territories of the Qing still living under a monarch. (Macau, which was returned to Beijing's control in 1999, was the first territory on the soil of either the Qing or the Ming Dynasty to come under permanent republican rule, following the abolition of the Portuguese monarchy in 1910).

These general features of anti-dynastic republicanism as a worldwide phenomenon—hostility to hereditary ruling houses and hostility to domination by people perceived to be foreigners—coalesced in China in 1911. Like their counterparts in other countries from the 18th century onwards, the supporters of the republican state-building project in China committed themselves to the defence of the nation and its culture against foreign incursions and to the ending of the structures of monarchical power. Each of these two agendas was placed in the service of the other. At the same time, those who were preoccupied with one agenda could be accused of compromising the other: opponents of structures of hereditary authority might be held to be supporting ideas "foreign" to Chinese tradition, and opponents of "foreign" influence might be seen as tacitly endorsing a reintroduction of hereditary power and could be criticised under the rubric of "feudalism". A situation where these two tendencies seem to coexist, which has often been presented as a crisis of tradition or a failure to create a proper modern state, can thus be interpreted as an inherent feature of anti-dynastic republicanism, which is obliged to forge a structure that seeks to dismantle the structures of monarchy while preventing the country from seeming to adulterate its cultural practices with "foreign" elements.

Anti-foreignism has been a problem for republican movements since the revolutions in the Americas. How were boundaries to be drawn to divide republicans in the Americas from others who participated in the same trans-Atlantic elite cultural world? How was the fact that republican ideology was not born in the Americas but was imported from outside (in Ancient Rome and Greece and in Renaissance Italy and elsewhere in late Medieval Europe) to be handled?[28] Resistance to foreign states—the Spanish, French and British empires, and neighbouring peer republics—had to be given a substance. There needed to be national cultures that would distinguish the republic from those of the foreigners whom it opposed, whether these be the national cultures of other republics or those of the imperial monarchies. Rejection of monarchy alone would not provide the foundation for a comprehensive anti-foreignism. Without powerful marks of distinctiveness, there was always a danger of being absorbed into neighbouring states or being reabsorbed into the empire.

Yet the intensity of commitment to either anti-monarchism or anti-foreignism varied from person to person. A cosmopolitan anti-monarchist might be relatively untroubled by foreigners and their ways; a xenophobe might be less troubled by monarchical institutions provided they were home-grown. Some people might have joined the American revolution because they wished to end monarchical rule, while others may have joined because they wanted to end control by the British; overthrow of the monarchy in Britain might have satisfied the former, and the establishment of an American royal family might have satisfied the latter. The problem was how these two positions might be reconciled. A further problem was created by neighbouring republics: what was to prevent one state from being absorbed by its neighbour, especially if neither political ideology nor cultural practices divided them? And how was the declaration of new republics within a republic to be prevented?

The competition between the forces of anti-monarchism and anti-foreignism—which could unite in the cause of revolution but could divide once the revolution has succeeded—becomes a central political and intellectual problem for republican regimes. One solution to this problem is to articulate traditions of home-grown republicanism that identify the native tradition as anti-monarchical and identify monarchy with foreign rule. This necessarily involves a struggle against elements in the native tradition which are pro-monarchy. Native supporters of monarchy (especially where the monarchy concerned has been defined as originally foreign) who seem to be active in the cause of defending the state against subjection to the power of outsiders present a particular problem, and their support for monarchy has to be downplayed in favour of the idea that their primary commitment is to the local cultural tradition. This is a particularly acute issue when such individuals are also promoting technological modernization, especially when such modernization involves technologies that are seen to be foreign.

The republican who is indifferent to local culture and the critic of foreign influence who drifts into monarchism represent the two extremes that most endanger the project of patriotic republicanism. In the case of the former, his or her opposition to the institutions of dynastic monarchy will always run the risk of being perceived as weakening his or her commitment to the project of opposing foreign rule. [29] In the case of the latter, his or her opposition to foreign power always runs the risk of seeming too attached to native traditions that were formed in the monarchical era and which might ultimately favour the restoration of some type of hereditary power structure affiliated with the defence of native tradition. Equally, the anti-monarchical activists may worry that their anti-foreign peers will degenerate into parochial xenophobes, while the opponents of foreign rule may fear that the anti-monarchists will cease to be dedicated to the central principle of defending the nation's independence.

To maintain the alliance between these two differing agendas that are participating together in the project of republicanism, attention needs to be taken away from this foundational contradiction. One way of doing this is to construct the two types—the patriotic modernizer/internationalist and the anti-dynastic defender of the country's traditions—as paired figures. This allows the republic to appear to be neither a foreign import nor an obstacle to participation in the global cultural order. Furthermore, rather than making the relationship between monarchy and republic the key axis, the issue now becomes the relationship between how local culture and foreign influence are to be combined and how tradition and modernity interact. This is a problem in the organization of culture that is common to republics worldwide. In the case of China, however, the core issue has often been presented as the balancing of the claims of tradition with the demands of modernity and the balancing of the absorption of foreign influence with the maintenance of local culture. This plotting of the history of political thought has been one of the dominant ones in modern China. (The same narrative of tradition and modernity and local and foreign is found in accounts of modern Japan, but in Japan's case, the issue is not how to maintain a republic in a society with a long monarchical tradition, but how to maintain a monarchy in a society with strong republican tendencies). The modern history of China in this account is not one whose contours resemble those of other republican states, such as Chile or the United States or newer republics, but which is instead grouped with other societies where the force of tradition is held to contend with the demands of modernity, or where powerful foreign influences must be reconciled with equally powerful local ideas and practices. The durability of modern Chinese republicanism is less often noted than the theme of a conflict or balance between the modern and the traditional, the Chinese and the foreign.

The overthrow of the Qing Dynasty in 1911 was driven by a desire to put to an end to the dynastic monarchy order (and for some thinkers also a desire to replace a society of hierarchies of status with one of citizen equality), a desire to strengthen the state, and a desire to drive out the Manchus and to bring an end to the power of foreigners on Chinese soil. [30] For some, the republic was a fulfilment of Chinese tradition that had been repressed by a dynasty of foreign origin and also, more recently, by the incursions of overseas and overland imperialists. For others, it was a replacement of the institutions of monarchy with those of citizen government, understood either as a replacement of an outmoded political structure with one commensurate with the demands of the modern world, or as an attempt to bring to fulfilment utopian visions of an ideal political community that were articulated in the texts of the classics. For yet others it was a more radical stage in the project of the rejuvenation of the country that had begun in the 19th century but had often been frustrated by the supposed self-serving corruption of the old regime. Those whose motivation was the expulsion of the Manchus felt that this was the end of a colonial occupation that had lasted for almost three centuries; 19th-century ideologies of racial conflict also influenced this tendency to regard the Qing as a foreign occupying race. Concern with the expanding power of the new industrial empires; a sense of the danger of China being dismembered by the forces of global imperialism gave a further impetus to the republican cause.

The success of the republican project—in the very simple sense that monarchy was never re-established—led to a reading of the republican revolution as a product of a specific series of short-term, medium-term and long-term historical tendencies. [31] Disagreements over the proper direction of the republic were significant, and violent struggles for state power were their concrete embodiment, but the republic formed the pre-eminent framework within which these disputes were articulated. This entailed a basic common understanding, which in turn allowed a shared narrative to be created regarding what had produced the republic. The writers who are included in this book are the ones which began to emerge in the course of the 20th century as those considered to be decisive figures in the transformation of a monarchical empire into a citizen republic. From the 1950s through to the 1970s, the list of significant figures was beginning to be consolidated; whether they were evaluated positively or negatively might vary, but the lineup of significant people—and events—had begun to fix itself in the national narratives, not only in the People's Republic of China, but also in other Sinophone societies, and to a significant extent in the Anglophone and other Europhone worlds as well. [32]

The major alternative to this common narrative about the events and the thinkers who had contributed to the formation of the Republic in this period was the leftist accounts of Chinese history which focused on the role of the rebellious working class in the creation of modern China. In these accounts, the major impetus towards change came from mass rebellions that had sought to overthrow the established order, or which were active in the struggle against the incursions of imperialists. The Communist Party, having triumphed in its war with their Nationalist Party rivals—both parties claimed to be the true inheritors of the revolution which overthrew the Qing in 1911—presented itself in the official accounts of modern Chinese history that it sponsored after 1949 as the successor to this tradition of popular revolt. [33]

By the late 20th century the story of rebellions by the working masses had largely been moved off centre stage in the dominant narratives of modern Chinese history. Instead, the core story—we may call it the core mobilizing narrative—has become that of the struggle of people of vision and ethical responsibility to produce a strong country built on moral foundations. To a great extent, this narrative recuperates one that began to be articulated in the middle decades of the 20th century when righteous Confucian officials from imperial times came to be cast as forebears of the patriotic 20th-century intellectuals devoting their lives to the cause of building a strong republic, particularly in the face of foreign attack. To accomplish this recuperation, a link needed to be created between dissenting but upright officials of the imperial era and the republican present. The issue here was how to uncouple the imagery of the morality of the traditional imperial official from loyalty to the monarchical order that the republic was trying to overthrow. Paradoxically, the longer the republic lasted, and the more the ethics of imperial officialdom passed into memory, the easier it was to present upright officials as motivated by concerns other than those of devotion to the dynasty. In this way, a moral continuity between republic and empire could be established, without the republic being seen as having failed in its mission to destroy the cultural structures of dynastic power.

It would be mistaken to present this as something that was easily accomplished or uncontroversial. Intellectual controversies in the 1920s and 1930s were intense and, as the civil war intensified, intellectual opponents often ended up in rival political camps. This was partly the result of dissensions about the way the project of the republic should unfold and how the twin objectives of national liberation and national strengthening should be accomplished. In addition, there was tension between those who continued to immerse themselves in the corpus of classical texts, and to see themselves as inheritors of scholarly debates dating to the imperial era, and those who identified more profoundly with the cause of liberal or revolutionary change. This was not a simple opposition. Political and intellectual radicals calling for complete overthrow of the old order might derive their iconoclasm from engagement with the classical corpus; more conservative figures might derive their commitment to the preservation of traditional Chinese culture from a reading of English literature and political theory.

The middle decades of the 20th century saw the fleshing out of an account of the landmark events in Chinese intellectual history and a depiction of the people who were held to be the key figures in that story; as already noted, that list retains much of its force in the present, and might be said to form the dominant narrative that informs the way in which many Chinese intellectuals conceptualize their own history. Like all such dominant narratives, it is open to contestation and even to radical challenge. What it illuminates, however, is the consensus that has emerged about the relationship between the story of the state since the 17th century and the critical turns in thinking about the proper direction of society and politics that have accompanied that state story.

Like all revolutions, the overthrow of the Qing order produced a group of people lamenting the fall of the old system, a group of people anxious to build a new one, and a group of people who observed the changes of the times without wishing to commit themselves to either of the other two positions. As in other revolutions, the number of issues and individuals about whom there was any kind of general consensus was small.

Among the few figures about whom there was some degree of consensus in this era were the two 17th-century thinkers who appear in the first section of this book, Huang Zongxi and Gu Yanwu[34]. Both Huang and Gu were born and spent their early years under the Ming Dynasty, but lived through the establishment of the Qing Dynasty, which they both refused to serve. Both were engaged in critical reflection on the political and intellectual legacies of the Ming by which they were shaped, but about which they were ambivalent. Twentieth-century writers, both Chinese and non-Chinese, have been generally enthusiastic about the intellectual achievements of both Huang and Gu. People looking for historical antecedents for the traditions of both careful empirical scholarship and restraint on the power of rulers that are thought to foretell both modern academic practice and modern concepts of politics could find them in the writings of these two men. Anti-traditionalists might see in Gu and Huang a critical attitude to received wisdom (especially received wisdom backed by the power of the state) which began the unpacking of the dominant canon of knowledge that reached its height in the 20th century. People concerned with the classical inheritance saw the work of Gu and Huang as the beginning of a process of putting classical knowledge on firm textual or empirical grounds, enabling it to be the object of solid and reasonable belief. People who felt that the

Ming Dynasty had been overtaken by a form of Confucian philosophy too dominated by metaphysical speculation that was too far removed from either careful study of original texts or concrete political concerns, Gu and Huang mark a break, presaging a new, more careful type of research-focused Confucianism that would be the most prestigious form of scholarship in the Qing era. For people who felt that Qing scholarship had ultimately become too extreme in its critique of the philosophical Confucianism of the Ming and Song Dynasties, Gu and Huang could be understood as still loyal to the traditions of the great philosophers of the earlier times. People who felt that historical learning rather than philosophical speculation or close reading of the classics (which were seen as the embodiment of sacred wisdom) was the foundation for scholarly activity saw Gu Yanwu's scholarship as heralding a new type of historically-oriented scholarship that would also flower in the Qing and even more so in the 20th century. Nationalists, on the other hand, saw in Huang and Gu's resistance to the Manchus the origin of the movement to overthrow the dynasty that would triumph in 1911, with the added advantage that Huang's critique of unrestrained royal power seemed also to betoken the agendas of 19th and 20th-century republicans.

One major American scholar of Chinese thought and history argued that the 17th century contributed new approaches to Chinese culture that would find their fruition in the 19th century. [35] This view, which is rather similar to that enunciated by the late Qing and early Republican era scholar Liang Qichao, holds that in broad scholarly terms, Ming and Qing China was moving more or less in tandem with Western Europe in the same era. If the 17th century seemed to entail the same crisis in political systems that was seen in Western Europe in the same period, it can be argued that the Qing state was much better than its European peers at re-establishing itself in the 18th century, and that to some extent, the immense expanding power of the Qing state in the 18th century was able to procure the loyalty of scholars who might have taken a more resolutely oppositional stance in the 17th century. At the same time, a critical tradition of independent scholarship that focused on close textual study of the classics in a style pioneered by Gu Yanwu in particular precipitated a new approach to learning which called into question the re-established philosophically oriented orthodoxy derived from the Song period. Scepticism about the authenticity of some of the classics prompted a new interpretation of Confucian thought which cast Confucius as a more prophetic figure whose thought might be used to justify a reformist approach to established institutions. Wei Yuan, the third figure whose writings are presented in this book, was a follower of this tradition, while at the same time committing himself anew to a vision of scholarship as being something that had to be geared to the needs of the practical management of the world. Wei lived at a time when the empire had reached its greatest physical extent, but also when problems of administration and the preservation of order were beginning to show. Problems in the governance of the empire were understood by Wei to involve a combination of both empirical and politically committed study of the classics. Wei Yuan also lived in an era when the problems of the maritime regions of China were beginning to be critical to the empire's geostrategic balance, and when information about the wider maritime world derived from contact with the British and other traders living on the South Coast was beginning to filter in to the Qing state. Lin Zexu, with whom Wei Yuan was closely associated, is best known as the person who was involved with the Opium War with the British, and his opposition to drugs and to foreign military and economic pressure made him an important symbol for mid 20th century patriotism, when he was seen as an enlightened official whose wisdom and knowledge were placed at the service of national strengthening. Lin Zexu was also praised for his interest in foreign knowledge and in helping to increase awareness of other societies in Qing China; the sections of his writings re produced here are an example of this.

The balance of power began to shift in the mid 19th century thanks to a combination of internal and external pressures. Senior Qing officials such as Li Hongzhang, Zeng Guofan and Zhang Zhidong who were active from the mid 19th century to the century's end were simultaneously involved in the suppression of large-scale internal rebellion and in the first major state sponsored adoptions of Western industrial technology. They articulated a philosophy of emphasizing traditional Chinese ethical teaching while adopting western technology, a philosophy generally known in English as 'self-strengthening', which combined loyalty to the Qing court with an emphasis on technical modernization.

The defeat of the Qing Dynasty by Japan in 1894 led to a more radical approach to reform, one that stressed the need for institutional change. Thinkers associated with this reform movement were distinguished by their dissenting approach to Confucian texts, following the same school of ideas which had influenced Wei Yuan in the early 19th century. The defeat of this movement by its highly placed opponents in the Qing court led to an intensification of calls for a significant overhaul of the Chinese political system, calls that included the demand for the establishment of constitutional monarchy and also, for those committed to the cause of republican revolution, the expulsion of the Manchus and the end of dynastic rule.

Unlike the thinkers and writers that appear in the first three sections of the book, the Nationalist revolutionary Sun Yat-sen was not distinguished for his Confucian scholarship and had been largely educated outside China. Sun, like other revolutionaries including Zou Rong and Chen Tianhua, whose writings also appear later in this book, he was profoundly affected by his foreign experience, and his political thinking combined opposition to the monarchical state with a complex view of Chinese culture as something that needed to be defended and to be reformed.

With the establishment of the republic, the critique of the old order moved beyond a simple call for the expulsion of the Qing and the abdication of the emperor. Serious political change, it was now argued, required cultural change. Individuals who were associated with the "New Culture Movement", as it was known, included key early figures in the communist movement such as Chen Duxiu, Qu Qiubai and Li Dazhao, whose writings are presented towards the last section of this volume. All three were learned men and were respected for their knowledge. They called for an overhaul of the traditional cultural order. In the case of Qian Xuantong, a radical language reformer, this overhaul was to include the transformation of the Chinese written language.

The cultural radicalism of these four writers represented a major tendency in cultural and political thinking for much of the 20th century, and the Communist movement has generally presented itself as carrying out the mission of these radical critics of the old order. For several decades, the progression of political thought—from Huang Zongxi and Gu Yanwu to Wei Yuan and Lin Zexu to the Self-Strengtheners to the late 19th century reformers to the republican revolutionaries to the advocates of the New Culture movement—has seemed like a movement towards ever-increasing levels of radical enlightenment. Each stage in this history has to a great extent been portrayed as superseding the one before it, the New Culture movement being the climax of the development. As the republic has become more and more an entrenched reality in Chinese political and intellectual life, being at the time of writing exactly a century old, we may argue that the repudiation of the intellectual systems of the imperial era has given way to a structure of thought in which the patriotic commitment of historical figures is judged less by their attempt to overcome the ideologies of imperial era Confucianism in the name of technical modernization than by their efforts to animate the project of technical strengthening with a set of spiritual values supposedly shared by Chinese people through the centuries. Although for many intellectuals in present-day China these issues form part of a still unresolved debate about the roles that tradition and modernity and/ or Chinese and foreign values should have in contemporary society, one can equally argue that this debate is an expression of the profound commitment that Chinese people have had to the idea of a republic in the course of the last 100 years. In this republican idea, a cultural inheritance profoundly shaped by the concepts and institutions of monarchy is successfully assimilated to an anti-monarchical political idiom. While it is often said that the long history of imperial rule in China has made the abolition of dynastic monarchy a painful and disorienting experience, it can also be observed that the unwillingness to reinstate monarchy even in the mild form of a figurehead sovereign betokens a much older tradition of commitment to meritocratic rule represented by China's long history of government by officials chosen by competitive examination. It may well be that in 1911 this tradition found a way to liberate itself from the last major vestige of hereditary power that was attached to it, by deploying the global technology of republican revolution. It may be that rather than plotting a story about modernity and tradition, or about the relationship between empire and nation-state, the thinkers whose writings are presented here tell us something about the interpenetration—pervasive in the present—between monarchical and republican ways of organizing and representing political power, in which monarchies must resist and appropriate the structures of republics, and republics must resist and appropriate the structures of monarchies.

(The original draft of this section was completed on the 10th of October, 2011, the 100th Anniversary of the Wuchang Uprising.)

Notes

1. In fact, in a newspaper article published at the time of the 2011 royal wedding, the

popular British academic historian Simon Schama contrasted the long-term survival of the British monarchy with the demise of many other dynastic regimes in modern times, including the Qing. Schama attributes the staying power of the British royal family to its rejection of autocracy, a viewpoint common amongst British historians who see the monarchical tradition as part of the broad history of British liberty. See Simon Schama, "Dynastic lessons from the familiar Windsor family flourish", The Financial Times April 29, 2011. A similar display of support for the British monarchy can be found in an article by the British Labour Party politician Tristram Hunt in the same newspaper (generally thought of as a platform for the expression of the ideas of the British economic elites) . See Tristram Hunt, "Love and leverage in an age of global royalty", *The Financial Times April* 27, 2011.

2. Alexander Woodside has pointed to the difficulties faced by the Qing state in the early 20th century in its attempt to establish a house and a college of nobles that would match similar institutions in Japan and Britain. See Alexander Woodside, *Lost Modernities: China, Vietnam, Korea, and the Hazards of World History.* Cambridge: Harvard University Press. 2006, p. 54.

3. Studies of this subject are extremely numerous. Among the most compelling is Jonathan Scott, *England's Troubles: Seventeenth-Century English Political Instability in European Context.* New York: Cambridge University Press, 2000.

4. Scholars concerned with historical comparison have sought to examine the commonalities and differences between the transition from the Ming Dynasty to the Qing and the crisis faced by the Stuart Dynasty in England, Scotland, Ireland and Wales in the mid 17th century. See, for example, Jack A. Goldstone, "East and West in the Seventeenth Century: Political Crises in Stuart England, OttomanTurkey, and Ming China" *Comparative Studies in Society and History* Vol. 30, No. 1 (1988), pp. 103-142. Frederic Wakeman argued that the Chinese world recovered sooner from the crisis of the 17th century than any other major world power. See p. 36 of Frederic Wakeman's "China and the Seventeenth Century World Crisis" in Frederic E. Wakeman (ed. Lea H. Wakeman), *Telling Chinese History: A Selection of Essays.* Berkeley: University of California Press, 2009, pp. 27 – 43. (This essay was originally published in 1986)

5. See Frederic Wakeman "The Ming-Qing Transition: Seventeenth-Century Crisis or Ax-

ial Age Breakthrough?" in Jóhann Páll Árnason, Shmuel Noah Eisenstadt and Björn Wittrock (eds), *Axial Civilizations and World History* Leiden: Brill, 2005, pp. 509–528. See also Wm. Theodore de Bary *Waiting for the Dawn: A Plan for the Prince*. New York: Columbia University Press, 1993.

6. Examples of late Qing and early Republican intellectuals influenced by the ideas of dissenting political thinkers from the Ming-Qing transition period include Zhang Shizhao, Zhang Binglin and Liang Qichao. See for example p. 35 of Leigh K. Jenco *Making the Political: Founding and Action in the Political Theory of Zhang Shizhao*. Cambridge: Cambridge University Press, 2010. For the influence of political thinking from the Ming-Qing transition era on Liang Qichao (a monarchist who eventually accepted the establishment of the republic), see pp. 73–74 of Hao Chang *Liang Ch'i-ch'ao and Intellectual Transition in China*. Cambridge, Massachusetts: Harvard University Press, 1971.

7. This point is adapted from an observation by Alexander Woodside in *Community and Revolution in Modern Vietnam* Boston: Houghton Mifflin, 1976, p. 15) noting that the patriotic heroes from the past invoked in modern Vietnamese nationalism are very often kings who resisted foreign invaders, whereas modern Chinese nationalists have tended to cite scholars loyal to dynasties conquered by non-Han dynasties as exemplars of patriotism.

8. See the writings of Zou Rong and Chen Tianhua presented in this volume.

9. Zhang Binglin is one example of a thinker who saw no conflict between the republic and the traditional Chinese cultural inheritance. For some of Zhang's thinking about republicanism, see Kenji Shimada (trans. Joshua Fogel), *Pioneer of the Chinese Revolution: Zhang Binglin and Confucianism*. Stanford: Stanford University Press, pp. 35–54.

10. Alexander Woodside suggests on page 8 of *Community and Revolution in Modern Vietnam* that the idea of revolution had as great a force for 20th-century Chinese intellectuals and political activists as the idea of nation for their peers in Japan or the idea of community for their Vietnamese counterparts.

11. A powerful recent study of the force of the commitment to republicanism in China after 1911 is David Strand's *An Unfinished Republic: Leading by Word and Deed in Modern China*. Berkeley: University of California Press, 2011.

12. The interest shown in China in the 1990s in the mid-19th century Self-Strengthening official Zeng Guofan is one symptom of this. Marxist historiography had attacked Zeng as a traitor and an agent of ruling-class oppression. See Yingjie Guo and Baogang He, "Reimagining the Chinese Nation: The 'Zeng Guofan Phenomenon'", *Modern China*, Vol. 25, No. 2 (Apr. , 1999), pp. 142 - 170.

13. This lineage is traced—with qualifications—by Suisheng Zhao in *A Nation—state by Construction*: *Dynamics of Modern Chinese Nationalism*. Stanford: Stanford University Press, 2004.

14. The campaigns against feudal thinking in the more radical phases of republican revolution in China in the 20th century were often associated with the idea that institutions and practices from the dynastic era persisted after 1911. While popular writing on China often suggests (directly or indirectly) that politics in the Chinese republics involves the persistence of imperial-era practices (with references to the leaders of China's republics as "emperors"), academic writing in English at least has often been more concerned with the transition from empire to nation-state than with the transition from dynastic monarchy to republic. See, for example, Peter Zarrow, *China in War and* Revolution, 1895 - 1945. London: Routledge, 2005, pp. 54 - 60.

15. The pre-eminent exponent of this approach to the history of republican nations is Benedict Anderson. See "Creole Pioneers", pp. 47 - 66 of Anderson's *Imagined Communities*: *Reflections on the Origins and Spread of Nationalism* (2nd edition) London: Verso, 1991.

16. For an account of the global transitions of this period, see Benedict Anderson, *Under Three Flags*: *Anarchism and the Anti-colonial Imagination* London: Verso, 2005.

17. Parallels between the 19th and 20th-century history of the Qing and other Eurasian land-based empires are articulated in Pamela Crossley, *the Manchus*. Oxford: Blackwell, 1997, pp. 177 - 188.

18. One example of the many works in this vein is Emil Brix, "The Role of Culture in the Decline of the European Empires" in Emil Brix, Klaus Koch and Elisabeth Vyslonzil (eds), *The Decline of Empires* Vienna: Verlag für Geschichte und Politik, 2001, pp. 9 - 20.

19. See footnote 13.

20. For a sense of the political intensity of debates about the classics in the Qing, see Ben-

jamin A. Elman, *Classicism, Politics, and Kinship: The Ch'ang-chou School of New Text Confucianism in Late Imperial China*. Berkeley: University of California Press, 1990.

21. The selection of the texts of Wei Yuan and Lin Zexu in this volume reflects the salience of these concerns for many Chinese intellectuals in the present.

22. A good sense of the pervasiveness of these themes can be found in Gloria Davies' account of the intellectual scene in China in the 1990s and early 2000s. See Gloria Davies, *Worrying about China: The Language of Chinese Critical Inquiry*. Cambridge, Massachusetts: Harvard University Press, 2007.

23. This issue is usually expressed in the relationship between *daotong* (orthodox lineage of the way) and *zhengtong* (legitimate political succession from ruler to ruler) .

24. For example, the Qing loyalist scholars Zheng Xiaoxu and Luo Zhenyu both joined the Manchukuo project. For biographical information on Luo Zhenyu, see the entry under Lo Chen-yu in Howard Boorman (ed.), *Biographical Dictionary of Republican China* Vol. 2, New York: Columbia University Press, 1968. On Zheng Xiaoxu, see the entry under Cheng Hsiao-hsü in Howard Boorman (ed.) Biographical Dictionary of Republican China Vol. I, New York: Columbia University Press, 1968.

25. The different accounts of Chinese history presented by Mao Zedong, Chiang Kai-shek and Hu Shi could perhaps be seen as constituting views from the left, right and centre respectively, representing radical, conservative and liberal variants of republicanism.

26. A good sense of the relationship between universalistic visions and nationalism in modern Chinese culture between the late Qing and the mid-20th century can be found in John Fitzgerald *Awakening China: Politics, Culture, and Class in the Nationalist Revolution*. Stanford: Stanford University Press, 1996.

27. Perhaps the most influential description of modern Chinese intellectual history that is organized around the opposition between traditional Chinese culture and the structures of modernity is Joseph Levenson's *Confucian China and Its Modern Fate: A Trilogy* Berkeley: University of California Press, 1968. For a discussion of a contemporary Chinese thinker critical of the opposition between tradition and modernity in the historiography of modern Chinese thought see Viren Murthy, "Modernity Against Modernity: Wang Hui's Critical History of Chinese Thought," Modern Intellectual History Vol. 3 No. 1, 2006.

28. The best-known account of the relationship between North American republican thought and its European antecedents is J. G. A. Pocock *The Machiavellian Moment*: *Florentine Political Thought and the Atlantic Republican Tradition*. Princeton: Princeton University Press, 2003. Pocock is perhaps more interested in the continuity of republican thought in the North Atlantic than in the question of how the idea of the republic was to be "Americanized".

29. This was arguably a crucial line of dispute in the Chinese Civil War, with the Communists arguing that the Nationalists were betraying the Chinese people by supporting the interests of international capital, and the Nationalists arguing that the Communists were betraying the Chinese people by supporting the interests of international Bolshevism.

30. See the writings of Zou Rong and Chen Tianhua in this volume.

31. A good account of the interpretations of the structure of modern Chinese history is found in the introduction to William T. Rowe's *China's Last Empire*: *The Great Qing*. Cambridge, Massachussetts, Belknap Press, 2009.

32. A good sense of the formation of the "cast of characters" who would be seen as having created the intellectual foundations of modern China can be derived from the selection of thinkers whose works were chosen for inclusion in anthologies such as Wm Theodore de Bary's *Sources of Chinese Tradition*, first published by Columbia University Press in New York in 1960. The writers deemed appropriate for inclusion in this anthology were those that prominent mid 20th-century Chinese intellectual historians had deemed to be key thinkers. The list of writers excerpted in this present volume to some extent matches the selection by de Bary and other prominent anthologists of Chinese thought, both in China and abroad.

33. A sense of the types of historical writing produced in China during the first two decades of Maoist rule can be gleaned from Albert Feuerwerker (ed.), *History in Communist China*. Boston: MIT Press, 1969.

34. As with the other writers discussed in this section, a list of sources appears in the relevant chapter of the book.

35. See p. 516 of Frederic Wakeman, "The Ming-Qing Transition: Seventeenth-Century Crisis or Axial Age Breakthrough?", cited in footnote 5.

二、反集权帝制

（一）反集权帝制概论

The Critique of Centralised Imperial Authority:

Gu Yanwu (1613 - 1682) and Huang Zongxi (1610 - 1695).

People looking back on the development of Chinese political thought since the 17th century from the vantage point of the modern Chinese republics hold Huang Zongxi and Gu Yanwu in high esteem. Huang Zongxi is often seen as having initiated the critique of monarchical power that is central to the desire to establish, if not a republic, then at least a form of monarchy constrained by a constitution. Gu Yanwu is likewise admired for his ideas about political organisation, and also for his prodigious learning, his commitment to a project of knowledge based on critical empirical research, and his commitment to study being geared to the practical needs of the governed. Both men were born in the declining years of the Ming Dynasty, an entity to which they gave formal loyalty but whose faults they sought to understand and enumerate, and they both resisted the incoming government of the Manchu Qing Dynasty. This opposition to a government that modern Chinese nationalists have regarded as a foreign state has also made them powerful exemplars of the tradition of scholar patriotism which many modern Chinese intellectuals see themselves as inheriting.

Whether the political ideas of Huang and Gu were forerunners of modern Chinese nationalism, republicanism or constitutional monarchy, or whether they were working within the broad structures of dynastic political morality as it had evolved over the centuries, is a matter of controversy, but it is an issue of questionable importance. Gu Yanwu's thought was invoked both by officials who sought to defend the Qing state and by people who favoured a republic. What is interesting, however, is to what extent the arguments of both Gu and Huang about the need to limit the power of rulers stem from a tendency among an official class chosen for their educational attainments (and not by birth) to resist hereditary power. This brings to our attention two differing tendencies in both administrative monarchies and in citizen republics: support for the idea of impartial government based on administrators who govern communities with reference to a set of impartial principles (based on equality of all people in the face of those principles), support for the idea of durable local self-government, based on a group of community leaders with established and enduring ties to that community (in practice often a hereditary local elite). The discussion by Gu Yanwu that is excerpted here, about the imperial system of prefectures and counties—that is the system of territorial administration by functionaries appointed by the centre—hinges on a central problem of Chinese political theory in the imperial era, namely how the ideal system of decentralised power with local leaders in more or less permanent positions that supposedly existed in antiquity in China should interact with the system of regularised administration created by the empire. This was a problem that was much discussed in the early years of the republic.

Huang Zongxi's sense that the power of the sovereign should be subject to limitation has been invoked in the 20th century as a sign of the importance of a tradition of liberalism in China which involved both intellectual pluralism and the critique of established power. It might be observed that if Gu Yanwu and Huang Zongxi represent a tradition that has some analogues to the forms of anti-monarchical thought that contributed to republicanism in other parts of the world, it may be because they were living in an age when many states experienced crises, crises that may have raised similar questions for political theorists. One argument about the differing fates of these traditions of thought in China and in Western Europe that were affected by 17th-century problems in state systems is that the Qing imperial state proved better able to re-establish its authority than, for example, its English counterpart, which was a much weaker and more vulnerable entity, one that was really only able to acquire substantial power over its subjects in the 19th century. Significantly, it was the 19th century that saw Qing scholars regain interest in the works of Gu Yanwu, and he became an important influence on thinkers who would be increasingly concerned with the problem of dealing with foreign powers, such as the British empire.

Sources and Further Reading

Good biographical information on Huang Zongxi and Gu Yanwu can be found on pp. 351 – 354 and pp. 421 – 426 of Arthur W. Hummel (ed.), *Eminent Chinese of the Ch'ing Period*, Taipei: Ch'eng-Wen Publishing Company, 1967.

Examples of the ways in which Chinese scholars from the era of the Chinese republics perceived and helped to articulate the role of Gu Yanwu and/or Huang Zongxi can be found in Liang Ch'i-ch'ao, *Intellectual Trends in the Ch'ing Period* (translated by Immanuel C. Y. Hsu), Cambridge, Massachussetts: Harvard University Press, 1959—an account that comes from the viewpoint of an opponent of the Neo-Confucian scholarship of the Song and Ming Dynasties; Liang Qichao, *Zhongguo Jinsanbainian Xueshushi* (A history of Chinese scholarship in the last 300 years), Taipei: The Commercial Press of Taiwan, 1968, Volume One—an account by a scholar who supports the Neo-Confucian scholarship of the Song and Ming eras, and Hou Wailu, *Jindai Zhongguo Sixiang Xueshuo Shi* (A history of doctrines and thought in Modern China), Shanghai: Life Publishing, 1947. An example of the incorporation of Gu and Huang into the patriotic narrative of the revolution from the early People's Republic of China is Yang Tingfu, *Mingmo Sanda Sixiangjia* (Three great thinkers of the late Ming). Influential late 20th and early 21st-century accounts of the place of thinkers from the Ming-Qing transition in the history of modern Chinese thought include Li Zehou, *Zhongguo Jindai Sixiang Shilun* (An essay on the history of modern Chinese thought), Beijing: People's Publishing, 1979, and Wang Hui, *Xiandai Zhongguo Sixiang de Xingqi* (The rise of modern Chinese thought), Beijing: SDX Joint Publishing Company, 2004.

A good sense of the broad historical context can be gained from the sections on the Ming-Qing transition in the following works: William T. Rowe, *China's Last Empire: The Great Qing* Cambridge, Massachussetts, Belknap Press, 2009; F. W. Mote, *Imperial China* 900 – 1800, Cambridge, Massachussetts: Harvard University Press, 1999, and Jonathan Spence *The Search for Modern China* (2nd ed.), New York: W. W. Norton, 1999, (probably the rendering of modern Chinese history in English that has been the most commonly used in university courses over the last two decades). The most detailed English-language account of the Ming-Qing transition is Frederic Wakeman, *Great Enterprise: The Manchu Reconstruction of Imperial Order in Early Seventeenth Century China* (2 volumes), Berkeley: University of California Press, 1986. Key studies of Huang, Gu and the late Ming / early Qing intellectual world include Benjamin A. Elman, *From Philosophy to Philology: Intellectual and Social Aspects of Change in Late Imperial China*, Los Angeles: UCLA Press, 2001, and Frederic Wakeman's essay "The Ming-Qing Transition: Seventeenth-Century Crisis or Axial Age Breakthrough?" in Jóhann Páll Árnason, Shmuel Noah Eisenstadt and Björn Wittrock (eds), *Axial Civilizations and World History*, Leiden: Brill, 2005, as well as Wakeman's essays in the collection Frederic E. Wakeman (ed. Lea H. Wakeman), *Telling Chinese History: A Selection of Essays*, Berkeley: University of California Press, 2009. A key study of Huang Zongxi which traces the process of his canonisation by late Qing and early Republican era advocates of reform and revolution, and also places his work firmly in its historical context, is Lynn A. Struve, "Huang Zongxi in Context: A Reappraisal of his Major Writings", *Journal of Asian Studies*, Vol. 47, No. 3, (1988), pp. 474 – 502. Wm Theodore de Bary provides a translation of Huang Zongxi's key work *Mingyi Daifang Lu*, (the source of the two samples of Huang's writings given below). See Wm Theodore de Bary, *Waiting for the Dawn: A Plan for the Prince*, New York: Columbia University Press, 1993. Joseph Levenson's "The Abortiveness of Empiricism in Early Ch'ing Thought", which appears in Volume 1 of his *Confucian China and Its Modern Fate: A Trilogy* (Berkeley: University of California Press, 1968) is the account of early Qing thought that has exerted the greatest influence on Anglophone understandings of Chinese political and philosophical thinking in the years since WWII. Much of the scholarship of Elman, Wakeman, Struve and de Bary arises in dialogue with, or critique of, Levenson's observations.

（二）反集权帝制文献

（1）日知录[1]（节选）

顾炎武[2]

《日知录》卷 6〈爱百姓故刑罚中〉

人君之于天下，不能以独治也。独治之而刑繁，众治之而刑措[3] 矣。古之王者不忍以刑穷天下之民也，是故一家之中，父兄治之；一族之间族子治之。其有不善之萌，莫不自化于闺门之内；而犹有不帅教者，然后归之士师。然则人君之所治者约矣。然后原父子之亲、立君臣之义以权之，意论轻重之序、慎测浅深之量以别之，悉其聪明、致其忠爱以尽之。夫然，刑罚焉得而不中乎？是故宗法立而刑清。天下之宗子各治其族，以辅人君之治，罔攸兼于庶狱[4]，而民自不犯于有司。风俗之醇，科条之简，有自来矣。《诗》曰："君之宗之。"吾是以知宗子之次于君道也。

《日知录》卷 7〈管仲不死子纠[5]〉

君臣之分，所关者在一身，华裔之防，所系者在天下。故夫子之于管仲，略其不死子纠之罪，而取其一匡九合之功，盖权衡于大小之间，而以天下为心也。夫以君臣之分，犹不敌华裔之防，而《春秋》之志可知矣。[6]

有谓管仲之于子纠未成为君臣者，子纠于齐未成君，于仲与忽则成为君臣矣。狐突之子毛及偃从文公在秦[7]，而曰："今臣之子名在重耳，有年数矣。"[8] 若毛、偃为重耳之臣，而仲与忽不得为纠之臣，是以成败定君臣也，可乎？又谓桓兄纠弟，此亦强为之说。[9] 论至于尊周室、存华夏之大

功，则公子与其臣区区一身之名分小矣。虽然，其君臣之分故在也，遂谓
之无罪，非也。[10]

《日知录》卷7〈周室班爵禄〉

为民而立之君，故班爵之意，天子与公、侯、伯、子、男一也，而非
绝世之贵。代耕而赋之禄，[11]故班禄之意，君、卿、大夫、士与庶人在官一
也，而非无事之食。是故知天子一位之义，则不敢肆于民上以自尊，知禄
以代耕之义，则不敢厚取于民以自奉。不明乎此，而侮夺人之君，常多于
三代之下矣。[12]

《日知录》卷8〈法制〉

法制禁令，王者之所不废，而非所以为治也。其本在正人心，厚风俗
而已。故曰："居敬而行简，以临其民。"[13]周公作《立政》之书曰："文王
罔攸，兼于庶言、庶狱、庶慎。"又曰："庶狱、庶慎，文王罔知于兹。"[14]
其丁宁后人之意可谓至矣。秦始皇之治天下事，勿大小皆决于上，上至于
衡石量书，日夜有呈，不中呈不得休息，而秦遂以亡。太史公曰："昔天
下之网尝密矣，然奸伪萌起，其极也，上下相遁，至于不振。"[15]然则法禁
之多，乃所以为趋亡之具，而愚闇之君犹以为未至也。

……

前人立法之初，不能详纠事势，豫为变通之地。后人承其已弊，拘于
旧章，不能变革，而复立一法以救之，于是法愈繁而弊愈多，天下之事至
于从腔[16]，其究也眊而不行[17]，上下相蒙，意为无失祖制而已。

《日知录》卷9〈守令〉

所谓天子者，执天下之大权者也。其执大权，奈何以天下之权寄之天
下之人，而权乃归之天子？自公卿大夫至于百里之宰，一命之官，莫不分
天子之权，以各治其事，而天子之权乃益尊。后世有不善治者出焉，尽天
下一切之权收之在上，而万几[18]之广，固非一人之所操也，而权乃移于法，

于是多为之法以禁防之。虽大奸有所不能逾，而贤智之臣亦无能效尺寸于法之外，相与兢兢奉法，以求无过而已。于是天子之权不寄之人臣，而寄之吏胥[19]，是故天下之尤急者，守令亲民之官。而今日之尤无权者莫过于守令，守令无权而民之疾苦不闻于上，安望其致太平而延国命乎！《书》曰："元首丛脞哉，股肱惰哉，万事堕哉。"[20] 盖至于守令日轻，而胥吏日重，则天子之权已夺，而国非其国矣，尚何政令之可言耶！削考功之繁科，循久任之成效，必得其人，而与之以权，庶乎守令贤而民事理，此今日之急务也。

注释：

1.《日知录》是明末清初著名学者顾炎武的代表作品之一。书名取之于《论语·子张篇》。子夏曰："日知其所亡，月无忘其所能，可谓好学也已矣。"《日知录》内容宏富，贯通古今。三十二卷本《日知录》有条目 1019 条。《日知录》的内容《四库全书总目》分作十五类，即经义、政事、世风、礼制、科举、艺文、名义、古事真妄、史法、注书、杂事、兵及外国事、天象术数、地理、杂考证。关于写作此书的目的，顾炎武本人说得很明白，他说："别著《日知录》，上篇经术，中篇治道，下篇博闻，共三十余卷。有王者起，将以见诸行事，以跻斯世于治古之隆。"撰写《日知录》，"意在拨乱涤污，法古用夏，启多闻于来学，待一治于后王"。这说明，《日知录》是寄托作者经世思想的一部书，内容大体分为三类：经术、治道、博闻，而核心则是"治道"。本书节选《日知录》中〈爱百姓故刑罚中〉等五篇，则从其抨击君主体制、宣扬民本思想之处着眼。本文选自黄汝成集释、秦克诚点校《日知录集释》，岳麓出版社 1994 年版。

2. 顾炎武（1613—1682）本名继坤，改名绛，字忠清；南都败后，改炎武，字宁人，号亭林，自署蒋山佣，学者尊称为亭林先生。汉族，南直隶苏州府昆山（今属江苏）人 。明末清初著名的思想家、史学家、语言学家。与黄宗羲、王夫之并称为明末清初三大儒。明末诸生，青年时发愤为经世致用之学，并参加昆山抗清义军，败，幸而得脱。后漫游南北，屡谒明陵，卒于曲沃。康熙间被举鸿博，坚拒不就。其学以博学于文，行己有耻为主，合学与行、治学与经世为一。著作繁多，以毕生心力所著为《日知录》，另有《音学五书》《亭林诗文集》《天下郡国利病书》等。

3. 措：安排、实施。

4. 语见《尚书·立政》："文王罔攸兼于庶狱；庶狱庶慎，为有司职牧夫是训用违，

......"意思是，文王不兼管各种教令，各种狱讼案件和各种禁戒，用与不用只顺从主管和牧民的人。

5. 事见《论语·宪问》，公子纠为其弟齐桓公所杀，管仲与召忽同为公子纠的家臣，召忽自杀以殉其主，而管仲却做了齐桓公的宰相。子路问孔子说："齐桓公杀了公子纠，召忽自杀以殉，但管仲却没有自杀，不能算是仁德之人吧?"孔子说："桓公多次召集各诸侯国的盟会，不用武力，都是管仲的力量啊。这就是仁德。"

6. 杨宁评：夫子于管仲之罪，只存而不论，不曾说仲之无罪。校记：华裔之防。抄本"华裔"作"夷夏"。又，"犹不敌华裔之防"。抄本"华裔"作"夷夏"。

7. 毛，狐毛。偃，狐偃。狐毛为狐偃之兄，都是晋文公重耳之舅。周惠王二十一年（公元前656年）晋国内乱，太子申生被迫自杀，公子重耳、夷吾出亡。毛、偃二人随重耳出亡，又助重耳归晋继君位，佐晋文公成霸业。文公，即晋文公重耳。

8. 原注：汉、晋以下，太子诸王与其臣皆定君臣之分，盖自古相传如此。

9. 杨宁评：此程子之言，实不然。

10. 校记：论至于尊周室存华夏之大功。抄本"存华夏"作"攘夷狄"。

11. 原注：《黄氏日钞·读王制》曰：必本于上农夫者，示禄出于农，等而上之，皆以代耕者也。

12. 雷学淇注：周之班爵禄，有本制，有加礼。《孟子》于侯国举本制，而不言加礼，所以抑七国也。于天子之臣举加礼，而不官本制，所以申王朝也。

13. 语见《论语·雍也篇》："居敬而行简，以临其民。"意思是，治国理政，只要立身恭敬，严格依礼办事，便可简约行之，不求全责备。

14. 见《尚书·周书》。

15. 语见《史记·酷吏列传》卷六十二。

16. 脞：细碎。

17. 原注：语出《汉书·董仲舒传》。师古曰："眊，不明也。"

18. 几：事务，特指政务。

19. 吏胥："胥"指的是一种基层的办事人员，即政府将平民按户口加以控制，并从中选拔出"有才智者"加以管理。"吏"本是指替天子管理臣民、处理政务的人，即"官"。一般认为，汉代以后"吏"逐渐专指小吏和差役，即没有官位的官府工作人员。有人这样形容它与"官"的区别："官如大鱼吏小鱼，完粮之民且沮洳，官如虎，吏如猫，具体而微舐人膏。"由于两者都是指代官府的各类办事人员和差役，后世遂有人将胥、吏并称。

20. 语见《尚书·皋陶谟》。丛脞，细碎无大谋略。

译文：

日知录（节选）

顾炎武

《日知录》卷 6〈仁爱百姓人民，刑罚才会有效〉：

一国君主统治国家的本意，并不是独裁统治。因为独裁统治用刑必然繁重，而分权治理则用刑才会恰当。古代帝王不忍心以加重刑法来约束天下人，是因为每个家庭中有父亲和兄长来规范家庭成员，每个宗族之内有族长来规范本族人。即使有了罪恶的萌芽，也都于家庭和家族之内清理掉了。如果家法族规不能解决问题，才归到官府解决。虽然上有君主统治国家之法，但下有家族孝悌教化的引导、忠君大义的规范；确立有尊卑等级的理念和审慎的行为规范的判断标准，以召唤人的良知为出发点，使人们本着忠义和友爱精神处事。果真是这样了，刑罚还能不发挥其意义和效果吗？所以，家族的宗法严明了，国家刑罚就会减少。整个国家的每个家庭宗族都做到有效的管理，以此来辅佐君主治理国家，君主不必去兼管各种政令和刑狱，人民自然就不会触犯官府的法律。民风由此而淳厚，国家刑罚由此减轻。《诗经》中有句："君主统治之，宗族管理之。"对此我们可以这样理解，宗族管理之作用相当重要，仅次于君主统治之作用。

《日知录》卷 7〈关于管仲不为公子纠效死的评价〉：

君臣之间的名分关系，只以君主一人为至尊，而国家对外的主权和尊严则关乎全体国民。由此孔子评价管仲不效死公子纠之事时并不计较其不效死子纠的过失，而只看他为秦国匡正天下的功劳业绩，这是因为在大事小事之间要有所权衡取舍，考虑问题要以国家和人民利益为重。由此思路可见君臣关系中的名分和臣下对君主的效忠并没有国家主权和尊严重要，这就是孔子在编修《春秋》时的观点。

有人说，管仲不效死于公子纠是因为公子纠在齐国还未当上国君，公子纠与管仲的关系还不能算是君臣关系，而管仲与齐桓公的关系才是君臣关系。当年狐突的两个儿子狐毛和狐偃随公子重耳在秦流亡时，曾这样说："如今我们称臣于公子重耳有许多年了。"狐毛和狐偃可以称臣于公子重耳，而管仲和召忽却不能称臣于公子纠，这是以王子是否后来继位而确定他们是否是君臣的名分，难道这样可以吗？还有人说，齐桓公是长兄而公子纠是弟弟，所以管仲不能称臣于公子纠。这样的说法很牵强。如果从尊崇周王室、保全国家民族大局利益角度论之，公子纠与管仲的君臣名分就显得太微不足道了。虽然这样说，但管仲与公子纠之间的君臣关系不能说完全没有，说管仲这样处理完全没有过失，也不太妥当。

《日知录》卷7〈周室班爵禄〉

一国君主的设立是为了天下百姓的，与贵族的封侯授爵出自一个道理。在此意义上，君主的王位与公、侯、伯、子、男贵族的爵位一样，并非绝对高贵的象征。而国家俸禄等物质待遇，追根寻源，都出自于耕田人的租赋。在此意义上，君主、公卿士大夫贵族以及庶民官僚所得到的俸禄，并不是无所事事、不劳而获的物质待遇。真正懂得一国之君皇位的真实含义，就不敢凌驾于人民之上妄自尊大；明白从皇帝到各级贵族官僚的俸禄都是来自耕田人的租赋这个道理，就不敢为贪图一己享受而搜刮民脂民膏。夏商周三代以后，很多人不懂得这个道理，而狭隘地轻视由其他途径获得王位的君主。

《日知录》卷8〈法制〉

英明的君主使用法律和禁令，并非用以维系统治，只是来规范人们的思想，倡导淳厚民风。古人云："治国理政，只要立身恭敬，严格依礼办事，便可简约行之，不求全责备。"周公曾编修《立政》一书，书中有言："周文王建立统治，却并不亲自兼管各种政令，只是按照各主管和地方官的意见去办理各类狱讼案件和禁戒。"还说："各种狱讼案件和各种禁戒，周文王并不多做了解。"周公反复讲此番话，其嘱托后世子孙之意已达到

极致了。秦始皇时统治天下，政事无论大小都亲自处决，诸如度量衡之
法、禁书之令等，公文政令日夜传发不停，政令不落实便不停息，秦由此
则短命而亡。司马迁曾感叹道："秦始皇时控制国家的法网密布，但彼时
虚伪和狡诈蜂起，达到极致。上下相互欺瞒，最终导致国家衰败。"法律
和禁令虽然多，却成为迅速灭亡的原因。而愚蠢闭塞的君主却认为，国家
速亡的原因是法律政令还不够多的缘故。

......

从前的君主最初立法，并非针对处理很具体的情况，只是作为某种预
备措施。后人则根据自己所面临的弊端，机械地加以运用，解决不了问题
又不能加以革新，只好再设立一条法令去弥补此法之缺。于是法律政令越
来越多，弊病也越来越多，国家政事也就越来越复杂麻烦。究其原因，法
律政令多含混不明，行之不通，上下互相欺瞒，却都还以为是按照祖制行
事了。

《日知录》卷 9〈守令〉

什么是天子？就是掌握国家最高权力的统治者。而怎么可以由天子一
人掌控国家最高权力，却不把国家权力分配给国家的臣民呢？上至公卿大
夫，下抵国家任命的县令，每一职任都在分掌天子的权力，各自履行自己
的职责，这样天子的权力才能实现，天子的尊严才能显出。

后世出现许多不会治理国家的统治者，把国家一切权力都掌控在手
中，但国家政务太繁多了，凭个人肯定是无法处理的。于是就把权力转变
为法律政令，多设法律政令对下面加以禁止和防范。虽然这样可以限制奸
臣作乱，但贤明有为的臣子也被这些繁琐的法律政令所限制，难以有所作
为。只能是兢兢业业遵纪守法，但求无过而已。这时，天子的国家权力没
有分配于臣下的手中，而掌握在执行监察、考功的小官手中。治理国家最
关键的是那些热爱百姓的地方守令官，现在最大的问题是这些守令官最没

有权力。地方守令官手中无权，百姓的疾苦如何能够上报到天子，又如何指望国家的长治久安！《尚书》有歌词："君王琐碎啊！大臣就懈怠啊！诸事就荒废啊！"因为地方守令权力地位越来越轻，而执行监察、考功的小官权力越来越大，如此天子的权力实际上已经被侵夺了。国家都不是原来意义上的国家了，还谈何国家政令的有效实施！削减监察考功这类繁琐法规条令，允许政绩卓著的地方官久任其职，胜任之人才必然辈出，再委之以重任。可以肯定，地方守令官贤明，地方行政就会治理，此乃当今最为至关重要的事情。

（2）郡县论[1]（节选）

顾炎武[2]

郡县论一

知封建之所以变而为郡县[3]，则知郡县之敝[4]而将复变。然则将复变而为封建乎？曰：不能。有圣人起，寓封建之意于郡县之中[5]，而天下治矣。

盖自汉以下之人，莫不谓秦以孤立而亡。不知秦之亡，不封建亡，封建亦亡；而封建之废，固自周衰之日而不自于秦也。封建之废，非一日之故也，虽圣人起，亦将变而为郡县。方今郡县之敝已极，而无圣人出焉，尚——仍其故事[6]，此民生之所以日贫，中国之所以日弱而益趋于乱也。

何则[7]？封建之失，其专在下；郡县之失，其专在上。古之圣人，以公心待天下人，胙之土而分之国[8]；今之君人者，尽四海之内为我郡县犹不足也，人人而疑之，事事而制之[9]。科条文薄日多于一日[10]，而又设之监司[11]，设之督抚[12]，以为如此，守令不得以残害其民矣[13]。不知有司之官[14]，凛凛焉救过之不给[15]，以得代为幸[16]，而无肯为其民兴一日之利者，民乌得不穷[17]，国乌得不弱？率此不变[18]，虽千百年，而吾知其与乱同事，日甚一日者矣。然则尊令长之秩[19]，而予之以生财治人之权，罢监司之任，设世官之奖[20]，行辟属之法，[21]所谓寓封建之意于郡县之中，而二千年以来之敝可以复振。后之君苟欲厚民生，强国势，则必用吾言矣。

郡县论三

何谓称职？曰：土地辟，田野治，树木蕃[22]，沟洫修[23]，城郭固，仓廪实[24]，学校兴，盗贼屏[25]，戎器完[26]，而其大者则人民乐业而已。

夫养民者，如人家之畜五牸然[27]：司马牛者一人，司走刍豆者复一人[28]，又使纪纲之仆监之[29]，升斗之计必闻之于其主人，而马牛之瘠也日甚[30]。

吾则不然。择一圉人之勤干者[31]，委之以马牛，给之以牧地，使其所出常浮于所养，而视其肥息者赏之[32]，否则挞之[33]。然则其为主人者，必乌氏也[34]，必桥姚也[35]。

故天下之患，一圉人足办，而为是纷纷者也。不信其圉人，而用其监仆，甚者并监仆又不信焉，而主人之耳目乱矣。于是爱马牛之心，常不胜其吝刍粟之计，而畜产耗矣。故马以一圉人而肥，民以一令而乐。

郡县论六

今天下之患，莫大乎贫。用吾之说，则五年而小康，十年而大富。

且以马言之：天下驿递往来，以及州县上计京师[36]，白事司府[37]，迎候上官，递送文书，及庶人在官所用之马，一岁无虑百万匹[38]，而行无虑万万里。今则十减六七，而西北之马骡不可胜用矣。以文册言之[39]：一事必报数衙门，往复驳勘必数次[40]，以及迎候、生辰、拜贺之用，其纸料之费索诸民者，岁不下巨万。今则十减七八，而东南之竹箭不可胜用矣[41]，他物之称是者，不可悉数。

且使为令者得以省耕敛[42]，教树畜，而田功之获[43]，果蓏之收[44]，六畜之孳[45]，材木之茂，五年之中必当倍益。从是而山泽之利亦可开也。夫采矿之役，自元以前，岁以为常，先朝所以开之而不发者，以其召乱也。譬之有窖金焉，发于五达之衢[46]，则市人聚而争之；发于堂室之内，则唯主人有之，门外者不得而争也。今有矿焉，天子开之，是发金于五达之衢也；县令开之，发金于堂室之内也。利尽山泽而不取诸民，故曰：此富国之策也。

注释：

1. 《顾炎武文集》〈郡县论〉。郡县论共九论，本书选其论一、论三和论六。是顾炎武探讨地方行政制度改革的一组论文。此组文章在讨论从封建制到郡县制发展历程的基础上指出郡县志之弊，提出了"寓封建制之意于郡县之中"的主张，具有明显的进步意义。其中也明显表达出作者反封建专制体制、倡导民本主张的政治思想倾向。本文摘引自"明清八大家文选丛书"《顾炎武文集》，钱仲联主编，张兵点校，苏州大学出版社 2001 年版。

2. 见《日知录》篇注释。

3. 封建：指西周分封制，由天子分封同姓王、功臣或就不首领为诸侯，赐以山川土地，建立邦国。郡县：秦统一中国后推行的郡县两极地方行政体制，统称郡县制。

4. 敝：衰败。

5. 在郡县志中加入封建制的内容。顾炎武曾明确主张，郡县若称职，可以"任之终身"，可传于子弟；若不称职，则严加惩处。

6. 仍：沿袭。故事：旧的规章制度。

7. 何则：什么原因呢？

8. 胙：赐给。

9. 制：制约、控制。

10. 科条文簿：法令条规和公文案卷。

11. 监司：监察地方属吏之官。

12. 督抚：总督和巡抚。

13. 守令：郡称守，县称令。统指郡县的长官。

14. 有司：指各级官吏，主要指地方长官。

15. 凛凛焉：恐惧的样子。救：止。给：及。

16. 得代：得到代替。

17. 乌得：怎能。

18. 率：沿袭、遵循。

19. 秩：指官吏的等级。

20. 世官：世代沿袭的官职。

21. 辟属之法：由县令直接委任属吏的方法。辟：委任；属：指县令属吏，如主簿、尉、博士、驿丞、司仓等。

22. 蕃：繁殖、生长。

23. 洫：沟渠。

24. 仓廪：储存粮食的仓库。

25. 屏：除去。

26. 戎器：武器装备。

27. 五牸：即五畜，指牛羊猪鸡犬。牸：本指雌性的牲口。

28. 刍：喂牲口的草。

29. 纪纲之仆：即管事的仆人。纪纲：管理。

30. 瘠：瘦。

31. 圉人：养马的人。

32. 息：繁殖。

33. 挞：鞭打，处罚。

34. 乌氏：乌支倮，人名，善养马。见《史记．货殖列传》。

35. 桥姚：人名，以养马牛羊致富。见《史记．货殖列传》。

36. 上计：战国、秦汉时，年终，地方官本人遣吏至京师上计簿，将全年人口、钱粮、盗贼、讼狱等事报告朝廷。

37. 白事：即言事。白：告。明告其事。司府：官府。

38. 无虑：大略、大概。

39. 文策：公文。

40. 驳勘：驳回复查。

41. 竹箭：泛指竹子，造纸的材料。箭：此指竹的一种，即箭竹，产于江南。

42. 耕敛：耕种和收获。

43. 田功：农事。

44. 瓝：瓜类植物的果实。

45. 孳：繁殖。

46. 五达之衢：通五方的道路。

译文：

郡县论（节选）

顾炎武

郡县论一

我们知道，郡县制是由封建制变更而来，由此便可推论，如果郡县制出现问题也要加以变更，那么是否完全变回封建制呢？答案当然是否定的。真有英明的君主出现，将郡县制加以改良，加入封建制的内容，国家就会治理好。

汉朝之后，人们都说秦朝之所以短命，在于失去了六国贵族的支持而陷于孤立。但是没有考虑到，秦朝灭亡是必然的，不实行封建制灭亡，就是实行封建制也要灭亡。而封建制的崩溃，应该从周朝衰败之日就开始了，并非开始于秦朝。所以说，封建制的灭亡过程不是一天之内可以完成的，即使封建制由伟大英明的圣人创建和维护，终将为郡县制所取代。到了今天，郡县制已经相当衰败了，只是没有英明君主出现，旧体制还在运行，这就是中国人民日趋贫穷、国家愈加衰落和混乱的根本原因。

这是为什么？因为封建制的弊端在于各诸侯国的专权，而郡县制的缺陷在于皇帝专权。古时的圣人以天下为公为出发点，将国家土地封赐给臣下治理；今天的皇帝，把全国领土都置于郡县的管理之下还嫌权力不够集中，怀疑每一位臣下，每项政事都加以严格控制。法令条规、公文案卷愈加繁琐，而且设有监察机构加以监督，设有总督巡抚加以掌控，以为有了这样监督控制，郡县的长官就不会欺压管辖之内的百姓了。却不曾想到，这样一来地方之官心怀恐惧，唯恐过失得祸，明哲保身，哪里还顾得上为辖区百姓的利益着想。这样一来，人民怎能不日趋贫穷，国家怎能不越来越衰落？如此下去而不图变革，虽然郡县制千百年延续至今，我们看到治理上的弊病伴随其间，国家混乱也就日甚于一日。如果能给予地方长官更多的尊严和独立性，给予其更多的地方财政和人事权力，撤除监察机构的控制，允许政绩出色的地方官僚的官职地位得以世袭，允许地方官直接任命下属官员，也就是把封建制的内容加入郡县制之中，这样的话，郡县制两千年的弊病便可解决。今后若有真心想励精图治、富民强国的君主，肯定要采用我的这个治国策略。

郡县论三

对于地方官，什么是称职的标准？回答是：辖区内疆土得到很好的开辟治理，农业林业兴旺，水利系统完善，城池防备坚固，粮食囤积充盈，大力兴办教育事业，清除盗贼，加强武备。这些都做得出色，辖区人民就会安居乐业。

统治管理百姓如同农家饲养家畜。如果有一个饲养牲畜的人，再另设一个人监管喂马牛的饲料，然后再派一个人对他进行监督，时时向主人汇报他的饲养工作情况，他饲养的牲畜肯定是越养越瘦。我就不会这样做。我会选一位精于饲养牲畜的人，把牛马全部交给他饲养，分给他牧地，由他一个人管理。还要考虑到他的支出能力要超出他所负担的限度。如果他饲养的牛马越来越肥壮，而且不断繁殖增加，我就给他奖赏，相反就处罚他。而作为主人，一定要像古时善于养马的乌倮和以饲养牲畜而致富的桥姚那样精通牲畜的饲养和管理。

饲养牲畜就像管理国家地方政务，本来一个好的饲养员完全可以胜任，却搞得那般复杂。对饲养员不信任而又派个管家去加以监督，甚至连管家也不信任，这样一来主人（君主）的观察和判断的能力就乱了。其结果，使其爱马牛（仁爱百姓）之心常被算计饲料花费（管理环节上的算计）所干扰，反使畜产减产（百姓遭殃）。其实饲养牲畜任用得力饲养员一人就足可以办好，地方政务的管理是同样的道理，放手任用一个得力地方官足以管理好一方的政务。

郡县论六

目前，国家最大的问题是贫穷，如果采用我的治国方略，则五年之内必达到小康水平，十年之内便可富强昌盛。

单以马匹使用一项计：全国的驿站马匹的使用，从地方州、县每年派人到京师上报财政、讼狱诸事，下级向上级汇报工作，出差官员的迎来送往，往返公文传递，以及官府工作人员日常使用马匹，一年算下来不少于百万马匹，而行程得上万万里路了。整个损耗如果减去六七成，西北地区的马骡畜力则取之不尽、用之不竭。

再看公文行移运作的消费：地方上每发生一件事，必然上报上级官府，就此一事的批驳复查不下多次，而且官府上的迎来送往、生辰庆贺，以及例行的那些日常走访交际的应酬，仅仅这些方面用纸都要从百姓身上出。仅这些就是一大笔花费。如果现在能把这些耗费减去七八成，东南地区造纸省出来的竹子多得都无法计算。诸如此类的节省项目就太多了。

使令地方官大力发展农业生产，发展林业畜业，这样农业和农副业的收获，林业、畜牧业的收获，五年之内必然翻增数倍。而且还可以从开发山川河湖等国土资源中获利。开采矿业在元朝之前很普遍，明朝时国家加以控制，是担心矿徒聚众作乱闹事。用一个形象的比喻：矿业就像窖藏的金子，把它开发在四通八达的大道上，人们就会奔来抢夺；把它开发于住户庭院内，就只归房主所有，外人无法争夺。看今日国家之矿藏，如果以皇帝名义国家开采，就像把金子开发在大道之上；如果地方官府开采，就像把金子开发于私人庭院之内。你就是把国家的山川河湖的资源都采光了，人民也获不着利。所以说，处理好开发山川河湖国土经济资源问题，也是使国家富强的一大国策。

(3) 原君[1]

黄宗羲[2]

黄宗羲《明夷待访录》卷一

有生之初，人各自私也，人各自利也。天下有公利而莫或兴之，有公害而莫或除之。有人者出，不以一己之利为利，而使天下受其利；不以一己之害为害，而使天下释其害。此其人之勤劳，必千万于天下之人。夫以千万倍之勤劳，而己又不享其利，必非天下之人情所欲居也。故古之人君，量而不欲入者，许由、务光是也[3]；入而又去之者，尧舜是也；初不欲入而不得去者，禹是也。岂古之人有所异哉？好逸恶劳，亦犹夫人之情也。

后之为人君者不然。以为天下利害之权皆出于我，我以天下之利尽归于己，以天下之害尽归于人，亦无不可。使天下之人不敢自私，不敢自利，以我之大私为天下之公；始而惭焉，久而安焉，视天下为莫大之产业，传之子孙，受享无穷。汉高帝所谓"某业所就，孰与仲多"者[4]，其逐利之情，不觉溢之于辞矣。

此无他，古者以天下为主，君为客；凡君之所毕世而经营者，为天下也。今也以君为主，天下为客；凡天下之无地而得安宁者，为君也。是以其未得之也，屠毒天下之肝脑，离散天下之子女，以博我一人之产业，曾不惨然。曰："我固为子孙创业也。"其既得人之也，敲剥天下之骨髓，离散天下之子女，以奉我一人之淫乐，视为当然。曰："此我产业之花息也。"然则为天下之大害者，君而已矣，向使无君，人各得自私也，人各得自利也。呜呼！岂设君之道固如是乎？

古者天下之人爱戴其君，比之如父，拟之如天，诚不为过也。今也天下之人怨恶其君，视之如寇仇，名之为独夫，固其所也。而小儒规规焉以君臣之义无所逃于天地之间，至桀、纣之暴，犹谓汤、武不当诛之，而妄传伯夷、叔齐无稽之事[5]，视兆人万姓崩溃之血肉，曾不异夫腐鼠。岂天地之大，于兆人万姓之中，独私其一人一姓乎？是故武王，圣人也；孟子之言，圣人之言也。后世之君，欲以如父如天之空名，禁人之窥伺者，皆不便于其言，至废孟子而不立，[6] 非导源于小儒乎？

虽然，使后之为君者，果能保此产业，传之无穷，亦无怪乎其私之也。既以产业视之，人之欲得产业，谁不如我？摄缄縢，固扃鐍，一人之智力，不能胜天下欲得之者之众，远者数世，近者及身，其血肉之崩溃在其子孙矣。昔人愿世世无生帝王家[7]，而毅宗之语公主，亦曰："若何为生我家[8]！"痛哉斯言！回思创业时，其欲得天下之心，有不废然摧沮者乎！

是故明乎为君之职分，则唐、虞之世，人人能让，许由、务光非绝尘也；不明乎为君之职分，则市井之间，人人可欲，许由、务光所以旷后世而不闻也。然君之职分难明，以俄顷淫乐不易无穷之悲，虽愚者亦明之矣。

注释：

1. 《原君》：是明末清初文学家、思想家黄宗羲的代表作之一，是作者《明夷待访录》中之首篇。作者认为封建君主以天下为私有，掌天下利害之权，实为天下之"大害"，应破除以"君臣之义"为至上的观念。论说简明、犀利，逻辑性较强，行文中含有痛切之情。

2. 黄宗羲（1610—1695），字太冲，号南雷，尊称为南雷先生，晚年自称梨洲老人，学者称梨洲先生。浙江余姚人。明末清初经学家、史学家、思想家、地理学家、天文历算学家、教育家。黄宗羲学问极博，思想深邃，著作宏富，与顾炎武、王夫之并称明末清初三大思想家（或清初三大儒）；与弟黄宗炎、黄宗会号称浙东三黄；与顾炎武、方以智、王夫之、朱舜水并称为"清初五大师"。黄宗羲亦有"中国思想启蒙之父"之誉。黄宗羲多才博学，于经史百家及天文、算术、乐律以及释、道无不研究。尤其在史学上成就很大。清政府撰修《明史》，"史局大议必咨之"（《清史稿》480卷）。而在哲学和政治思想方面，更是一位从"民本"的立场来抨击君主专制制度者，堪称中国思想启蒙第一人。他的政治理想主要集中在《明夷待访录》一书中。

3. 许由、务光：传说中的高士。唐尧让天下于许由，许由认为是对自己的侮辱，就隐居箕山中。商汤让天下于务光，务光负石投水而死。

4. 汉高帝：《史记·高祖本纪》载汉高祖刘邦登帝位后，曾对其父说："始大人常以臣无赖，不能治产业，不如仲（其兄刘仲）力，今某之业所就，孰与仲多？"

5. 伯夷、叔齐无稽之事：《史记·伯夷列传》载他俩反对武王伐纣，天下归周之后，又耻食周粟，饿死于首阳山。

6. 废孟子不立：《孟子·尽心下》中有"民为贵，社稷次之，君为轻"的话，明太祖朱元璋见而下诏废除祭祀孟子。

7. 《南史·王敬则传》载南朝宋顺帝刘准被逼出宫，曾发愿："愿后身世世勿复生天王家！"

8. 毅宗：明崇祯帝，南明初谥思宗，后改毅宗。李自成军攻入北京后，他叹息公主不该生在帝王家，以剑砍长平公主，断左臂，然后自缢。

译文：

原 君
黄宗羲

黄宗羲《明夷待访录》卷一

　　人类社会出现之后，人就变得自私自利了。对公众有利的事无人兴办，对公众有害的事也无人革除。这时有人站出来，他不以一己之利为利，却愿使天下人获得利益；不以自己的祸患为患，而想让天下人免除祸患。他付出的勤苦辛劳，必定比天下人多千万倍。虽然付出千万倍的勤苦辛劳，而自己却又不享受其利，这肯定不是天下常人所情愿做的。所以古人对君主之王位，有人经过考虑后不愿就位，像许由、务光等人；有人就位后又离位的，像尧、舜等人；还有人起先不愿就位而最终却未能离位的，就像大禹。难道说古代人有什么不同吗？喜好安逸，厌恶劳动，和我们平常人没有两样。

　　后代做人君的却不是这样了。他们认为天下的利害大权都出自自己，而将天下的利益都归于自己，将天下的祸患都加之于他人，也不认为有什么不妥的。让天下的人不敢自私自利，而将自己无限扩大的私利当做天下的公利。开始时对此还觉得惭愧，时间久了也就心安理得了。将天下看作一己之广大的私产，传之子孙，享受无穷。正如汉高祖所说的"我的家业之宏富广大，我二哥怎比得了呢？"追逐利益的思想意识不觉已溢于言表了。

　　这没有其他原因，古人把国家和人民放在主要位置上，而把君主放在从属位置上，君主一世的所作所为都应当是为天下百姓。现代人却把君主摆在首要位置上，反把国家与人民放在从属位置，所有使天下各地得不到安宁的原因，都在于有了君主。在他未得到皇位时，不惜屠戮、戕害天下百姓，拆散天下人子女，以达到家天下目的而毫不觉得惨痛，说："我这是为我子孙后代创业。"当他得到皇位后，就敲诈剥夺民脂民膏，离散天下人的子女，以供奉自己一人的荒淫享乐，还视此为理所当然，说："这些都是我的家业和财富。"由此以见，作为天下最大的祸害，当非君主莫属了！当初若没有君主，人们尚可以想自己之所想，得自己之所得。难道设立君主的道理本该如此吗？

古时候天下人爱戴自己的君主，把他比作父亲，拟作苍天，确实不为过分。如今天下人怨恨、憎恶自己的君主，将他视为仇敌，称为"独夫"，这原本就是君主的本来面目。但那些迂腐的儒生，死抱着儒家陈旧的说教，认为君臣名分是永恒的，是与天地共存的。甚至像夏桀、商纣那样残暴的君主，竟然说商汤、周武王不应杀他们。还编造传播伯夷、叔齐的那些无从查考的忠君故事，把千千万万人民的血肉横飞的尸体视为腐鼠。天地如此之广阔，亿万人民之中岂能唯独侍奉君主一人一姓？所以说灭了商纣的武王是圣人，孟子赞美武王的话，就是圣人的立言。后代君主妄图凭皇帝如天如父的尊贵虚名和空洞的尊称，来禁绝他人窥测皇位的企图，都会感到孟子的话对自己不利，由此而废除了孟子配祀孔子的资格，此类事不是那些迂腐的儒生造成还能是谁？

这样，后代君主都愿能保住这份皇家基业并代代相传，本着如此之愿望，把国家当作一己之私有也就不是什么奇怪的事了。你既然有着把皇位看作自家家业而严格掌控的强烈欲望，他人想得到这份家业的欲望又有什么不同呢？于是将其牢牢把握，就像用绳、锁束牢加固。但是个人的智谋与力量毕竟不及天下众多窥测皇位者的智谋与力量。皇位的维系远的不过几代，短暂的仅限于自身，帝王们灭顶之祸常就显现在子孙的身上。曾有君主说，愿后世子孙世世代代都不要生在帝王之家；而崇祯皇帝对女儿说："你为何偏生在我家啊？"这话说得真够惨痛！回想其祖上创业时志在得天下之雄心，能不黯然沮丧吗？

尧、舜时代的人懂得作君主的职任和分量，所以人人都能禅让王位，许由、务光在那时也称不上是什么超凡脱俗之人。不懂得作君主的职任与分量，就连市井布衣也都个个想当皇上，许由、务光的明智也就绝迹于后世了。也许，人们未必都能真正懂得君主的职任与分量，但是不值得用片刻的荒淫享乐换取无穷的悲哀这个简单道理，再愚蠢的人也不会不懂吧。

（4）原 臣[1]

黄宗羲[2]

　　有人焉，视于无形，听于无声，以事其君[3]，可谓之臣乎？曰：否。杀其身以事其君，可谓之臣乎？曰：否。

　　夫视于无形，听于无声，资于事父也[4]，杀其身者，无私之极则也，而犹不足以当之，则臣道如何而后可？曰：缘夫天下之大，非一人之所能治，而分治之以群工[5]。故我之出而仕也，为天下，非为君也，为万民，非为一姓也。

　　吾以天下万民起见[6]，非其道，即君以形声强我，未之敢从也[7]，况于无形无声乎？非其道，即立身于其朝，未之敢许也，况于杀其身乎？不然，而以君之一身一姓起见，君有无形无声之嗜欲，吾从而视之听之，此宦官宫妾之心也。君为己死而为己亡，吾从而死之亡之，此其私昵者之事也。是乃臣不臣之辨也[8]。

　　世之为臣者昧于此义，以谓臣为君而设者也[9]，君分吾以天下而后治之，君授吾以人民而后牧之，视天下人民为人君囊中之私物。今以四方之劳扰，民生之憔悴，足以危吾君也，不得不讲治之牧之之术[10]；苟无系于社稷之存亡[11]，则四方之劳扰，民生之憔悴，虽有诚臣，亦以为纤芥之疾也。夫古之为臣者，于此乎，于彼乎？

　　盖天下之治乱，不在一姓之兴亡，而在万民之忧乐。是故桀纣之亡，乃所以为治也，秦政、蒙古之兴[12]，乃所以为乱也；晋、宋、齐、梁之兴亡，无与于治乱者也[13]。为臣者轻视斯民之水火[14]，即能辅君而兴，从君而亡，其于臣道固未尝不背也。夫治天下犹曳大木然，前者唱邪，后者唱许[15]。君与臣，共曳木之人也；若手不执绋[16]，足不履地，曳木者唯娱笑于曳木者之前[17]，从曳木者以为良[18]，而曳木之职荒矣。

　　嗟乎！后世骄君自恣[19]，不以天下万民为事。其所求乎草野者[20]，不过欲得奔走服役之人。乃使草野之应于上者，亦不出夫奔走服役。一时免于寒饿，遂感在上之知遇，不复计其礼之备与不备，跻之仆妾之间而以为当然。万历初，神宗之待张居正[21]，其礼稍优。此于古之师傅未能百一[22]，当时论者骇然居正之受无人臣礼。夫居正之罪，正坐不能以师傅自待，听指使于仆妾[23]。而责之反是，何也？是则耳目浸淫于流俗之所谓臣者以为鹄矣[24]，又岂知臣之与君，名异而实同耶？

注释：

1. 《原臣》选自黄宗羲《明夷待访录》。十七世纪已是中国封建社会的末期，思想也开始冲出专制主义的牢笼。本篇对君、臣、民三者的关系提出了新的看法，认为君和臣一样，是为万民治理天下的，臣应该为万民服务而不为一家一姓服务。这既是对君主集权体制的抨击，也是"民本"思想的继承和发展。原臣：从根本上推论关于臣的道理。原：推论其本原。

2. 见《原君》篇注释。

3. 《礼记·曲礼上》："为人于者……听于无声，视于无形。"指父母不在跟前，儿子也要想到父母的教诲。这里是说，君主的心意即使不通过言语和容色表达出来，臣子也要善于体会。

4. 资于事父：即"资于事父以事君"，语出《礼记·丧服四制》，又见《孝经》。意思是用事父之道以事君。资：凭借。

5. 群工：指群臣，百官。

6. 以……起见：为……着想。

7. 即：即使。以形声强我：意思是有明确的表示强制我去做某事。

8. 这就是臣和不是臣（而是宦官宫妾）的区别。

9. 以谓：以为。谓：通"为"。

10. 讲：研究。

11. 系：关系。

12. 秦政：秦始皇，姓嬴名政。蒙古：指元朝。

13. 与：关涉。

14. 水火：比喻极端的痛苦。《孟子·梁惠王》："今燕虐其民，王往而征之，民以为将拯己于水火之中也。"

15. 《淮南子·道应》："今夫举大木者，前呼邪许，后亦应之，此举重劝力之歌也。""邪"和"许"都是象声词。

16. 绋：大绳子。

17. 前一个"曳木者"比喻臣，后一个"曳木者"比喻君。

18. 从：纵使，即使。本句"曳木者"比喻君。

19. 自恣：放纵自己。

20. 草野：指民间。

21. 万历：明神宗朱翊钧的年号（1573—1620）。张居正：万历时的宰相。

22. 师傅：指古代太师、太傅、太保一类的官，是最高的官位，即所谓的"帝王之师"。受：指接受神宗的礼遇。

23. 坐：因。听指使于仆妾：指张居正与太监冯保的关系。

24. 浸淫：逐渐受影响。鹄：箭靶的中心。这里引申为准则、标准。

译文：

原 臣
黄宗羲

有一种人，在君主还没有在神色及言语上表示意思的时候，便臆测到其想法，以这样的方式侍奉君主，这样算得上是臣子了吗？答案是：不可以。那么牺牲自己的性命以侍奉君主，这样算得上是臣子吗？答案是：不可以。

还没有在神色及言语上表示意思的时候，便臆测到其想法，这是用来侍奉父母的；为对方牺牲自己的性命，是无私最高的境界，但这样做并非算得上是好臣子。那么为臣之道该如何才算可以呢？答案是：因为天下太广大了，并非君主一人所能治理，所以才把它分给百官分工管理。因此，我们出来做官，是为国家服务，而不是只为君主一人服务；是为天下百姓工作，不是为一朝一姓的皇帝工作。

我是从天下百姓的利益出发。如果不为百姓，就是国君明令强制我去做事，我也不敢听从，更何况没有明确的指令呢？如果不是为百姓，给我在朝廷加官封爵，我也不敢从命，更何况为国君牺牲自己的性命呢？如果不是为百姓，只为国君一人一姓的利益，国君有任何喜好嗜欲，我都悉心加以观察了解，曲意逢迎，这就成了宦官仆妾一样了。国君为一己的私利而身死家亡，我就追随他身死家亡，这只是私人之间亲密感情使然，并不是为臣之道的标准。

当今之世作臣下的并不了解此为臣之道，而认为臣下之职就是为了君主而专设。是国君把土地分给我，然后使我去治理；是国君把人民赐给我，然后命我去领导，这就把国家和百姓当成了君主的私人财产。到如今，因为国家各处贫穷纷乱，人民生活困苦，危害到君主的权威利益，才不得不研究统治管理的方法。如果没有关系到朝廷的存亡，国家再贫穷纷乱、人民再困苦，即使是忠心的臣子，也会认为比起君主的利益这些只是微不足道的小问题罢了。古代做臣子的，是以天下万民为重呢，还是以君主一己之利益为重呢？

其实国家的安定混乱，关键不在于皇室一家一姓的兴亡，而是在于全国老百姓的忧患安乐。因此夏桀、商纣的灭亡，我们称之为国家走向稳定治理；秦始皇和蒙古人建立了统治，我们反称之为乱政；晋、宋、齐、梁各姓王朝的短暂兴亡，与天下兴亡、国家安定毫无关系。做臣子的如果不重视百姓的疾苦，即使能辅佐君王兴起，效忠国君牺牲性命，仍然与真正的为臣之道背道而驰。治理国家如同大家一起抬运巨型木材，在前面的人喊："嘿！"在后面的人跟着喊："嚯！"君主和臣下如同前后两个协力抬运木头的人，如果手不抓紧绳子，脚不站稳，后面的人只想着如何讨好前面的人，就算前面的抬木者非常卖力称职，这个木材终究是无法运走的。

唉！后世的君主多自以为是，不把天下百姓的利益当回事，他们于民间为自己选拔臣子，只不过是想要找供他驱使的人。得以应选任职之臣下，也只能干那些供君主驱使服役的事情。这些人因得任官职而能免于挨饿受冻，便感谢君主的知遇之恩，不再考虑这样做是否合乎君臣关系的真谛，而甘心成为君主的仆妾并无怨言。明朝万历初年，明神宗给予张居正比较高的礼遇，古时君主对待自己老师的礼遇像这样高的一百例中未能有一例。但当时人们论及此事都震惊于张居正居然接受这样的礼遇，是有失臣子对君主应有的尊重。要我说，张居正真正的过失在于恰恰不能理直气壮地充当神宗的老师，而受后宫宦官的左右。而后来却以无视皇帝、权高震主而治张居正罪。为什么？这是人们的思想意识长时期受旧式为臣之道的影响。无法想象其实臣下与君主虽名称不同，而效力国家、服务百姓的实质却是完全相同的。

三、放眼看世界

（一）放眼看世界概论

Viewing the World:

Lin Zexu (1785 – 1850) and Wei Yuan (1794 – 1856) .

Not quite a hundred years after the death of Gu Yanwu, the Qing scholar Wei Yuan was born. The intervening century had seen the Qing state grow to an unprecedented size through conquests in Central Asia. It incorporated roughly three times the physical area that had been ruled from Beijing in the Ming Dynasty, most of it in Central Asia. These conquests had been accomplished with the help of—and had helped to create—a loyal administrative elite, which by and large accepted the claim of the Qing ruling house to the mantle of patron and defender of the various cultural traditions of the empire, including those of Confucian scholarship. An orthodox Confucianism based on Song-Dynasty interpretations of the classics was supported by the state, although a critical tradition—tracing some of its lineages back to Gu Yanwu—called aspects of this orthodoxy into question, in part through close study of the texts of the classics in line with traditions that were held to date to the Western Han Dynasty. At the same time, partly in response to the challenges of holding together the territorial structure that the Qing had created in the late 18th and early 19th centuries, a tradition of scholarship with a focus on concrete problems of governance, referred to in English as statecraft scholarship, became more prominent. Wei Yuan came to be strongly associated with this tradition which, like the tradition of empirical textual scholarship, could be traced back to Gu Yanwu.

The careers and the thought of Wei Yuan and Lin Zexu (who was older than Wei Yuan and more politically powerful but part of the same intellectual tradition, albeit less significant as a scholar) can be seen as involving the intersection of three different issues that had arisen from the developments of the 18th century and the challenges that were presented by new circumstances in the 19th century. One was the question of how the state should be administered, given its vast size and the complexity of its physical structures. Both Wei Yuan and Lin Zexu were interested in issues relating to the history, geography and administration of the territories in Central Asia which had been added to the Qing state in the 18th century (problems of war and defence naturally arose in their discussions of problems of state and territory). Another was the question of the maritime world. Historians have recently argued that the 18th century saw a boom in economic activity along the Chinese coast and into Southeast Asia that was driven by, and contributed to, the economic prosperity of the Qing state. One consequence of this was an increased engagement with states that had a strong interest in maritime commerce with the Qing, among whom the British became more and more significant from the early decades of the 19th century onwards. The final question involved the question of how the Chinese classics should be understood and how they should be related to the tasks of government.

For those who see the major story of the history of the Qing from the 19th century onwards as a matter of the twin issues of how traditional Chinese culture should adapt to modern structures and how China was to deal with people, ideas and objects that originated in the West, the chief importance of the careers of Wei Yuan and Lin Zexu lies in their involvement with the rising power of the British, and with the development of knowledge of the technologies, culture and institutions of Western Europe. Modern Chinese nationalism has taken Lin Zexu as one of its great heroes because of his involvement with the campaign to stop the commerce in opium, which led to the Opium War with the British. The Opium War, which led to the creation of new trading centres on the China coast and the establishment of a British colony in Hong Kong, has been used in the conventional periodization of Chinese history to mark the initiation of a new, modern era. In this narrative of Chinese history, the key features of the careers and thought of Wei Yuan and Lin Zexu lies in their perceived role as patriotic pioneers of the cause of adopting new knowledge for the strengthening of the country, the cause that has been the proper mission of upright officials between the 19th century and the present. The texts that are reproduced in this book are often seen as some of the first attempts to provide readers in Qing territory with information about the world of Western Europe that was the product of scholarly investigations done by men with traditional Chinese academic training. For those who adhere to a reading of modern Chinese history that is focused on the division between the traditional and the modern or between Chinese and Western learning, their writings either constitute the beginning of a new era or represent an example of the continuation of the old; they are seen either as pioneers of the modern enterprise of engaging with the learning of the west, or exponents of an established tradition of scholarship which analysed all phenomena within the moral and intellectual frameworks of the Confucian classics.

Lin and Wei's writings can be seen as the product of the intersection of the three key issues outlined above. First, they reflect the concern of those in the tradition of statecraft scholarship with the acquisition of knowledge relevant to the successful governance of the empire, especially as this e- volved in the context of the expanded imperial territory created by the Qing conquests in Central Asia. This involved the expansion of knowledge, in- cluding knowledge derived from sources outside the traditional canons of Chinese textual learning. This statecraft tradition was also concerned with the question of community self-governance as a way to maintain and fulfil Confucian ethical visions and to ensure the stability of the state, something that may have influenced their account of political institutions outside Chi- na, such as the British parliament. Second, they stress the importance of both the maritime world and the influences entering the Qing from the east- ern seaboard. Finally, their approach to texts and to the role of insights from the critical scholarship on the classics in their analysis of problems in the world in which they lived can be seen in their descriptions of phenome- na in foreign countries, which are presented according to intellectual tem- plates that can be found in Chinese histories and geographies from this peri- od that drew their inspiration from classical scholarship and contributed to legacies that would appear later in the 19th and 20th centuries.

Both republicans and monarchists have found it possible to assimilate the legacies of Wei Yuan and Lin Zexu. For the former, their commitment to the strength of the state, their questioning attitude to established knowle- dge, their interest in critical forms of scholarship and their attempt to re- sist foreign incursion can be seen as forerunners of republicanism. For the latter, their commitment to the dynasty and its institutions and their belief in a society organised around established local structures of authority, coupled with their willingness to integrate foreign knowledge into traditional conceptual and moral frameworks, makes them into supporters of monarchy—whether that support be conceived of as favouring the preservation or the modernization of monarchy's institutions. Wei and Lin could be seen as predecessors either of the Self-Strengthening officials who dominated the Qing state between the 1860s and the 1890s or the more radical Confucian reformers of the late 1890s.

Sources and Further Reading

Good biographical information on Lin Zexu and Wei Yuan can be found on pp. 511 – 515 and pp. 850 – 852 of Arthur W. Hummel (ed.), *Eminent Chinese of the Ch'ing Period*, Taipei: Ch'eng-Wen Publishing Company, 1967.

For a good account of the Opium War and of Wei Yuan and Lin Zexu's careers more broadly, see William T. Rowe, *China's Last Empire: The Great Qing*, Cambridge, Massachussetts, Belknap Press, 2009; this account takes the perspective that the Opium War was decisively important in China's encounter with the West and in China's modern history more generally. A classic account of Wei Yuan and Lin Zexu's careers within the frameworks of the "Western Impact" school is Immanuel C. Y. Hsü, The Rise of Modern China (fifth edition) New York: Oxford University Press, 1995. A good account of the Opium War can be found in Frederic Wakeman's article "The Canton trade and the Opium War" in John K. Fairbank (ed.), *The Cambridge History of China*, Volume 10, Part 1 Late Qichao, Cambridge: Cambridge University Press, 1978.

Accounts of Wei Yuan's place in Qing scholarly traditions can be found in Liang Ch'i-ch'ao, *Intellectual Trends in the Ch'ing Period* (trans. Immanuel C. Y. Hsu), Cambridge, Massachussetts: Harvard University Press, 1959. A more recent placing of Wei Yuan's scholarship in the tradition of Qing textual scholarship is Benjamin A. Elman, *From Philosophy to Philology: Intellectual and Social Aspects of Change in Late Imperial China*, Los Angeles: UCLA Press, 2001. An excellent description of the thought of Wei Yuan in the context of Statecraft thought can be found in the essay by Susan Mann Jones and Philip A. Kuhn, "Dynastic decline and the roots of rebellion " in John K. Fairbank (ed.), *The Cambridge History of China*, Volume 10, Part 1 *Late Ch'ing*, Cambridge: Cambridge University Press, 1978. Jane Kate Leonard, *Wei Yuan and China's Rediscovery of the Maritime World*, Cambridge, Massachusetts: Harvard University Press, 1984, contextualises Wei Yuan in terms of the Qing Dynasty's relationship with Southeast Asia. Representative of the older concept of Wei Yuan and Lin Zexu's thought within the history of modernisation and the "impact of the west" paradigm are Ssu-yü Teng and John K. Fairbank, *China's Response to the West: A Documentary Survey*, 1839 – 1923 Cambridge, Massachusetts: Harvard University Press, 1954 and the essay "The Beginnings of China's Modernization" in Kwang-Ching Liu (ed. Yung-Fa Chen and Kuang-che Pan), *China's Early Modernization and Reform Movement: Studies in Late Nineteenth-Century China and American-Chinese Relations*, Vol. 1, Taipei: Academia Sinica, 2009.

（二）放眼看世界文献

（1）四洲志[1]（节选）

林则徐[2]

英吉利国总记（节选）

英吉利又曰英伦，又曰兰顿。先本荒岛，辟地居处始自弗兰西[3] 之人。因戈瓦伦[4] 产锡最佳，遂有商舶往贸。于耶稣末纪年以前，蛮分大小三十种。居于西者曰墨士厄[5]，居于北者曰木利庵斯[6]，居于南委力斯[7] 者曰西鲁力斯[8]，居于糯尔及萨濩[9] 者曰委力斯、曰矮西尼[10]，居于腹地景[11] 及弥特色斯者曰萨濩、曰埂底伊[12]。尚有诸蛮，俱居于弥特色斯。旧皆茹血、衣毛、文身。唯脉士厄数种，渐兴农事，创技艺，制器械，修兵车，各蛮效之。旋被意大里国征服，旋叛旋抚。

至耶稣纪年百五十年[13]（汉孝桓帝和平元年），分英地为七大部落[14]：曰景，曰舒色司[15]，曰依掩那司[16]，曰委屑司[17]，曰落藤马兰[18]，曰伊什[19]，曰麻可腊[20]。与邻部塞循各自治理[21]。八百年间（唐德宗贞元十六年），委屑司之伊末[22] 遂并和七部为一国[23]，始名英吉利，建都兰顿。从此不属意大里[24]。又二百年（宋真宗咸平三年），为领墨攻击，遂属领墨[25]。其后叛服不常。公举壹货为王[26]。传至显利二代王[27]，先得爱伦[28]，次得斯葛兰[29]。显利四代即弃加特力教，而尊波罗特士顿教[30]。至显利七代王[31]，娶依来西白刺[32] 为国郡，始革世袭之职，皆凭考取录用。开港通市，日渐富庶，遂为欧罗巴大国。

职官：

有律好司[33]衙门，管理各衙门事务，审理大讼。额设罗压尔录司[34]四人，厄治弥索司[35]四人，爱伦厄治弥所司一人，录司[36]二十一人，马诡色司[37]十九人，耳弥司[38]百有九人，委尔司高文司[39]十八人，弥所司[40]二十四人，爱伦弥所司三人，马伦司[41]百八十一人，斯葛兰比阿司[42]十六人，即在斯葛兰部属选充，三年更易；爱伦比阿司二十八人，即在爱伦部属选充，统计四百二十六人。有事离任，许荐一人自代。凡律好司家人犯法，若非死罪，概免收禁。

有巴厘满[43]衙门，额设甘弥底阿付撒布来[44]士一人，专辖水陆兵丁；甘弥底阿付委士庵棉[45]士一人，专司赋税，凡遇国中有事，甘文好司至此会议。有甘文好司[46]理各部落之事，并赴巴厘满衙门会议政事。由英吉利议举四百七十一名，内派管大部落者百四十三名，管小部落者三百二十四名，管教读并各技艺馆者四名。由委尔士议举五十三名[47]，内派管大部落者三十名，管小部落者二十三名。由爱伦议举百有五名，内派管大部落者六十四名，管小部落者三十九名，管教读并各技艺馆者二名。统共六百五十八名，各由各部落议举殷实老成者充之。与国中有事，即传集部民至国都巴厘满会议。嗣因各部民不能俱至，故每部落各举一二绅耆至国会议，事毕各回。后复议定公举之人常往甘文好司衙门办事，国家亦给以薪水。

有布来勿冈色尔[48]衙门掌理机密之事，供职者先立誓后治事。

有加密列冈色尔[49]衙门，额设十二名，各有执事，曰法士律阿付厘特利沙利[50]（管库官），曰律占色拉[51]（管官），曰律布来西尔[52]（管印官），曰不列士顿阿付冈色尔[53]（管官），曰色吉力达厘阿付士迭火厘火伦厘拔盟[54]（管官），曰色吉力达厘阿付士迭火哥罗尼士奄窝[55]（管官），曰占色拉阿付厘士支厥[56]（管官），曰法士律阿付押弥拉尔底[57]（管官），曰马士达依尼罗付厘曷南士[58]（管官），曰布力士顿阿付离墨阿付观特罗尔[59]（管官），曰占色腊阿付离律治阿付兰加司达[60]（管官）。

占色利[61]衙门专管审理案件，额设律海占色腊[62]一名，司掌印判事之职；委士占色腊[63]一名，司判事之职；马士达阿付离罗士[64]十一名，司判事之职。每判事，二人轮值，周而复始。扼冈顿依尼拉尔[65]司理算法之职。

有经士冕治[66]衙厂专司审理上诉案件，额设知付质治[67]一名，布依士尼质治[68]三名。

有甘文布列[69]衙门专审理职官[70]争控之案，额设知付质治溢士知加[71]衙门专审理田土婚姻之案，额设知付马伦[72]一名，布依士马伦[73]三名。

有阿西士庵尼西布来阿士[74]衙门，额设撒久[75]六，每撒久设质治[76]二名，共十二名，专司审讯英吉利人犯。每年二次。有依尼拉尔戈达些孙阿付厘比士[77]衙门，每年审讯各部落人犯四次。有舍腊达文[78]衙门。此官职掌原缺。有历[79]衙门，每年派马落[80]百人，稽查各部落地方是否安静，归则具结一次。

······

政事：

凡国王将嗣位，则官民先集巴厘满衙门会议。必新王必背加特力教而尊波罗特士教始即位。国中有大事，王及官民俱至巴厘满衙门公议乃行。大事则三年始一会议，设有用兵和战之事，虽国王裁夺，亦必由巴厘满议允。国王行事有失，将成行之人交巴厘满议罚。凡新改条例，新设职官、增减税饷及行楮币[81]，皆王颁巴厘满转行甘文好司而分布之。惟除授大臣及刑官，则权在国王。各管承行之事，得失勤怠，每岁终会核于巴厘满，而行其黜陟。

······

注释：

1.《四洲志》由林则徐组织编译。将英国人穆瑞（Hugh Murray）编著的《地理大全》（*The Encyclopedia of Geography*）择要译出，经精心编辑而成。简要叙述了世界五大洲 30 多个国家的地理、历史和政治状况，是近代中国第一部相对完整、比较系统的世界地理志书。林则徐编译《四洲志》主要目的在于通过了解世界情况，寻求抵抗英国侵略的方策。《四洲志》实为开风气之先的创举，而编译组织者林则徐也因此举被后人称为中国开眼看世界第一人。《四洲志》于 1842 年被魏源辑入《海国图志》，至今未发现其原始版本。本篇引自魏源《海国图志》卷五十，〈大西洋欧罗巴州·英吉利国总记（原本）〉，岳麓书社 1998 年出版的点校注释本。

2. 见上篇林则徐奏疏注释。

3. 弗兰西：指高卢（Gaul）。

4. 戈伦瓦：康沃尔（Cornwall）。

5. 墨士厄：指贝尔加埃（Belgae）人。

6. 指市里甘特（Brigantes）人。

7. 南委力斯（South Wales），南威尔士。

8. 西鲁力斯，指锡鲁雷（Silures）人。

9. 萨濩（Suffolk），又作萨贺，即萨福克。

10. 矮西尼（Iceni），指伊切尼人。

11. 景（Kent），肯特。

12. 埂底伊（Cantii），指坎蒂伊人。

13. 据《海国图志》注，此处误译，提前了几百年。

14. 七大部落：即公元七世纪英国历史上的"七国时代"。

15. 疏色斯（Sussex），苏萨克斯。

16. 依掩那司（East Englas），东英格拉斯。

17. 委屑司（Wessex），韦萨克斯。

18. 落藤马兰（Northumberland），诺森伯兰。

19. 伊什（Essex），埃塞克斯。

20. 麻可腊（Mercryc/Mercia），默克里克。

21. 据《海国图志》注，英文原著并无此语。

22. 伊末（Egbert），埃格伯。

23. 今译爱格伯特，于 827 年曾一度在名义上统治七国。

24. 据《海国图志》注，英文原著亦无此语。

25. 1017 年丹麦克努特政府攻占英国全境，即宋真宗天禧九年。

26. Edward the Confessor，今译爱德华（1042—1066），英国国王。

27. 显利二代：今译亨利二世（1133—1189），英国国王（1154—1189）建立金雀花王朝。

28. 今译爱尔兰。

29. 今译苏格兰。

30. 据《海国图志》注，英国放弃天主教改尊新教，应该晚于此时。

31. 今译亨利七世，通称亨利·都铎（1457—1509），英国国王（1485—1509），建立都铎王朝。

32. 依来西白剌（Elizabeth），伊丽莎白。

33. 律好司（House of Lords），贵族院，上议院。

34. 罗压尔录司（Royal dukes），大公（封公爵王子）。

35. 厄治弥索司（Archbishops），大主教。

36. 录司（Dukes with English Titles），英衔公爵。

37. 马诡色司（Marquesses），侯爵。

38. 耳弥司（Earls），伯爵。

39. 委尔司高文司（Viscounts），子爵。

40. 弥所司（Bishops），主教。

41. 马伦司（Barons），男爵。

42. 比阿司（Peers），贵族。

43. 巴厘满（Parliament），议会、国会。

44. 甘弥底阿付撒布来（Committee of Supply），预算委员会。

45. 甘弥底阿付委士庵棉士（Committee of Ways and Means），财政委员会。

46. 甘文好司（House of Commons），众议院、下议院。

47. 今译威尔士。

48. 布来勿冈色尔（Privy of Council），枢密院。

49. 加密列冈色尔（Cabinet Council），内阁会议。

50. 法士律阿付厘特私沙私（First lord of the Treasury），首相。

51. 律古占色拉（lord Chancellor），大法官。

52. 律布来西尔（Lord Privy Seal），掌玺大臣。

53. 不列士顿阿付冈色尔（President of the Council），枢密院议长。

54. 色吉力达厘阿付土迭火厘火伦厘拔盟（Secretary of State for the Home Department），内政大臣。

55. 色吉力达厘阿付士迭火哥罗尼士奄窝（Secretary of State for Colonies and War），殖民地和陆军大臣。

56. 占色拉阿付厘士支厥（Chancellor of Exchequer），财政大臣。

57. 法士律阿付押弥拉尔底（First Lord of the Admiralty），海军大臣。

58. 马士达依尼罗付厘曷南士（Master-general of the Ordnance），军械大臣。

59. 布力士顿阿付离墨阿付观特罗尔（President of the Board of Control），监督大臣。

60. 占色腊阿付离律治阿付兰加司达（Chancellor of the Duchy of Lancaster），代表英王龄兰开斯特公。

61. 占色利（The High Court of Chancery），最高法院。

62. 律海占色腊（Lord Chancellor），大法官。

63. 委士占色腊（Vice-Chancellor of England），英格兰副大法官。

64. 马士达阿付离罗士（Master of Rolls），记录推事。

65. 扼冈顿依尼拉尔（Accountant-General），主计。

66. 经士冕治（King's Bench），高等法院。

67. 知付质治（Chief Justice），审判长。

68. 布依士尼质治（Puisné Judge），陪席推事。

69. 甘文布列（Court of Common Pleas），高等民事法庭。

70. 职官应为民事。

71. 溢士知加（Exchequer），税务法院。

72. 知付马伦（Chief-baron），审判长。

73. 布依士马伦（Puisné Baron），陪席推事。

74. 阿西士庵尼西布来阿士（Court of Assize and Nisi Prius），巡回裁判法庭。

75. 撒久（Circuit），巡回裁判所。

76. 质治（judge），推事。

77. 依尼拉尔戈达些孙阿付厘比士（Court of General Quarter Sessions of the Peace），
   季度法庭。

78. 舍腊达文（the sheriff's tourn），州（郡）法庭。

79. 历（leet），（封建领主设立的）民事法庭。

80. 马落（Manor），领主。

81. 即由政府金融机构发行的纸币。

译文：

四洲志（节选）

林则徐

英吉利国总记（节选）

英国又称英伦，也称伦敦。早先英伦三岛是蛮荒之地，高卢人是最初
在这里开辟土地定居于此的。康沃尔地区因为盛产锡，而开始有了商船往

来贸易。在公元纪年之前，这里居住的土著民部落大大小小有三十余族。居住于西部地区的是贝尔加埃人，居住于北部地区的是市里甘特人，居住于南威尔士的是锡鲁雷人，居住在萨福克的是伊切尼人，居住在肯特的是坎蒂伊人。另外还有些部族，都居住在弥特色斯。古代落后时，人们食生肉，以野兽皮毛为衣，而且流行文身的习俗。只有脉士厄等几个部族开始发展农业和手工技术，制造机械和兵车等等，而其他部族也相继效法。随后英伦三岛被罗马人征服，各部族人时时掀起反抗，反对罗马人的统治。

到公元一百五十年（相当于中国汉朝孝桓帝和平元年），英伦三岛上分出七个相互割据大部落，分别是：肯特部、苏萨克斯部、东英格拉斯部、韦萨克斯部、诺森伯兰部、埃塞克斯部和默克里克部。相互独立，各自治理。到公元八百年时（相当于唐代德宗贞元十六年），韦萨克斯部的埃格伯把七国合并为一国，开始称为英格兰，在伦敦建都。从此摆脱罗马帝国的统治。又过了二百年（相当于宋朝真宗咸平三年）为丹麦攻击，此后从属于丹麦。这期间英国人有时屈从有时反叛，丹麦人的统治并不稳定。后来英伦各部共同推举爱德华为英国国王，传位到英王亨利二世时，先吞并爱尔兰，后来又吞并了苏格兰。到了英王亨利四世时，即放弃了天主教，而皈依基督教。到英王亨利七世时，娶伊丽莎白为王妃。开始革除世系制，所有政府官职一律通过考试录用。开港通商，越来越发达强盛，逐渐成为欧洲的大国。

英国国家机构及官职设置：

英国国家设有上议院（贵族院），统理国家各机构事务，审理裁决重大诉讼案件。上议院设员为：设大公四个席位，设大主教四个席位，设爱尔兰大主教四个席位，设英格兰授衔公爵席位四员，设侯爵十九个席位，设伯爵一百零九个席位。设威尔士授衔子爵十八个席位，设主教二十四个席位，设爱尔兰主教席位三员。设男爵一百八十一个席位。设苏格兰贵族十六个席位，此十六席由苏格兰地区选送，三年一更换。设爱尔兰贵族席位二十八个，此二十八席也由爱尔兰地区选送。上议院总共设有四百二十六个席位。上议院议员如因时离任，允许其推荐一人接替其职任。上议院议员家属犯罪，如果不是死刑，可豁免监禁之罚。

英国国家另设有国会（议会），国会下设常任机构预算委员会，负责掌管海军和陆军的编制问题；另一个常任机构为财政委员会，专门负责国家的财政税收事务。遇到国家有重大事务，下议院（众议院）的议员便集中到国会开会集议。

下议院主要统理联邦国家各地区的地方事务，而且定期在国会召集会议。下议院设立的席位：英格兰占四百七十一席，其中中央地区占一百四十三个席位，地方共占有三百二十四个席位，文教艺术部门占四个席位。下议院中，威尔士占据五十三个席位，中央地区占三十个席位，地方占二十三个席位。爱尔兰占据一百零五个席位，中央地区占六十四个席位，地方占三十九个席位，文教艺术部门占两个席位。下议院一共有六百五十八个席位，分别由各地选拔当地具有经济实力和品德敦厚者出任。每逢国家有大事，即通知各地议员集中到国会开会集议。平时各地议员不可能逢事必到齐，就由各地选举一两名德高望重的议员到国会定期参加会议，会议一结束，即各回各地。后来由各地议会选举专人，定期来国会议事，由国家支付薪水。

英国还设有枢密院，掌管国家机密重事，枢密院的所有职员都要先宣誓，然后方可任职工作。

还设有内阁会议机构，设阁员十二名，各自有其行政职掌。有首相、大法官、掌玺大臣、枢密院议长、内政大臣、殖民地陆军大臣、财政大臣、海军大臣、军械大臣、监督大臣及代表英国国王的兰开斯特公。

设有最高法院专管审理案件，设有大法官一名，专司掌印裁决审判；设英格兰副大法官一名，掌裁决审判事务；设秘书十一名，协管裁决审判事务。设有讼狱，分别由两员秘书任事，十二人轮流，周而复始。另设主计一员，主管诉讼统计之类事务。

设有高等法院，专管审理判决上诉案件，设有审判长一名，副审判长三名。

设有高等民事法庭，专门审理判决民事诉讼案件。下设税务法院，专门审理土地产案及婚姻诉讼案件。设有审判长三名。

另设有巡回裁判法庭，下设巡回裁判所六个，每一巡回裁判所设法官，六个巡回裁判所共十名法官，专门审理判决英国犯人。每年开庭两次。还设有季度法庭，每年四次开庭，审判各地区犯人。还设有州（郡）级法庭。设有封建领主的民事法庭。每年派各地封建领主百余人，巡回勘察各部落地区治安是否安定，考察归来后，作详尽报告。

……

政事运作程序：

每逢国王即位时，召集上议院、下议院议员在国会集议。新任国王必须信奉基督教而非天主教，方可即位。每逢国家有大事，国王与上议院、下议院议员共同议定，方可执行。国家大事，每三年会同公议决定。如果遇到与他国战争或媾和之军国重事，虽然国王做出决议，必须经由国会准允方可执行。倘国王行政事有失误，对此事主要责任人交由国会裁判处罚。凡是有关修改法律条款、新设官职、增加或减免税务和军饷，及发行货币等事项，皆由国王颁令，由国会具体执行。只有任免大臣和刑法官员由国王直接任命。所有官僚的工作，诸如业绩与失误，勤奋与否，每年由国会考稽，最终确定其升迁或贬斥。

……

（2）粤东章奏一[1]（节选）

林则徐[2]

道光十九年十二月十一日：

……

臣等查粤东二百年来，准令诸夷互市，原系推恩外服，普示怀柔，并非内地赖其食用之资，更非关榷利其抽分之税。况自上冬断绝英夷贸易以来，叠奉谕旨，区区税银，何足记论？大哉谟训，中外同钦。臣等有所秉承，无所用其瞻顾。惟将各国在粤贸易，一律停止，则有尚须从长计议者。

窃以封关禁海之策，一以杜绝鸦片之来源，虽若确有把握，然专断一国贸易，与概断各国贸易，揆理度势，迥不相同。盖鸦片出产之地，皆在英吉利国所辖地方，从前例禁宽时，原不止英夷贩烟来粤，即别国夷船，亦多以此为利。而自上年缴清趸船[3]烟土以后，业经奏奉恩旨，概免治罪，即未追究前非。此后别国货船，莫不遵具切结，层层查验，并无夹带鸦片，乃准进口开舱。惟英吉利货船，聚泊尖沙嘴，不遵法度，是以将其驱逐，不准通商。今若忽立新章，将现未犯法之各国夷船，与英吉利一同拒绝，是抗违者摈[4]之，恭顺者亦摈之，未免不分良莠，事出无名。设诸夷者禀问何辜？臣等即碍难批示。

且查有英吉利在外国，最称强悍，诸夷中惟美利坚及佛朗西尚足与之抗衡，然亦忌且惮之。其他若荷兰、大小吕宋[5]、连国[6]、瑞国[7]、单鹰[8]、双鹰[9]等国，到粤贸易者，多仰英夷鼻息。自英夷贸易断后，他国皆欣欣向荣。盖逐利者喜彼绌而此赢，怀忿者谓此荣而彼辱。此中控驭之法，似可以夷治夷，使其相间相睽，以彼此之离心，各输忱而内向。若盖与之绝，则觖望[10]之后，转易联成一气，勾结图私。《左传》有云：彼则惧而协以谋我，故难间也。[11]我朝之驭夷，故非其比。要亦罚不及众，仍宜示以大公。且封关云者，为断鸦片也。若鸦片果因封关而断，亦何惮而不为？惟是大海茫茫，四通八达，鸦片断与不断，转不在乎关之封与不封。

即如上冬以来，已不准英夷贸易，而臣等今春查访外洋信息，知其将货物载回夷埠，转将烟土换至粤洋。并闻奸夷口出狂言，谓关以内法度虽严，关以外汪洋无际，通商则受管束，而不能禁违；不通商择不受管束，而正好卖烟。此种贪狡之心，实堪令人发指。是以臣等近日不得不于各海口倍加严拿，有一日而船烟并获数起者。可见英夷货去烟来之言，转非虚拟。

·······

　　至于备火船，练乡勇，募善泅之人，则臣等自上年至今，皆经筹商办理，惟待相机而动。即各山淡水，上年本以派弁守之。始则夷船以帆布兜接雨水，几于不能救渴；继而觅诸山麓，随处汲取不穷，则已守不胜守，似毋庸议。

　　总之驭夷宜刚柔互用，不必视之太重，亦未便视之太轻。与其泾渭不分，转至无所忌惮，何若薰莸[12]有别，俾皆就我范围；而且用诸国则不啻殴渔[13]，此际机宜，不敢不慎。况所杜绝者惟在鸦片，即原奏亦云：凡有夹带鸦片夷船，无论何国，不准通商。则不带鸦片者，仍皆准予通商，亦以明甚。彼各国夷人，原难保其始终不带，若果查出夹带，应即治以新例，不但绝其经商，如其无之，自不在峻拒之列也。

······

注释:

1. 此篇奏折是林则徐出任两广总督主持禁烟事的第二年（道光十九年十二月）所上，其主要内容是关于通商政策上区别对待各国，以达到孤立英国和有效禁绝鸦片的目的。本篇摘引自魏源《海国图志》卷七十八，〈筹海总论二·粤东章奏一〉，岳麓书社 1998 年出版的点校注释本。

2. 林则徐（1785—1850），汉族，福建侯官人（今福建省福州），字元抚，又字少穆、石麟，晚号俟村老人、俟村退叟、七十二峰退叟、瓶泉居士、栎社散人等。是清朝后期杰出的政治家、思想家和诗人，是中华民族抵御外辱过程中伟大的民族英雄，其主要功绩是虎门销烟。官至一品，曾任江苏巡抚、两广总督、湖广总督、陕甘总督和云贵总督，两次受命为钦差大臣。林则徐出任两广总督时曾主持编译《四洲志》，为中国开眼看天下第一人。其主张严禁鸦片、抵抗西方的侵略、坚持维护中国主权和民族利益深受全世界中国人的敬仰。

3. 趸船：无动力装置的平底船，固定在岸边、码头，以供驳船停靠，上下旅客、装卸货物。

4. 摈：排斥、遗弃。

5. 吕宋：西班牙。

6. 连国：丹麦。《海国图志》为嗹国，又称领墨。

7. 瑞国：瑞典。

8. 单鹰国：德国。《海国图志》为普鲁社国。

9. 双鹰国：奥地利。

10. 触望：不满、怨恨。

11. 语见《左传·桓公》："我张吾三军，而被吾甲兵，以武临之，彼则惧而协以谋我，故难间也。"

12. 薰莸：薰，香草；莸，臭草。香草与臭草要有所区别，比喻分清好坏。

13. 殴渔：殴，同"驱"。

译文：

粤东章奏一（节选）

林则徐

道光十九年十二月十一日：

......

臣下通过调查得知，广东开通为对外通商口岸已二百年了。与海外各国通商之本意是对臣服大清王朝的海外各国展示恩惠和关怀，并非我大清国经济命脉依赖于此，更不是看上其微小的关税之利。况且自去年冬天与英国断绝贸易以来，皇上屡屡下达圣旨强调不要在乎关税小利。皇上的英明论断何等伟大，四海遵奉，臣下贯彻执行，毫不含糊。只是将各国在广东的贸易全部封闭，此事应该从更长远的利益加以考虑。

我个人认为，封关海禁政策，一方面断绝外国人的利益之所在，另一方面杜绝鸦片入口的来源。虽然效果显著，然而断绝一国贸易与封闭与所有国家的贸易从理论上和当前形势来讲都是截然不同的。因为，鸦片出产之地都在英国管辖的地区。从前正常通商时，确实不仅仅是英国在广东贩卖鸦片，其他国家商船也多从贩卖鸦片中获利。但自去年查缴各国船坞储存鸦片之后，经由皇上批示一律赦免其罪，而且对以往贩烟行为不予追究。此后其他国家的商船全都依照禁烟法令行事。在经过严格查验后，并没有发现夹带鸦片的情况下，准许其进关开仓卸货。只有英国商船，聚集在尖沙嘴一带，不遵守禁烟法令，所以将其驱逐，不准其进港通商。现在如果突然推行新法，将现在没有违反禁烟法令的各国商船与英国商船一同拒绝通商，等于是违反禁烟者禁止通商，未违反禁烟者也禁止通商，不分好坏一律对待，有失原则。如果没有违反禁烟法令的国家抱怨为何禁止他们通商，我们的确无法明确应对。

据调查，英国在海外，最为强大，海外各国中只有美国和法国能与英国抗衡，但也心存惧怕。其他国家像荷兰、西班牙、丹麦、瑞典、德国和奥地利等来广东贸易的国家，都听从英国的指手画脚。自从断绝了与英国的贸易之后，其他各国都兴高采烈的。从利益上讲，是能从英国对我国贸易的损失中获得好处。而对英国怀有怨愤的国家，则幸灾乐祸。这实际上类似于以夷治夷的对外控制之法，使各国互相牵制，造成他们之间的矛盾，他们就都来讨好我大清国了。如果把他们一律断绝，令他们全都失去希望，反而使他们联合在一起，相互勾结而牟利。《左传》中有这样一句话："把敌方逼迫太甚使之惧怕，他们就会相互勾结来与我对抗，到那时想离间他们便很困难了。"我大清王朝驾驭海外各国的情况还不同于《左传》中所讲的那样。关键是不要惩罚太广，要表示出公平。而且，封闭贸易的目的就在于禁止鸦片入口。如果鸦片真的能够因封闭贸易而禁绝，那还顾虑什么？问题是海洋太广阔了，四通八达，鸦片是否能禁绝，并不在于是否封闭贸易。

去年冬天到现在，一直不准英国来华贸易，我于今年春天调查海外各国情况，得知英国已将货物运回自己的港口，而把鸦片运到广东沿海。英国奸商口出狂言说，广东关口之内禁烟之法虽严格，但海关以外海域太广阔了，规规矩矩通商受法令的约束，不敢违反；但不通商而走私则不受法令的约束，正好利用这个漏洞贩卖鸦片。这种贪婪和狡诈真令人愤怒啊！由此臣下最近不得不在广东各海口严查抓捕，有时于一天之内逮捕数艘贩卖鸦片的船只。可见英国运走货物、运来鸦片的说法属实，并不是传闻。

……

关于筹备军舰、训练部队、招募擅长游泳的人这些措施，我从去年到现在，都已筹备商议办妥，见机行动。广东各个山上的淡水水源，我已于今年派兵控制。由此，英国商船开始用帆布接雨水，几乎都不能维持饮用，而后他们到各个山麓寻找水源，已经坚持不下去了，这些都不必讲了。

总而言之，驾驭外国列强应该刚柔并用，不必把他们太看重了，但也不可轻视他们。如果不能分清好坏敌友，反而使对方无所顾忌。不如把他们区别对待，使他们在我们的掌控之中；而且对付各国不仅仅是驱逐笼络那般简单，其中讲求的策略，要谨慎从事才是。何况所要禁绝的只是鸦片，就像上篇奏本所说的：凡有于货物中偷偷夹带鸦片的船只，无论哪国的，都不准通商。而没有夹带鸦片的船只，一律准许通商，已经非常明确了。各国的商船，本来很难保证他们不夹带鸦片，如果查出夹带鸦片的，应该按照禁烟新法令加以惩处，不是仅仅不准通商的问题了。而那些没有夹带鸦片的各国商船，就不应该严厉拒绝其通商。

……

（3）海国图志叙[1]（节选）

魏源[2]

《海国图志》六十卷，何所据？一据前两广总督林尚书所译西夷之《四洲志》[3]，再据历代史志，及明以来岛志，及近日夷图、夷语[4]，钩稽贯串，创榛辟莽，前驱先路[5]。大都东南洋、西南洋，增于原书者十之八；大、小西洋、北洋、外大西洋增于原书者十之六。又图以经之，表以纬之，博参群议以发挥之。

何以异于昔人海图之书？曰：彼皆以中土人谭西洋，此则以西洋人谭西洋也。是书何以作？曰：为以夷攻夷而作，为以夷款夷而作[6]，为师夷长技以制夷而作。《易》曰："爱恶相攻而吉凶生，远近相取而悔吝生，情伪相感而利害生。"[7] 故同一御敌，而知其形与不知其形，利害相百焉；同一款敌，而知其情与不知其情，利害相百焉。古之驭外夷者[8]，诹以敌形，形同几席；诹以敌情，情同寝馈[9]。

然则执此书即可驭外夷乎？曰：唯唯，否否！此兵机也，非兵本也；有形之兵也，非无形之兵也。明臣有言："欲平海上之倭患，先平人心之积患。"人心之积患如之何？非水，非火，非刃，非金，非沿海之奸民，非吸烟贩烟之莠民。故君子读《云汉》、《车攻》[10]，先于《常武》、《江汉》[11]，而知《二雅》[12]诗人之所发愤；玩卦爻内外消息[13]，而知大《易》作者之所忧患[14]。愤与忧，天道所以倾否而之泰也[15]，人心所以违寐而之觉也[16]，人才所以革虚而之实也。

昔准噶尔跳踉于康熙、雍正之两朝，而电扫于乾隆之中叶[17]。夷烟流毒，罪万辈夷。吾皇仁勒，上符列祖，天时人事，倚伏相乘。何患攘剔之无期？何患奋武之无会？此凡有血气者所宜愤悱，凡有耳目心知者所宜讲画也。去伪，去饰，去畏难，去养痈[18]，去营窟[19]，则人心之寐患祛，其一。以实事程实功，以实功程实事，艾三年而蓄之[20]，网临渊而结之[21]，毋冯河[22]，毋画饼[23]，则人材之虚患祛，其二。寐患去而天日昌，虚患去而风雷行。传曰："孰荒于门，孰治于田？四海既均，越裳是臣。"[24]叙海国图志。

注释：

1.《海国图志叙》作于 1842 年。魏源在《海国图志叙》中首先提出"师夷长技以制夷"的口号，他认为必须学习西方"船坚炮利"的军事技术，才能抵御敌人的侵略。同时他又认为为了反对外国侵略，使国家强盛，首先必须改革国内弊政。

2. 魏源（1794—1857），清代启蒙思想家、政治家、文学家，近代中国"睁眼看世界"的先行者之一。名远达，字默深，又字墨生、汉士，号良图，汉族，湖南邵阳隆回人，道光二年举人，二十五年始成进士，官高邮知州，晚年弃官归隐，潜心佛学，法名承贯。魏源认为论学应以"经世致用"为宗旨，提出"变古愈尽，便民愈甚"的变法主张，倡导学习西方先进科学技术，总结出"师夷之长技以制夷"的新思想。

3. 林尚书，即两广总督林则徐。清制，凡总督皆加兵部尚书衔。1839 年林则徐请人翻译英人慕瑞（HughMurray）所著《世界地理大全》，辑成《四洲志》。魏源编辑《海国图志》时，曾根据《四洲志》作为主要参考资料，并根据史志、岛志等加以扩编而成。

4. 史志，指二十四史中的四夷传、《通典》中的《边防典》、《通志》中的《四夷传》、《通考》中的《四裔考》等。明以后岛志，如黄衷《海语》、张燮《东西洋考》、利玛窦《坤舆图说》、艾儒略《职方外纪》及清王大海《海岛逸志》等。夷图，指外文地图；夷语，指外文著作。

5. 创榛辟莽，指开辟荒芜，做前人没有做过的工作。前驱先路，是说他自己领先撰写别人没有写过的书籍。

6. 款：讲和。

7. 语见《易·系辞》。

8. 驭：统率；控制。

9. 诹：咨询，了解。寝馈，寝食，吃住。

10. 《云汉》、《车攻》均为《诗经》中的篇名。《云汉》，《诗经·大雅》的首篇。原句"倬彼云汉，昭回于天。"云汉在诗中之意为银河。全诗通过比较详尽的叙写，具体深入地反映了西周末期那场大旱的严重，抒发了宣王为旱灾而愁苦的心情。《车攻》，《诗经·小雅》中的名篇。叙述周宣王在东都会同诸侯举行田猎的情形。二篇之引在于歌颂周宣王内修政事的文治业绩。

11. 《常武》、《江汉》：《诗经·大雅》篇名。两篇是歌颂周宣王兴衰拨乱的赫赫武功。

12. 《二雅》，指《诗经》中的《大雅》、《小雅》。上述四首诗，均在《二雅》中。

13. 爻，组成《易》卦的基本符号。《易·系辞》："爻象动乎内，吉凶见乎外。"原句意为，爻象在卦内起了变化，吉和凶就表现出来了。

14. 《易·系辞》："《易》之兴也，其于中古乎！作《易》者其有忧患乎！"

15. 《易·否卦》："上九，倾否，先否后喜。"否，《否卦》坤下乾上，《泰卦》乾下坤上，《否卦》反转来就是《泰卦》。否是闭塞，泰是亨通。这里是说发愤与忧虑可以变闭塞为亨通。

16. 违，作脱离解；寐，作蒙昧无知解。违寐，脱离蒙昧无知的状态。

17. 准噶尔，厄鲁特蒙古一部族，游牧于金伊犁河流域。跳踉，即跳梁，这是指该部上层贵族噶尔丹等勾结沙俄，制造分裂，侵袭青海、西藏，不断破坏统一。清朝为平息准噶尔叛乱，从康熙二十九年（1690）至乾隆二十二年（1757），多次用兵，始将其平定。

18. 痏：毒疮。养痏，是指明知毒疮在身，不肯开刀，让它愈养愈大。这里比喻墨守旧章，遗患无穷。

19. 营窟：指营谋私利。

20. 《孟子·离娄上》："犹七年之病，求三年之艾也。"艾可以灸人病，愈陈愈好。这里是比喻对外要有多年的准备。

21. 《汉书·董仲舒传》："临渊羡鱼，不如退而结网。"这里是说有好机会还要做好实际工作。

22. 《论语·述而》："暴虎冯河，死而无悔者，吾不与焉。"《论语正义》注："无舟渡河为冯河。"毋冯河，是说不要去干冒险的行动。

23. 《三国志·魏志·卢毓传》："选举莫取有名，名如画地作饼，不可啖也。"毋画饼，是说不要只图名而不务实。

24. 见韩愈所作《越裳操》。据《后汉书·南蛮西南夷列传》记载："交趾之南有越裳国。周公居摄六年，制礼作乐，天下和平，越裳以三象重译而献白雉。"作者此处引用韩愈诗句的意思是：只要老百姓安居乐业，天下无不均的现象，敌人就会向我们称臣。

译文：

海国图志叙（节选）

魏 源

《海国图志》全书共六十卷，其编纂所依据的材料基本上建立于两个来源：其一，据两广总督林则徐所编译的《四洲志》提供的材料。其次，据历代所修史书中有关海外的记述和明代以来所修各岛国的史志资料，以及海外出版的地图、海图和外文记载的有关资料等等。进行了大量的资料查询、核实与综合整理工作，终完成此前人未曾尝试之富于创建之作品。

总的来看，有关南太平洋地区方面的记载在原有资料的基础上增加了八成的内容，印度洋地区、渤海、黄海地区和大西洋方面的内容增加了六成。又辅助以海图、地图、表等材料，在广泛地参考了多方见识的基础之上创作而成。

若问本书与从前同类海外地理志方面的著作有何区别？回答是：从前这类图书都是以国人的眼界视角考查观察海外事务，这部书则是以海外人士的眼界视角观察讨论海外事务。若问此书编纂目的何在？回答是：为了利用西方列强的优势而对付西方列强，学习西方列强的先进技术而达到战胜西方列强目的。

《易经》有言："爱恶相攻而吉凶生，远近相取而悔吝生，情伪相感而利害生。"由此以见，同样是抵御外敌，了解其国势与不了解其国势，其效果相差千里；同样是与外敌修好，了解其国情与不了解其国情，其效果也是差之千里啊！

古人对付外敌的诀窍在于细致入微地了解外敌之国势，如同了解自己的茶几和卧席一样；了解外敌之国情与习性，就如同熟悉自己的起居饮食习惯一样。那么，有了这部书就解决了如何对付列强的问题了吗？并非如此！这部书所解决的只是战术方面的问题，并非制胜的战略方面的问题；只是给出了具体的作战之法，还不是用兵制胜的保证。明代有大臣曾说过：欲彻底平定东南沿海的日本海盗骚扰之患，必须先清除长期以来桎梏人心的蔽障。所谓人心蔽障是什么呢？并非水患、火灾；也不是争斗仇杀和财富的欲望所引发；更不是海盗和贩卖吸食鸦片的恶人所能制造。所以贤明的智者读《诗经》中各篇歌颂周王文治武功的篇章，就能从中感受到《大雅》、《小雅》作者们的感慨激奋；研究《易经》，以卜相的变化预测吉凶，就能体察出《易经》作者的忧患意识。有此激奋情绪和忧患意识，便可以改变天道，开创局面，使壅蔽化为畅通。人心便可冲破蒙昧而达到觉悟，人的才能便可真正发挥作用。

当年于康熙、雍正朝蒙古准噶尔部作乱，于乾隆朝中叶彻底平定，而现今西方鸦片之泛滥其罪孽甚于准噶尔叛乱不下千万倍。皇上开明勤政，振兴列祖列宗开创之基业，得天时人和之势，还怕鸦片之患不能革除？还怕文治武功之宏图大业不能实现？有血性的人都应振奋精神，发奋努力；有头脑良知的人都应出谋划策，宣传策动。革除虚假浮华之风，破除畏难懦弱情绪，敢于革新，去除结党营私之弊病，人心的蔽障就会消除。

　　首先，做扎实的工作以建立实际的功效，再以实际的功效带动实际工作的开展，持之以恒则必见成就。就如同渔家周密布网，不蛮干，不务虚，则人材的冗滥混杂之弊便可立除。而后，人心之蔽障除，则国势日渐昌盛；人材冗滥之弊除，则雷厉风行之作风盛。这就如同古人诗句中赞颂周公业绩的那样：人民安定乐业，举国上下治理有方，井然有序，则外敌自然前来朝拜称臣。

　　仅以上述议论做为《海国图志》序言。

（4）海国图志[1]（节选）

筹海篇三：议战（节选）

魏源[2]

海国图志卷二邵阳魏源重辑
筹海篇三议战

......

　　今日之事，苟有议征用西洋兵舶者，则必曰借助外夷恐示弱，及一旦示弱数倍于此，则甘心而不辞；使有议置造船械师夷长技者，则曰糜费，及一旦糜费十倍于此，则又谓权宜救急而不足惜；苟有议翻夷书、刺夷事者，则必曰多事。（嘉庆间，广东有将汉字夷字对音刊成一书者，甚便于华人之译字，而粤吏禁之。）则一旦有事，则或询英夷国都与俄罗斯国都相去远近，或询英夷何路可通回部，甚至廓夷[3]效顺，请攻印度而拒之，佛兰西、弥利坚[4]愿助战舰，愿代请款[5]而疑之。以通市二百年之国，竟莫知其方向，莫悉其离合，尚可谓留心边事者乎？

　　汉用西域攻匈奴，唐用吐番攻印度，用回纥攻吐番；圣祖[6]用荷兰夹板船攻台湾，又联络俄罗斯以逼准噶尔。古之驭外夷者，惟防其协寇[7]以谋我，不防其协我而攻寇也；止防中华情事之泄于外，不闻禁外国情形之泄于华也。然则欲制外夷者，必先悉夷情始；欲悉夷情者，必先立译馆翻夷书始；欲造就边才者，必先用留心边事之督抚始。

问曰：既款之后，如之何？曰：武备之当振，不系乎夷之款与不款。既款以后，夷瞰我虚实，藐我废弛，其所以严武备、绝狡启者，尤当倍急于未款之时；所以惩具文、饰善后者，尤当倍甚于承平之日。未款之前，则宜以夷攻夷；既款之后，则宜师夷长技以制夷。

夷之长技三：一战舰，二火器，三养兵、练兵之法。请陈国朝前事：康熙初，曾调荷兰夹板船以剿台湾矣，曾命西洋南怀仁制火炮以剿三藩矣，曾行取西洋人入钦天监以司历官矣[8]。今夷人[9]既以据香港、拥厚赀骄色于诸夷，又以开各埠、裁各费德色[10]于诸夷。与其使英夷德之以广其党羽，曷若自我德之以收其指臂？

考东、中二印度据于英夷，其南印度则大西洋各国市埠环之，有荷兰埠，有吕宋[11]埠，有葡萄亚[12]埠，有佛兰西埠，有弥利坚埠，有英吉利埠。每一埠地各广数百里，此疆彼界，各不相谋。各埠中皆有造船之厂，有造火器之局，并鬻船鬻炮于他国，亦时以兵船货船出租于他国。其船厂材料山积，工匠云辏[13]，二三旬可成一大战舰，张帆起柁，嗟咄立办。其出工匠各以材艺相竞，造则争速，驶又争速，终年营造，光烛天，声殷地。是英夷船炮在中国视为绝技，在西洋各国视为寻常。广东互市二百年，始则奇技淫巧受之；继则邪教毒烟受之，独于行军利器则不一师其长技，是但肯受害不肯受益也。

······

人但知船炮为西夷之长技，而不知西夷之所长不徒船炮也。每出兵以银二十员安家，上卒月饷银十员，下卒月饷银六员，赡之厚故选之精，练之勤故御之整。即如澳门夷兵仅二百余，而刀械则昼夜不离，训练则风雨无阻。英夷攻海口之兵，以小舟渡至平地，辄去其舟，以绝反顾，登岸后则鱼贯肩随，行列严整，岂专恃船坚炮利哉？无其节制，即仅有其船械，犹无有也；无其养赡，而欲效其选练，亦不能也。故欲选兵练兵，先筹养兵，兵饷无可议加，惟有裁并之而已。

粤省水师将及四万，去虚伍计之，不及三万。汰其冗滥，补其精锐，以万五千人为率。即以三万有余之粮，养万五千之卒，则粮不加而足。以五千卒分防各口炮台，与陆营相参；以万人分配战舰，可得三十余艘。无事日，令出哨外洋，捕海盗，缉烟贩；有事寇在邻省，则连艅赴援，寇在本省，则分艘犄角，可以方行南海矣。或曰：粤洋绵长三千余里，水师数万，尚虞不周，今裁汰大半，不弥形单寡乎？曰：水师多而不敷，以无战舰也，无战舰出洋，则口岸处处出防，以水师当陆师之用，故兵以分而见寡。今以精兵驾坚舰，昼夜千里，朝发夕至，东西巡哨，何患不周？是兵以聚而见多。英夷各处市埠，自大西洋至中国，首尾数万里，何以水师不过九万即能分守各国？又何以入寇之兵不过五十艘，而沿海被其骚动？况水师外，尚有本省绿营数万，何患其无兵分守？

⋯⋯

问：西洋与西洋战，亦互有胜负，我即船炮士卒一切整齐，亦何能保其必胜？曰：此为两客相攻言之，非为以客待主言之也。夫力不均、技不等而相攻，则力强技巧者胜；力均技等而以客攻主，以主待客则主胜，攻劳守逸。请言其状：夫海战全争上风，无战舰则有上风而不能乘。即有战舰，而使两客交哄于海中，则互争上风，尚有不能操券之势。若战舰战器相当，而又以主待客，则风潮不顺时，我舰可藏于内港，贼不能攻，一俟风潮皆顺，我即出攻，贼不能避，我可乘贼，贼不能乘我，是主之胜客者一。无战舰，则不能断贼接济，今有战舰，则贼之接济路穷，而我以饱待饥，是主之胜客者二。无战舰，则贼敢登岸，无人攻其后，若有战舰则贼登岸之后，舶上人少，我兵得袭其虚，与陆兵夹击，是主之胜客者三。无战舰，则贼得以数舟分封数省之港，得以旬日遍扰各省之地。有战舰则贼舟敢聚不敢散，我兵所至，可与邻省之舰夹攻，是主之胜客者四。故历考西洋各国交兵，凡英吉利往攻弥利坚本国，则弥利坚胜；以英吉利往攻俄罗斯本国，则俄罗斯胜；若英吉利与各国互战于海中，无分主客，则舵师能得上风者胜。

······

注释：

1. 《海国图志》魏源编著。1841 年 8 月，魏源在镇江与被革职的林则徐相遇，他受林则徐嘱托，立志编写一部激励世人、反对外来侵略的著作。他以林则徐主持编译的《四洲志》为基础，广泛搜集资料，编写成《海国图志》50 卷。此后一再增补，全书达到 100 卷。《海国图志》除根据林则徐所译《四洲志》外，更引证历代史志十四种，中外古今各家著述七十多种。《海国图志》系统地介绍世界各国的地理位置和历史沿革，并叙述各国的气候物产、交通贸易、文化教育等情况，还特别介绍西方先进军事生产技术（如战船、洋炮、火铳、火药、水雷、西洋器艺、望远镜制法等）。书中不仅介绍世界各国的情况，而且也阐明他自己对政治、经济和海防的见解。《海国图志》是一部划时代的著作，其"师夷之长技以制夷"对外战略思想的提出，打破了传统的夷夏之辨的传统对外政治思想理念，摒弃了九州八荒、天圆地方、天朝中心狭隘的史地观念，开辟了五大洲、四大洋的新的世界史地广阔知识领域，传播了西方近代科学知识、文化传统、社会制度、风土人情等，拓宽了国人的视野，领导了近代中国向西方学习的时代潮流。本篇引自魏源《海国图志》卷二，〈筹海篇三·议战〉，岳麓书社 1998 年出版的点校注释本。

2. 魏源：见《海国图志叙》注释。

3. 廓尔喀（Gurkha），即尼泊尔（Nepal）。

4. 佛兰西、弥利坚：法国、美国。

5. 款：归顺，服罪。

6. 圣祖：清朝康熙皇帝。

7. 协寇：协，合作，帮助。

8. 钦天监：官署名。旧时指掌为观察天象，推算节气，制定历法。明初沿置司天监、回回司天监，旋改称钦天监，有监正、监副等官，末年有西洋传教士参加工作。清沿明制，有管理监事王大臣为长官，监工、监副等官满、汉并用，并有西洋传教士参加。

9. 此处"夷人"指英国。

10. 费德色：英文音译而来，无从查考。应该是贸易上的优惠政策。

11. 吕宋：西班牙。

12. 即葡萄牙。

13. 云辏：辏，聚集。

译文：

海国图志

〈筹海篇三：议战〉（节选）

魏源

海国图志卷二邵阳魏源重辑
筹海篇三议战

......

目前的情况是，如果有人讨论征用西方兵舰事项，必然说这种想法是想借助外国列强的强势，而表示自己软弱，而一旦为形势所逼，做出数倍于此的示弱表现，也心甘情愿地去接受了；如果有人讨论制造兵舰学习西方先进技术，就会说是浪费，而对于十倍于此的真正浪费，却又说是紧急情况下的救急措施，不必可惜；如果有人讨论翻译西方书籍，以调查了解西方情况，就会说这样做是多此一举，没有必要。（嘉庆年间，在广东有人以汉语与英文语音对照编成一本书，非常方便华人进行外文翻译，广东官府却把此书禁刊了。）然而，一旦外交方面发生问题，不是询问英国首都与俄罗斯首都相距有多远，就是问从英国有没有道路通往新疆地区这类愚蠢问题；甚至尼泊尔想为我国效力要求进攻印度，却被拒绝；法国和美国愿意援助我国军舰，愿意与我国修好，却百般猜防。我国已有二百年对外通商的历史，却不知道西方各国的所在方位，不了解西方各国之间的关系，还能说是对边防事务的精通与关心吗？

汉朝时联合西域各国围困孤立匈奴；唐朝时利用土蕃攻打印度，又利用回纥打击土蕃；我朝康熙年间曾联络俄罗斯以平定蒙古准噶尔部的叛乱。古代时处理对外事务策略是，重点防范外国联合入侵者以阴谋颠覆我国，并不排斥外国联合我国以打击入侵者；禁止向国外泄露我国的情况，而没听说禁止国外的情况传入我国的。如果想要在外交上战胜西方各国，必须先从了解外国的情况开始；想要了解西方各国情况，必须从设立翻译机构翻译西方书籍开始；想要得到擅长边防事务的人才，必须从任用关心边防事务的都督与巡抚开始。

如果问：与外国修好时期应该如何做？回答是：加强国防，积极军备，并不取决于与西方各国是否修好。在外交和平时期，西方各国时时也在观察我国实力的虚实，若我们国防废弛，他们就会轻视我国。所以，尤其在外交和平时期，更要加强国防建设、杜绝阴谋狡诈之端倪，甚至比对外战争时期还要紧迫；更要严明法令、完善外交上的各项事务，比太平盛世时更要加倍努力。未与西方各国修好之时，对外策略是利用西方各国之矛盾，使之相互攻击；与西方各国修好之时的策略应该是学习西方各国先进的技术，以达到战胜他们的目的。

西方人的先进技术主要有三：第一是战舰，第二是枪炮，第三是养兵和练兵的方法。在此容我先陈述一下我清朝先前的有关事例。康熙初年曾调用荷兰的夹板船清剿台湾郑氏势力，又曾令南怀仁制造火炮，用以平定三藩之乱，还曾任用西方人在钦天监担任官职。现而今英国已经占据香港，仗其国力强大称雄于西方各国，而且用开商埠、贸易上的优惠笼络各国。与其让英国收买各国以壮大其势力，为什么我国不去施惠于各国而削弱英国的势力呢？

据考察，东印度与中印度已为英国所占据，而在南印度，欧美各国商埠环海岸分布。有荷兰商埠、西班牙商埠、葡萄牙商埠、法国商埠、美国商埠和英国商埠。各国商埠都有数百里之辽阔，相互疆界分明，互不干涉。而且各国商埠内都建有造船厂和制造枪炮的机构。都向其他国家出售船和枪炮，同时也出租军舰和货船。各国造船厂内，建造材料堆积如山，造船工匠众多。只需两三旬时间便可建造一艘大型军舰。造成即下水开航，投入使用。造船工匠都以技术质量相互竞争，制造过程讲究快，造出的船也讲究其航速。年复一年制造不止，声势红火。中国人视英国的军舰和大炮为极其先进的技术产品，而在国外这只是很平常的技术而已。广东通商二百多年了，我们仅仅引进了西方人的一些奢侈品、工艺品小玩意儿，然后西方宗教渗入，鸦片大量入口。而恰恰没有学习人家的先进国防工业和科技。这是甘心受害而不肯受益。

对于外国先进技术的认识，中国人仅限于军舰和枪炮，不知道西方先进的东西不仅仅是军舰枪炮，还在于养兵与练兵。英国每增加一名兵员先给士兵二十银元的安家费，然后上半月的军饷是十元，下半月的军饷是六元，如此优厚的经济待遇才能募得精兵；加上训练有素，才能军纪严明。如在澳门，英军只有二百名士兵，枪械昼夜不离手，严阵以待。操练勤奋，风雨无阻。英军进攻海口时，先乘小舟，上岸后即丢弃船只，破釜沉舟，以壮决战之志。登陆后列队行进，行列规整。这难道是仰仗军舰坚固和枪炮的先进吗？如果部队没有严明的纪律和战斗素质，仅靠军舰和武器装备的先进，根本没有用；如果士兵没有物质待遇的保障，想提高招募和训练士兵的水平，也办不到。想招募到精兵和严格练兵，就要先解决好军人的待遇问题。军饷问题并不是大问题，可以通过精简部队编制来解决。

驻防广东的海军将近四万人，去掉编制中虚报的人数，不到三万人。裁汰其中不称职的兵员，补充进精锐兵员，把广东海军编制确定为一万五千员。这样用三万兵员的军粮，养一万五千兵员，不用增加任何军粮而绰绰有余。用五千兵员分别驻守广东各口岸的炮台，与陆军相配合协作。以另外一万兵员分配给军舰，可以装备三十多艘战舰。没有战事时，军舰在海上巡逻，抓捕盗贼，缉查鸦片贩卖走私船；有战事时，邻省有敌入侵则前往增援，配合作战。本省有敌进犯，则协同布阵，南海完全可以在掌控之中了。

有人会说：广东省海岸线三千多里长，数万海军恐怕都不够用，如今淘汰裁员一大半兵员，海军力量是不是会减弱？回答是：过去海军兵员多却感觉兵力不够用，是因为没有军舰，没有军舰出海防御，只在各个口岸把守，把海军当成陆军使用，部队布防分散，所以总觉得兵力太少。现在以精锐海军兵员配上坚固军舰，昼夜奔驰千里，早上出发，晚上就可抵达，纵横巡逻，还怕会出现兵力不够的问题？因为只有把部队聚集在一起兵力才会充足。比如英国在世界各地开商港，从大西洋到中国长达数万里，而英国全国海军兵员只有九万人，如何能在世界范围内分别把守各地？而且英国入侵中国的海军只有五十艘军舰，为什么整个中国沿海都能被其扰乱？广东除了海军以外还有数万陆军绿营军，还担心什么兵力不够的问题？

......

如果问：西方各列强间相互海战，互有胜负，我国海军装备编制健全后如何能保证我们必胜？回答是：西洋各列强间海战只是两个客军在海上交战，不存在主军与客军对战的问题。两军作战实力和技能不相等的情况下，则作战实力和技能强的一方胜；两军作战实力和技能相当的情况下，客军进攻主军，以主军守备而迎战客军，则主军胜，因为进攻比防守消耗军力更多。

具体地讲，海军作战一定要争取上风之势，你没有军舰就算是占据上风的位置也无法利用。即使有了战舰，两军交战于海上，争夺上风之势，都不能肯定稳操胜券。如果战舰装备水平相当，而以主军迎战客军，一旦风势不利时，我们的军舰可以利用内港隐蔽，等风势有利时，再出动进攻，而敌方海军却无处隐蔽，我军可以利用敌军的漏洞，敌军却无法寻找我军的漏洞，这就是主军制胜第一点。没有军舰，就不能切断敌军的供给线。如今我们有军舰了，敌军的供给线就受到了威胁，军需供应会出现问题，相比之下我军则供给稳定。这是主军制胜的第二点。没有战舰敌军便敢登陆，因为无需顾虑来自海上的袭击。如果我们有战舰敌军登陆，则敌船上的人数少，我海军便可与陆军配合作战，乘其虚弱而进攻，这是主军制胜的第三点。没有战舰，敌海军就可以以几艘军舰分别封锁我国数省的港口，可以同时骚扰我数省。有了军舰则敌海军只能聚集，不敢分散，我海军则可以聚集数省之兵力联合攻击敌军，这是主军制胜的第四点。

所以考察历史上西洋海战战史，英国海军进攻美国本土作战，则美国海军胜；英国海军进攻俄罗斯本土作战，则俄罗斯胜；而英国与各国在海上交战，不分主军客军，则军舰舵师能抢得上风一方胜。

……

四、洋务运动

（一）洋务运动概论

The Self-Strengthening（"Foreign Affairs"）Movement：

Zeng Guofan (1811 – 1872), Li Hongzhang (1823 – 1901) and Zhang Zhidong (1837 – 1909) .

For many people in contemporary China the Opium War continues to be seen as the decisive moment that separates China's modern from its pre-modern history, precisely because it initiated a wave of international competition with powerful foreign states equipped with industrial technology. In this narrative, the next phase in the story of China's modern development is the actions taken by Qing officials from the 1850s onwards to strengthen the state with the adoption of foreign industrial technology. These actions can be seen as a successor to the project of adopting foreign and knowledge initiated by Lin Zexu and Wei Yuan and as one of the first major steps in the key project of the Chinese state conceived of as a modernising entity. This project involved the building of a strong state on the basis of modern technology, a technology which is supposed to serve, rather than undermine, the preservation of Chinese culture.

The leaders of this "Self-Strengthening Movement" as it is generally known in English (*Yangwu Yundong* or "Foreign Affairs Movement" in Chinese) were officials who came to prominence through their involvement in the repression of major anti-Qing revolts that occurred in the mid 19th century. This association with repression has given them a complex status in the historiography produced in the era of the 20th-century republics. For some, they are traitors who suppressed the anti-Manchu movements to which the republican revolution was an heir; furthermore, they are seen as having compromised the cause of defending the country against foreign domination by permitting foreigners to strengthen their position in China (unlike Wei Yuan and Lin Zexu, who were engaged in a patriotic battle for the defence of the country. For others, however, they are pioneers of patriotic modernization who opened up the path of introducing foreign learning that could be used to build a China that would be freed from the shackles of the imperial structure that had supposedly brought about the nation's humiliation in the modern era; they could also be cast as forward and outward-looking, being respected on the world diplomatic stage and supported in their endeavours by the leading industrial powers of their time. From another perspective, their commitment to Confucian learning—in particular, to an orthodox form of Confucian learning that rejected neither the scholarly accomplishments of Qing empiricist learning nor the philosophical, political and moral commitments of Song and Ming Confucianism—reinforced a tradition of thought that is still honoured in the present.

Like Wei Yuan, Zeng Guofan was from Hunan Province. He was an advocate of the same form of statecraft learning that Wei Yuan and Gu Yanwu advocated, which emphasized the moral strengthening of local communities, including their powers of self-defence and self-government. In-deed, it was Zeng's success in raising local militias to resist anti-Qing reb-els that led to his appointment by the Qing state as a key official in the sup-pression of the revolts of the mid-19th century. He was one of the key fig-ures in what has been referred to as a moment of dynastic restoration be-tween the early 1860s and the 1870s. Li Hongzhang also rose to power in this period, and was a driving force in the creation of a diplomatic service that was intended to help the Qing to negotiate its rights on the global stage; Li was the central figure in the Qing Dynasty's foreign relations be-tween the 1870s and the 1890s. Where Zeng was committed to a vision of Confucian moral purity based on fidelity to the orthodox Song Dynasty vi-sion of the duties of an upright scholar, and was admired for his learning, Li Hongzhang appears more pragmatic, and was able to use his government position to preserve personal control over the army (which he had led dur-ing the struggle against anti-Qing rebels) and to amass a vast personal for-tune during his time in office (unlike Zeng, who retained a modest lifestyle and surrendered power over the army that he had created). Both Zeng and Li supported the incorporation of foreign technology and economic struc-tures into the Qing system and advocated a strengthening of orthodox Con-fucian learning, even though Zeng helped to promote the ideas of Gu Yan-wu (who has often been seen—incorrectly—as a critic of Song and Ming Confucian philosophy), perhaps partly because his own view of a tradition of local self-governance based on a system of modified hereditary power in the leadership of local communities echoed positions enunciated by Gu.

Zhang Zhidong was younger than either Zeng or Li, and he was strongly associated with both the initiative to encourage foreign learning in China (as with the other Self-Strengtheners, this included encouraging students to go abroad to study,) and a reaffirmed commitment to orthodox

Confucianism. Zhang kept his distance from the radical Confucian reformers who enjoyed brief power in the 1890s (and who are the subject of the next section of this book), and supported the institutions of monarchy. This has led to critiques of his position by anti-dynastic republicans. At the same time, however, in his capacity as the founder of the institution which would later become Peking University, he stands as one of the key producers of the 20th-century intellectual order in China.

For those who see the modern Chinese republic as committed to constructive engagement with the outside world on an equal footing, Zeng Guofan, Li Hongzhang and Zhang Zhidong represent an openness seen as lacking in the stereotypically backward-looking and xenophobic anti-Christian and anti-foreign Boxer movement, which broke out in 1900. Equally, those who may have reservations about the damage done by radical utopians to either Chinese culture or the project of technical modernization may see the learned Zhang Zhidong—respectful of education wherever that education may be found—as a spiritual forefather of the late 20th-century vision of a strong China that combined modern technology with respect for Chinese cultural tradition. Rather than being reactionary defenders of the old order, the Self-Strengtheners begin to appear as ancestors of modern China, supporters of a Confucian heritage that had been subject to question by radical advocates of the Chinese enlightenment (such as the members of the New Culture movement). Their support for dynastic monarchy—a serious obstacle for radical republicans earlier in the 20th century—can be overlooked in favour of their articulation of the image of a fusion of Chinese and foreign, traditional and modern elements, a nexus that arguably constitutes a key part of contemporary state ideology in China.

Sources and Further Reading

Good biographical information on Zhang Zhidong, Li Hongzhang and

Zeng Guofan can be found on pp. 27 – 32, pp. 464 – 471 and pp. 751 – 756 of Arthur W. Hummel (ed.), *Eminent Chinese of the Ch'ing Period*, Taipei: Ch'eng-Wen Publishing Company, 1967.

A positive appraisal of the thought of Zeng Guofan in the larger tradition of Qing scholarship is given by Liang Qichao, *Zhongguo Jinsanbainian Xueshushi* (A history of Chinese scholarship in the last 300 years) Taipei: The Commercial Press of Taiwan, 1968, Vol. 2. Joseph Levenson examines Self-Strengthening thought in Volume 1 of his *Confucian China and Its Modern Fate*: A Trilogy (Berkeley: University of California Press, 1968).

William Rowe gives an excellent account of the debates about Self-Strengthening and the restoration of the Qing in *China's Last Empire*: *The Great Qing*, Cambridge, Massachussetts, Belknap Press, 2009; Immanuel C. Y. Hsü, *The Rise of ModernChina*, (fifth edition), New York: Oxford University Press, 1995, presents Self-Strengthening as incomplete modernisation. A good analysis from the Western Impact perspective is given in Ting-yee Kuo and Kwang-Ching Liu, "Self-strengthening: the pursuit of Western technology" in John K. Fairbank (ed.), *The Cambridge History of China*, Vol. 10, Part 1, Late Ch'ing, Cambridge: Cambridge University Press, 1978. A broad survey of Self-Strengthening from this perspective is Ssu-yü Teng and John K. Fairbank, *China's Response to the West*: *A Documentary Survey*, 1839 – 1923, Cambridge, Massachusetts: Harvard University Press, 1954.

The most famous full-length account of the early part of this period is Mary C. Wright, *The Last Stand of Chinese Conservatism*: *The T'ung-Chih Restoration*, 1862 – 1874, New York: Atheneum, 1967. Daniel H.

Bays examines the later phases in the development of the Self-Strengthening movement in his *China Enters the Twentieth Century: Chang Chih-tung and the Issues of a New Age*, Ann Arbor: The University of Michigan Press, 1978. Zhang Zhidong's relationship with Peking University is discussed in Xiaoqing Diana Lin, *Peking University: Chinese Scholarship and Intellectuals 1898-1937*, Albany: State University of New York Press, 2005. Y. C. Wang also places the Self-Strengthening movement in a wider context of interactions with the outside world in *Chinese Intellectuals and the West 1872-1949*, Chapel Hill: University of North Carolina Press, 1966. Sympathetic accounts of Li Hongzhang and Zeng Guofan as pioneers of China's modernization appear in Kwang-Ching Liu (ed. Yung-Fa Chen and Kuang-che Pan), *China's Early Modernization and Reform Movement: Studies in Late Nineteenth-Century China and American-Chinese Relations*, Vol. 1, Taipei: Academia Sinica, 2009.

（二）洋务运动文献

（1）奏陈新造轮船及上海机器局[1] 筹办情形折[2]（节选）

曾国藩[3]

窃中国试造轮船之议，臣于咸丰十一年七月复奏购买船炮摺内即有此说。同治元、二年间驻扎安庆，设局试造洋器，全用汉人，未雇洋匠。虽造成一小轮船，而行驶迟钝，不甚得法。二年冬间，派令候补同知容闳[4]出洋购买机器，渐有扩充之意。湖广督臣李鸿章自初任苏抚[5]，即留心外洋军械。维时，丁日昌[6] 在上海道[7] 任内，彼此讲求御侮之策，制器之方。四年五月，在沪购买机器一座，派委知府冯浚光[8]、沈保靖[9]等开设铁厂，适容闳所购之器亦于是时运到，归并一局。始以攻剿方殷，专造枪炮。亦因经费支绌，难兴船工。至六年四月，臣奏请拨留洋税二成，以一成为专造轮船之用。仰蒙圣慈允准，于是拨款渐裕，购料渐多。苏松太道[10]应宝时[11]及冯浚光、沈保靖等朝夕讨论，期于必成。

查制造轮船，以气炉、机器、船壳三项为大宗。从前上海洋厂自制轮船，其气炉、机器均系购自外洋，带至内地装配船壳，从未有自构式样造成重大机器、汽炉全具者。此次创办之始，考究图说，自出机杼。本年闰四月间，臣赴上海察看，已有端绪。七月初旬，第一号工竣，臣命名曰恬吉轮船，意取四海波恬、厂务安吉也。其汽炉、船壳两项，均系厂中自造。机器则购买旧者，修整参用。船身长十八丈五尺，阔二丈七尺二寸。先在吴淞口外试行，由铜沙直出大洋至浙江舟山而旋，复于八月十三日驶至金陵。臣亲自登舟试行到采石矶，每一时上水行七十余里，下水行一百二十余里，尚属坚致灵便，可以涉历重洋。原议拟造四号，今第一号系属明轮[12]，此后即续造暗轮[13]。将来渐推渐精，即二十余丈之大舰可伸可缩之烟囱，可高可低之轮轴，或亦可苦思而得之。上年试办以来，臣深恐日久无成，未敢率尔[14]具奏，仰赖朝廷不惜巨款，不责速效，得以从容集事，中国自强之道，或基于此。各委员苦心经营，其劳勋亦不可没也。

溯自上海初立铁厂，迄今逾三年，先后筹办情形，请为皇上粗陈其概。开局之初，军事孔亟[15]，李鸿章饬令先枪、炮两项，以应急需。惟制造枪、炮，必先有制枪制炮之器，乃能举办。查原购铁厂，修船之器居多，造炮之器甚少。各委员详考图说，以点、线、面、体之法求方圆、平直之用，就厂中洋器以母生子，触类旁通，造成大小机器三十余座。即用此器以铸炮炉，高三丈，围逾一丈。以风轮煽炽火力，去渣存液，一气铸成。先铸实心，再用机器车刮旋挖，使炮之外光如镜，内滑如脂。制造开花、田鸡等炮[16]，配备炮车、炸弹、药引、木心等物，皆与外洋所造者足相匹敌。到洋枪一项，需用机器尤多。如辗卷枪筒，车刮外光，钻挖内膛，旋造斜棱等事，各有精器，巧式百出。枪成之后，亦与购自外洋者无异。此四、五年间先造枪炮兼造制器之情形也。

该局在上海虹口暂租洋厂，中外错处，诸多不便，且机器日增，厂地狭窄，不能安置。六年夏间，乃于上海城南兴建新厂，购地七十余亩，修造公所。其已成者，曰气炉厂、曰机器厂、曰熟铁厂、曰洋枪楼、曰木工厂、曰铸铜铁厂、曰火箭厂、曰库房、栈房、煤房、文案房、工务厅暨中外工匠住居之室。房屋颇多，规矩亦肃。其未成者，尚须速开船坞以整破舟，酌建瓦棚以储木料，另立学馆以习翻译。盖翻译一事，系制造之根本。

……

——同治七年九月初二日

曾国藩日记[17]——同治元年五月初七日与幕府诸君谈夷务[18]（节选）

曾国藩

……与幕府诸君鬯谈[19]。眉生[20]言及夷务，余以欲制夷人，不宜在关税之多寡、礼节之恭倨上着眼。即内地民人处处媚夷、艳夷而鄙华，借夷而压华，虽极可恨可恶，而远识者尚不宜在此等着眼。吾辈着眼之地，前乎此者，洋人十年八月入京，不伤毁我宗庙社稷，目下在上海宁波等处助我攻剿发匪[21]，二者皆有德于我。我中国不宜忘其大者而怨其小者。欲求自强之道，总以修政事、求贤才为急务，以学作炸炮、学造轮舟等具为下手工夫。但使彼之所长，我皆有之，顺则报德有其具，逆则报怨亦有其具。若在我者，挟持无具，则曲固罪也，直亦罪也，怨之罪也，德之亦罪也。内地之民，人人媚夷，吾固无能制之；人人仇夷，吾亦不能用之也。

……

注释：

1. 上海机器局，江南机器制造总局的简称，于1865年9月20日在上海成立。上海机器局为清朝洋务运动中成立的军事生产机构，为晚清中国最重要的军工厂，也是近代最早的新式工厂之一。上海机器局1867年由虹口迁高昌庙，之后并不断扩充，成为清政府最大的军事工业，主要制造枪炮和修造轮船。

2. 该文是同治七年（1868）九月初二，曾国藩向清廷所上的奏折，对自己自咸丰十一年以来的洋务活动作了一个全面的回顾。在奏折中，他不仅认为仿造外洋船炮当是"中国自强之道。"还将"制造机器"，西方的"算学"、"图说"等纳入洋务的范畴，扩大了洋务的范围。（见《曾文正公全集·奏稿》卷三十。）曾国藩在筹议购买船炮的同时，也开始筹备"制洋器"。"制洋器"从思想到实践转化的决策过程，深深打上了曾国藩的印迹。他积极向朝廷动议，使思想转变为朝廷的政策。他及时筹办，将政策付诸实践，从而开启了其后各地设局办厂、"制洋器"的先河。此奏折乃砸向古老帝国三尺坚冰之上的一块巨石，中国涉足工业化的划时代宣言书，通篇言辞深沉，于平实中有倔强之气，饱含浓烈的忧患意识与书生热血。本文选自《曾国藩全集》奏稿十，岳麓书社，1993 年版。

3. 曾国藩（1811—1872），汉族，出生于湖南长沙府湘乡县荷叶塘白杨坪（现湖南娄底市双峰县荷叶镇天子坪村），原名子城，字伯函，号涤生；道光十三年（1833）参加湘乡县试考取秀才，道光十八年（1838）殿试考中同进士，从此一步一阶地踏上仕途之路。曾国藩官至两江总督、直隶总督、武英殿大学士，为清朝中晚期重臣；亦是湘军的创立者和统帅，并曾率湘军镇压了太平天国起义。曾国藩倡导洋务运动，拒绝盲目排外，主张学习并引进西方的工业技术，且支持派遣留学生赴海外学习；在治国、治军、治家、教育等方面都有重大建树。有评论说：曾国藩可被视为中国古代历史上的最后一人、近代历史上的第一人。这句话似已概括出曾国藩在历史变迁时期的作用和影响。

4. 容闳（1828—1912），字达萌，号纯甫，广东香山县南屏村（今珠海市南屏镇）人。容闳是中国近代史上首位留学美国的学生。1847 年，美国教育家勃朗（Rev. Samuel Robbins Brown）牧师带容闳等三名中国学生前往美国留学，但其后只有容闳一人留在美国升学。容闳 1850 年考入耶鲁学院，并于 1854 年获文学士毕业。返国后，容闳参加了师夷自强的洋务运动。其后容闳结识了康有为、梁启超等人，并于戊戌维新中支持维新派。1912 年 4 月 21 日，容闳于美国去世。1998 年，容闳诞辰 170 周年时，耶鲁大学所在州，康涅狄格州宣布，将 9 月 22 日（当年第一批中国幼童在美入学的日子）公订为"容闳及中国留美幼童纪念日"。位于纽约华埠的公立容闳小学也是为纪念容闳而命名。

5. 江苏巡抚。

6. 丁日昌（1823—1882），字禹生，又作雨生，号持静。广东丰顺人。20 岁中秀才，后为曾国藩幕僚。丁日昌是清朝洋务运动主要人物。丁日昌曾任苏淞太兵备道，两

淮盐运使，江苏布政使，江苏巡抚，福州船政大臣，福建巡抚，是近代军事家兼政
治家。丁日昌主张发展实业、加强军事建设；在外交方面：力主维护主权和收回利
权等；在文化教育方面：建议变八股为八科，改革科举制度；推动和促成派遣第一
批留美学童；挑选船政学堂优等生赴欧留学；组织翻译出版西方科技书籍和编撰府
志政书；主张在通商口岸创办报馆，倡导广设社学和义学。

7. 上海道，苏松太道的俗称，为清朝江苏省下属道级行政区划之一，辖管苏州府、松
   江府和太仓直隶州；顺治年间驻地为太仓，康熙时期驻地为苏州，雍正之后驻地为
   松江府下辖的上海县。自雍正之后，苏松太道道台衙门设在上海县城大东门内，今
   上海黄浦区（原南市区）的巡道街上。

8. 冯浚光（1830—1878），南海人，字竹儒，咸丰年间举人；同治年间，曾任苏松太
   道。

9. 沈保靖（1828—1903），江苏江阴人，字仲维，咸丰年间举人。同治十一年（1872），
   授江西广饶九南道，光绪七年（1881），迁福建布政使。

10. 见"上海道"注释。

11. 应宝时（1821—1890），浙江永康人，字敏斋，道光年间举人。同治四年，官苏松
    太道。

12. 明轮是一种船用推进器，形状类似车轮，装在船的两侧或尾部。明轮轮周上装有若
    干桨板，向后拨水使船前进。因轮的大部分在水面以上，故称"明轮"。近代明轮
    由机器转动，明轮船即是早期的一种机械动力船。

13. 暗轮是一种形状像风车或电风扇一样的螺旋桨装置。暗轮装在船尾与蒸汽机联在一
    起，作为轮船的推进器。由于螺旋桨全都淹没在水中，故称"暗轮"。

14. 轻率。

15. 非常紧急、急迫。

16. 田鸡炮是一种载于架子上的小战炮，形略似蛙，故名田鸡炮；也有说是迫击炮的前身。

17. 该文摘自《曾国藩日记》，该书记录曾氏自清道光二十一年（1841）正月初一至同
    治十一年（1872）二月初三长达 32 年的日记。日记详细记载他的工作和生活。该
    书由曾国藩门人王启原摘录，分十类编为两卷，上卷分为问学、省克、治道、军
    谋、伦理，下卷为文艺、鉴赏、颐养、品藻、游览。该文记载了曾国藩于同治元年
    五月初七日同幕僚宾友的一段谈论洋务的话，最集中、最典型地表现出他的洋务思
    想。实际上包含着如何对待和处理外国侵略问题的全部政策与策略，即：怀德弃
    怨，化敌为友；自我振作，师夷长技。曾国藩在该谈话中所表达的，亦不仅是他个
    人的思想，而是整个洋务派与洋务运动的思想基础和行动纲领。本文选自陈国庆、

张克平编著《曾国藩全集》，西北大学出版社，1994年版。

18. 清代后期指与外国有关的各种事务。"夷"是贬义词，将办理外国事务称为"夷务"，有对外国蔑视的意味。鸦片战争前后，"洋务"一词开始出现，并被用来表示所有的对外事务。相对于"夷"的贱称属性，"洋"可被视为一种中性的称谓。

19. 畅谈。

20. 即金安清（约1817—1880），原名国琛，字眉生，号傥斋，魏塘镇人，国子监生出身。曾任江苏泰州府同知，海安府通判，官至道员，深得曾国藩器重。光绪三年夏，上海机器印书局曾以《水窗春呓》为书名，出版其笔记。

21. 清廷对太平军的蔑称。太平军仍按汉族传统习俗蓄发，并主张恢复中国自古以来的蓄发传统。

译文：

奏陈新造轮船及上海机器局筹办情形折（节选）

曾国藩

有关中国自己试造轮船的商议，我在咸丰十一年七月复奏购买船炮折中，即已提及。同治元年和同治二年，当我统兵驻扎安庆期间，就曾设机器局试造西式武器，而且在制造过程中，我们任用的全部是国人，没有聘请西人。虽然建成了一艘小轮船，但其行驶缓慢；显然我们还没有掌握造船的奥秘。同治二年冬季，派候补同知容闳出国购买机器，并逐渐有了扩充的意愿。湖广总督李鸿章从开始担任江苏巡抚时起，即已开始注意外国的军械；那时，丁日昌也正好在上海道任上。李、丁二人相互探讨抵御外敌的策略，以及制造武器的方法。同治四年五月，在上海购买了一台机器，于是委派知府冯竣光、沈保靖等开设冶铁厂。而这时容闳购买的机器，也正好运到，于是就将机器合并一处，成为一局。最初，因为正在攻剿的紧张时刻，所以工厂就专门制造枪炮；同时也因为当时经费困难，也就没有再造轮船。到同治六年四月，我曾奏请拨留洋税二成，并从中提出一成，专门用作制造轮船的经费。深蒙圣慈准许，于是所拨款项，渐渐多起来；所购材料，也渐渐多了起来。加之苏松太道应宝时与冯浚光、沈保靖等日夜讨论，才得以按期完成。

制造轮船，最重要的大部件，是气炉、机器、船壳。以前上海洋人工厂自制轮船，所需的气炉、机器等都是从外国购买，然后运到内地，装配在船壳上；从来没有自行设计及制造过重要机器、气炉。这次自创办开始，我们就研究图纸，自己制造机器。今年闰四月时，我到上海进行了视察，发现各项工作都已准备就绪。七月上旬，第一艘轮船竣工，我为该船取名"恬吉号"，取意为四海风平浪静、工厂生产平安吉祥。该轮船上的汽炉和船壳，都是工厂自己制造的。机器则是购买的旧货，修理后重新用。该船全长十八丈五尺，宽二丈七尺二寸。我们首先在吴淞口外试航，并由铜沙直接驶向大洋，至浙江舟山后返回；又于八月十三日驶到南京。我曾亲自登船试航至采石矶；逆水时，每小时能行七十多里；顺水行时，航速则可达到，每小时一百二十多里。轮船整体还算坚固轻便，也可以远洋航行。原来我们打算建造四艘，现在所造的第一艘是明轮，以后即要陆续制造暗轮。将来越研究越精密；就是二十多丈的大舰上可伸可缩的烟囱，可高可低的轮轴，或许经过刻苦钻研，也能制造出来。去年试办以来，我担心，会在相当长的一段时间内做不出什么结果，所以就没有轻率地上奏。都是因为朝廷不惜拨出巨款，但同时也没有要求我们迅速做出成效，我们才能如此从容地办理这些事宜。中国的自强之路，或许要以此为基础。各部委员苦心经营，他们的功劳也是不可埋没的。

自上海建立铁厂，迄今已经三年多了。有关前后筹办的情况，已经向皇上简单地介绍过了。生产的初始阶段，由于军需急迫，李鸿章命令先造枪、炮，以作应急之用。但制造枪炮，一定要有制造枪、炮的机器，才可以开工制造。经调查发现，原购得的铁厂，修船的机器很多，但制造枪、炮的机器却非常少。各委员仔细研究了图纸，用点、线、面、体等方法求得方圆、平直，利用厂里的外国机器，通过以现有机器造新机器、进而再制造其他同类机器的方法，最终制造了三十多台大小机器。然后用这些机器铸造了高三丈、周长一丈的炮炉；再以风轮鼓风，去渣存液，达到一气铸成。先铸成实心，再用机器车刮旋挖，使炮身光亮如镜，里面则像油脂一样光滑。制造成开花、田鸡两类大炮，并配有炮车、炸弹、药引、木心等物，足以与外国制造的大炮相匹敌。至于制造洋枪，需要的机器尤其多。诸如辗卷枪筒，车刮外光，钻挖内镗，旋造斜棱等工艺，都各需精密机器，巧式百出。而制造出来的枪支，也与购自外国的没有什么差异。以上所述，即这四五年间制造枪炮兼造机器的情况。

该局原在上海虹口暂时租借外国的工厂，但因中外交错，有诸多不便之处；且机器越来越多，由于厂房狭小，已经无法安置。因此于同治六年夏，在上海城南购地七十余亩，兴建了新厂，建造了公所。现已建成的有：锅炉厂、机器厂、熟铁厂、洋枪楼、木工厂、铸铜铁厂、火箭厂、库房、栈房、煤房、文案房、工务厅及中外工匠的住房。房屋虽多，却井然有条。尚未建成的有：修船的船坞（船坞必须要尽快建好），储存木料的瓦棚；另外，还要设立学馆研习翻译，因为翻译关系到机器制造的根本。……

——同治七年九月初二日

译文：

曾国藩日记——五月初七日与幕府诸君谈夷务（节选）

曾国藩

……与几位幕僚进行畅谈。眉生谈到了洋务事宜。我认为，要约束洋人，不应当仅考虑关税的多少、仅在礼仪上的恭敬和傲慢等方面着眼。即使内地民众处处讨好、羡慕洋人，鄙视自己人，并借洋人欺压自己人，即使这些行为让人憎恶，但有远见的人仍不应该仅着眼于这些方面。我们要考虑的重点应是，此前洋人十年八月进入北京，并没有破坏我们的宗庙、国家。现在又在上海、宁波等地帮助我们攻剿太平军。在这两方面，洋人都对我国有恩。我们不应该忘记这些主要方面，而为一些不重要事情怨恨洋人。我们要想自强，总应以治理政务、任用有德行、有才能的人为当务之急；从学习制作炸药、火炮、建造船舰等机械技术入手。只要洋人的先进技术我们都能掌握，那么他们与我们友好，我们就有能力报恩，他们不顺从我们，我们也有能力抗拒。如果我们没有先进的技术与器具，那么做得不对固然是罪过，但做得对也会是罪过；怨恨他们是罪，有德于他们同样也是罪。内地的民众，如果人人都讨好洋人，我自然无力禁止他们这样做，但如果他们人人都仇视洋人，我也不会任用他们。……

（2）劝学篇[1]（节选）

张之洞[2]

内篇：循序第七

今欲强中国，存中学，则不得不讲西学。然不先以中学固其根柢，端其识趣[3]，则强者为乱首，弱者为人奴，其祸更烈于不通西学者矣。……今日学者，必先通经以明我中国先圣先师立教之旨，考史以识我中国历代之治乱、九州之风土，涉猎子集以通我中国之学术文章，然后择西学之可以补吾阙者用之、西政之可以起吾疾者取之。斯有其益而无其害。如养生者先有谷气[4] 而后可饫[5] 庶羞[6]，疗病者先审藏府[7] 而后可施药石，西学必先由中学，亦犹是矣。（华文不深者不能译西书）

外国各学堂，每日必诵耶苏[8] 经，示宗教也。小学堂先习蜡丁文[9]，示存古也。先熟本国地图，再览全球图，示有序也。学堂之书多陈述本国先君之德政，其公私乐章多赞扬本国之强盛，示爱国也。如中士而不通中学，此犹不知其姓之人、无辔之骑、无柁之舟，其西学愈深，其疾视中国亦愈甚，虽有博物多能之士，国家亦安得而用之哉！

……

外篇：游学第二

出洋一年，胜于读西书五年…… 请论今事。日本，小国耳，何兴之暴也？伊藤[10]、山县[11]、榎本[12]、陆奥[13]诸人，皆二十年前出洋之学生也，愤其国为西洋所胁，率其徒百馀人分诣德、法、英诸国，或学政治工商，或学水陆兵法，学成而归，用为将相，政事一变，雄视东方。不特此也。俄之前主大彼得[14]，愤彼国之不强，亲到英吉利[15]、荷兰两国船厂为工役十馀年，尽得其水师轮机驾驶之法，并学其各厂制造，归国之后，诸事丕变，今日遂为四海第一大国。不特此也。暹罗[16]久为法国涎伺，于光绪二十年与法有衅，行将吞并矣。暹王感愤，国内毅然变法，一切更始，遣其世子游英国学水师。去年暹王游欧洲，驾火船出红海来迎者，即其学成之世子也。暹王亦自通西文西学。各国敬礼有加，暹罗遂以不亡。上为俄，中为日本，下为暹罗，中国独不能比其中者乎？

至游学之国，西洋不如东洋：一路近省费，可多遣；一去华近，易考察；一东文近于中文，易通晓；一西学甚繁，凡西学不切要者，东人已删节而酌改之。中东情势风俗相近，易仿行。事半功倍，无过于此。若自欲求精求备，再赴西洋，有何不可？

......

注释：

1.《劝学篇》是张之洞在 1898 年发表的，其基本思想，是说教育首先要传授中国传统的经史之学，这是一切学问的基础，要放在率先的地位，然后再学习西学中有用的东西，以补中学的不足。1898 年 7 月 25 日，清廷将张之洞所著《劝学篇》颁发各省督、抚、学政各一部，令其广为刊布，努力劝导，"以重名教而杜卮言"。《劝学篇》标"中体西用"之旨。当变法维新之时，清廷颁发此书，意在强调维新变法将坚持维护封建制度之基本立场。但是，这一教育主张在客观上也促进了近代教育的发展。本文选自李忠兴评注，张之洞著《劝学篇》，中州古籍出版社，1998 年版。

2. 张之洞（1837—1909），字孝达，号香涛、香岩，汉族，直隶南皮（今河北南皮）人；咸丰二年（1852），十六岁中顺天府解元，同治二年（1863）廿七岁中进士，授翰林院编修；历任内阁学士、山西巡抚、两广总督、湖广总督、两江总督（多次署理，从未实授）、军机大臣等职，官至体仁阁大学士。1898 年，他发表刊行《劝学篇》，提出"旧学为体，新学为用"，自言其书主旨在"正人心，开风气"。正人心，即提倡三纲五常；开风气，即学习西方办实业、设学堂。张之洞是洋务运动的领袖人物之一，他着力扶持民族工业，开发矿山，筹建铁路，开设铁厂、兵工厂、纺织厂等，为中国民族工业，特别是重工业及近代军事的发展，做出了贡献。他重视教育，拟定新学制，创办新式学堂，在中国教育由传统向现代化迈进过程中，也做出了贡献。

3. 识见志趣。

4. 中医名词，指胃气；也可泛指饮食营养。

5. 饱食。

6. 多种美味。

7. 中医名词，人体内脏器官的总称。藏，通"脏"。

8. 耶苏：耶稣。

9. 蜡丁文：拉丁文。

10. 伊藤博文（1841—1909），日本长州（今山口县西北部）人。伊藤博文 1863 年留学英国学习海军，是日本近代政治家，明治维新元老。1885 年起四任日本首相。伊藤博文是中日甲午战争的主要策划者。1909 年 10 月 26 日在中国哈尔滨车站，被朝鲜民族主义者安重根刺死。

11. 山县有朋（1838—1922），日本军人，政治家。幼名辰之助，后改小助、小辅。明治维新后改名有朋，号含雪；历任陆军卿、参军、参谋本部长、内务大臣、农商大臣和内阁总理大臣（首相）。1909 年伊藤博文死后，成为日本最有权势的元老。

12. 榎本武扬（1836—1908），日本德川幕府海军将领，虾夷共和国的创建者。1862 年至 1867 年被派赴荷兰学习海军。回国后被德川幕府任命为海军副总裁，成为实际上的幕府海军指挥官。1868 年，率 8 艘军舰和部分陆军一路北上占领了北海道，并于同年 10 月成立了虾夷共和国，自任大总统。后向维新军请降。两年牢狱生活后，仍被破格录用，担任了政府高官。1908 年，榎本武扬病逝于东京。

13. 陆奥宗光（1844—1897），原名"阳之助"，是日本明治时代的政治家和外交官。陆奥宗光曾接受伊藤博文的建议，到欧美访问。1892 至 1896 年，他在伊藤博文内阁任外交大臣。中日甲午战争时，他在日本的外交政策方面扮演重要的角色，史称"陆奥外交"。1897 年，在夏威夷因病逝世。

14. 彼得一世，阿列克谢耶维奇·罗曼诺夫（Пётр Алексе́евич Рома́нов，1672—1725），人称彼得大帝，为俄罗斯帝国罗曼诺夫王朝沙皇（1682—1725），及俄国皇帝（1721—1725）。在位期间力行改革，他制定的西方化政策是使俄国变成一个强国的主要因素。

15. 英吉利即英国在中世纪时期国家和民族的统称。

16. 现东南亚国家泰国的古称。暹罗于 1949 年更名为"泰国"，意为"自由之国"。

译文：

劝学篇（节选）

张之洞

如今我们要使中国强盛、维护我们的纲常名教以及我们的政制（中学），就必须要学习西方进步的科学技术以及各种社会管理措施（西学）。但如果在学习西学的同时，不以中学为基础，并端正人们的识见志趣，那强者就会变成乱首，而弱者就会变成奴隶。而这样的结果，更劣于不精通西学的后果。当今的学者必须先要精通我国的政教、纲常伦理以及道德规范，以懂得我先圣先师所创教义的宗旨；要研究我国的历史，以了解我国历代的治国之道以及各地的风土人情；还要广泛研习诸子百家、佛道等宗教著作以及各种文学、戏曲作品，以了解我国的学术、文学。这之后，才应选学西学以弥补我们的不足并为我所用。我们要采用那些可以纠正我们政制中所存弊端的西方治国方法。这样做才对我们有益，并能避免采用西政所造成的损害。这就如同养生，一个人要先有食欲，而后才能享受大量的食物；一个人要治病，医生要先检查他的内脏，才可施用合适的药。而我们先学好中学，再学西学，也是这个道理。（中文不好，就不能将西方的书翻译成中文）。

在西方的学校，学生每天都要背诵圣经，以表示对基督教的尊重；初级学校要先学拉丁文，以保存其古老传统；学生要先熟悉本国的地图，再看世界地图，这是了解事物所应遵循的顺序；学校里的藏书，大多都是述说本国先君德政的书籍，无论公开还是私下演奏的音乐，大多是歌颂本国强盛的乐章，这些都突显了西方人的爱国情怀。如果一个中国的读书人不精通中国的国学，就如同一个人不知道自己的姓名，或说一个人骑没有缰绳的马、驶没有舵的船。这样的结果即是，他的西学知识越丰富，对中国的厌恶就会越深。这样的人，虽然他们都是博学且有能力的人，但我们的国家怎么能够任用他们呢？

……

在国内读西方书籍，读五年也不如到西方国家学习一年。……我们看看现在的情况。日本只是一个小国，但为什么在短时间内就能振兴呢？伊藤、山县、榎本、陆奥等人，二十年前都曾出洋留学。他们因自己的国家，为西方国家所胁迫，而感到愤怒。在他们的感召下，一百多名日本学生，分别前往德国、法国、英国等国学习。他们有的学习政治，有的学习工商，还有的学生学习水路兵法。学成归国后，这些学生都被任命为将军或政府部长。这样，日本实施了变革，即成为雄视东方的强国。不仅日本，俄国前君主大彼得，也因对其国力不强的情况感到愤怒，而亲自到英格兰、荷兰的船厂做工，而且一做就是十多年。在这十多年中，他充分了解了水师轮机的驾驶方法，并学习了各船厂的制造技术。回国之后，国内发生了大变革；如今，俄国即已成为世界第一大国。除此之外，还有暹罗（今泰国）。长期以来，法国一直贪婪地窥伺暹罗。光绪二十年，法国与暹罗发生了争端，并且马上就要吞并暹罗。暹罗国王对此大感愤怒，毅然在国内推动变法，一切重新开始，并派遣其已立为储君的儿子，去英国学习水师。去年暹罗国王游欧洲时，驾驶蒸汽机驱动的轮船出红海迎接国王的，就是其已经在英国完成学业的儿子。而暹罗国王本人也精通西文、西学；因此欧洲各国对国王也给予了很高的礼遇。这样，暹罗就避免了亡国之灾。纵观俄国、日本、暹罗的发展，难道中国不能向日本学吗？

至于可去留学的国家，西方国家不如日本。其原因有以下几点：一是日本离我国较近，路费便宜，所以可以派遣更多的学生去；一是由于离我国较近，所以去考察比较方便；一是相较于西文，日文与中文更加接近，因此较容易理解；再有，西学内容繁多，但所有那些不必要的内容，日本人都已经作了删节、取舍；加之中国与日本国情、风俗都接近，容易仿照学习，所以去日本学习，可以得到事半功倍的效果，没有比这样更好的了。如有人还想进一步学习西学，在日本学完后，也还可以再去西方国家学习。

......

（3）筹议海防折[1]（节选）

李鸿章[2]

......

兹总理衙门[3]陈请六条，目前当务之急与日后久远之图，业经综括无遗，洵为救时要策。所未易猝办者，人才之难得、经费之难筹、畛域[4]之难化、故习之难除，循是不改，虽日事设防，犹画饼也。然则今日所急，惟在力破成见以求实际而已。

何以言之？历代备边多在西北，其强弱之势、客主之形皆适相埒[5]，且犹有中外界限。今则东南海疆万余里，各国通商传教，来往自如，聚集京师及各省腹地，阳托和好之名，阴怀吞噬之计，一国生事，诸国构煽，实为数千年来未有之变局。轮船电报之速，瞬息千里！军器机事之精，工力百倍；炮弹所到，无坚不摧，水陆关隘，不足限制，又为数千年来未有之强敌。外患之乘，变幻如此，而我犹欲以成法制之，譬如医者疗疾不问何症，概投之以古方，诚未见其效也。庚申（咸丰十年，1860年）以后，夷势骎骎[6]内向，薄海[7]冠带[8]之伦，莫不发愤慷慨，争言驱逐。局外之訾议，既不悉局中之艰难，及询以自强何术？御侮何能？则茫然靡所依据。自古用兵未有不知己知彼而能决胜者，若彼之所长己之所短尚未探讨明白，但欲逞意气于孤注之掷，岂非视国事如儿戏耶！臣虽愚闷，从事军中十余年，向不敢畏缩，自甘贻忧君父。惟洋务涉历颇久，闻见稍广，於彼己长短相形之处，知之较深。而环顾当世[9]，饷力人才实有未逮，又多拘於成法，牵於众议，虽欲振奋而末由。易[10]曰："穷则变，变则通。"盖不变通则战守皆不足恃，而和亦不可久也。

谨就总理衙门原议，逐条详细筹拟切实办法，附以管见；略为引伸。

……总之，居今日而欲整顿海防，舍变法与用人，别无下手之方。伏愿我皇上顾念社稷生民之重，时势艰危之极，常存欿然不自足之怀，节省冗费，请求军实，造就人才，皆不必拘执常例；而尤以人才为亟要，使天下有志之士无不明于洋务，庶练兵、制器、造船各事可期逐渐精强。积诚致行，尤需岁月迟久乃能有济。目前固须力保和局，即将来器精防固，亦不宜自我开衅。彼族或以万分无礼相加，不得已而一应之耳。

……

…… 若外洋本为敌国，专以兵力强弱角胜，彼之军械强於我，技艺精於我，即暂胜必终败。敌从海道内犯，自须亟练水师。惟各国皆系岛夷，以水为家，船炮精练已久，非中国水师所能骤及。中土陆多於水，仍以陆军为立国根基，若陆军训练得力，敌兵登岸后尚可鏖战，炮台布置得法，敌船进口时尚可拒守；但用旗、绿营[11]弓箭刀矛抬鸟枪旧法，断不足以制洋人，并不足以灭土寇。即如直隶[12]练军屡经挑选整顿，近始兼习洋枪、小炸炮，以剿内寇尚属可用，以御外患实未敢信。各省抽练之兵大率类此，用洋枪者已少，用后门枪及炸炮者更少，其势只可加练而不可减练，只可添练洋器以求制胜，而不可拘执旧制以图省费。

……

…… 西国水陆战守利器，以枪炮水电为大宗。炮有前后门、生熟铁纯钢之分，枪有前后门、滑膛、来福之异，水雷有用触物、磨物、电气发火之别。……外国每造枪炮，机器全副购价须数十万金，再由洋购运钢铁等料，殊太昂贵。须俟中土能用洋法自开煤铁等矿，再添购大炉、汽锤，压水柜等机器，仿造可期有成。…… 至水雷一项，轰船破敌最猛……沪津各局现只能仿造其粗者，而电机、铜丝、铁绳、橡皮等件，仍购自外洋。须访募各国造用水雷精艺之人来华教演，庶易精进。至火器尽用洋式，炮子、火药两项亦系要需。……各省防江、防海需用洋枪炮之子药，均宜设局在内地仿造。否则事事购自洋商，殊无以备缓急。且闽沪津各机器局逼近海口，原因取材外洋就便起见，设有警变，先须重兵守护，实非稳著。嗣后各省筹添制造机器，必须设局於腹地通水之处，海口若有战事，后路自制储备，可源源运济也。

……

…… 近日财用极绌，人所共知。欲图振作，必统天下全局，通盘合筹，而后定计。…… 此外沿江沿海各省，皆令整顿货厘[13]盐厘[14]，每省每年限定酌拨数万两协济海防。以上数端，皆开源之事也。若夫裁艇船以养轮船，裁边防冗军以养海防战士，停官府不急之需，减地方浮滥之费，以裨[15]军实而成远谋，亦节流之大者。苟非上下一心，内外一心，局中局外一心，未有不半涂而废者矣。

注释：

1. 该文是李鸿章于同治十三年十一月初二日（1874 年 12 月 10 日）向清廷所上的奏折。清朝军队在鸦片战争中的屡次惨败和《南京条约》的严酷现实，促使清朝统治集团中的一些有识之士大胆发出了"师夷长技以制夷"的时代呐喊，初次提出了创建近代海军的草案。但昏庸的清朝政府并没有立即着手兴办近代海军海防大业。1856 至 1860 年，英法两国联合发动第二次鸦片战争。1874 年，日本寻找借口出兵侵犯台湾。在清朝统治集团内部引发了一场轰轰烈烈的"海防大讨论"。此时身任直隶总督兼北洋通商事务大臣的李鸿章呈交了洋洋万言的《筹议海防折》，急切陈述了海军海防大业的重要战略意义，要求大举兴办近代化的海军海防。在以李鸿章为杰出代表的务实派高级官员们的努力倡导下，清朝政府开始较为认真地筹划并采取了兴办海军海防的一些实际步骤。本文选自《李文忠公全集》奏稿卷 24。

2. 李鸿章（1823—1901），汉族，安徽合肥人，本名章桐，字子黻、渐甫，号少荃（泉）、仪叟，世人尊称李中堂。李鸿章曾任江苏巡抚、湖广总督、直隶总督兼北洋通商大臣、授文华殿大学士、筹办洋务，为晚清军政重臣、外交家，以及洋务运动的主要倡导者之一。道光二十七年（1847），李鸿章中进士，后并受业曾国藩门下；咸丰八年（1858）冬，入曾国藩幕府襄办营务。同治二年（1863），李鸿章率淮军镇压了太平天国和捻军；光绪十四年（1888）筹组建成了北洋水师。1894 年甲午海战，北洋水师败于日本；次年李鸿章赴日签订《马关条约》，之后曾立誓终身不履日土。李鸿章曾积极推进官办、商办军工企业的发展，亦曾推动建立同文馆及选派学生出洋留学等事宜。其著作后被合编为《李文忠公全集》。

3. 总理各国事务衙门的简称，1861 年 1 月 20 日由咸丰帝批准成立，是清政府为办洋务及外交事务而特设的中央机构。光绪二十七年（1901），据清政府与列强签订的《辛丑条约》第 12 款规定，总理衙门改为外务部。

4. 界限：范围；也用于比喻成见或宗派情绪。

5. 相等。

6. 马快跑的样子；也用于比喻迅疾、急促、匆忙。

7. 泛指海内外广大地区。

8. 帽子与腰带；也用于比喻指官吏、士绅。

9. 而全面观察当今的情势。

10. 《周易》。

11. 清朝常备兵之一。顺治初年，在统一全国过程中，清廷将收编的明军及其他汉兵，参照明军旧制，以营为基本单位进行组建，以绿旗为标志，故称为绿营。

12. 中国早期的行政区划，意指直属京师之地，明朝有南直隶与北直隶。南直隶相当于今江苏、安徽、上海两省一市。北直隶相当于今北京、天津两市、河北省大部和河南、及山东的小部地区。清朝初年，南直隶改称江南省，北直隶改称直隶省。

13. 厘金（厘税）的种类之一。厘金是十九世纪中叶至二十世纪三十年代征收的一种地方商业税，又称厘捐或厘金税。

14. 见"货厘"注释。

15. 弥补；补助。

译文：

筹议海防折 [1]（节选）

李鸿章

现在总理衙门陈请以下六条，当前急切应办的事以及日后长远的规划，都已包括在其中了；所陈请的这些，确实都是挽救时局的重要策略。

无法轻易且迅速办理的事，是人才还难以寻觅、经费还难以筹措、不同的意见还难以化解、旧的陋习还难以根除。但如果这样下去不予改正，虽然日事都有防备，还是如同画饼充饥。既然这样，那么今日我们急于要做的，只有努力破除成见，以求把实际的事情做好。

为什么这么说？历代我们守备的边疆大多在西北，那里各方力量的强弱、我与外邦的状况，都恰好相等，特别是那里有国界。如今我国的东南海疆有万余里，各国通商传教的人士，来往自如。而且这些外国人士，聚集在京师以及各省腹地；表面上，他们做出为和好而来的姿态，而背地里，却心怀吞并我们的计谋；一个国家出现了事端，多国都来挑拨煽动。这确实是数千年来，从未出现过的局面。如今轮船的航速、电报的传送速度，都非常快，真可谓瞬息千里。军事装备以及机器制造的精密程度，使其威力较之以前的旧装置，高了百倍；如今的炮弹，可以摧毁各种设施，水上、陆上的关口，已经不能完全阻止外敌了。我们今天面对的，是数千年来都未曾遇到的强敌。如今外敌对我的侵犯，较以往已有很大变化，而我们却仍然要用现行的法规去应对；这就如同医生治病，不问是何种病症，一律使用传统药方，而这样做实在是无效的。庚申（咸丰十年，1860年）以后，外敌势力快速向我内地广大地区推进，我国习于礼教的民众，人人都感到愤怒、都意气激昂，都争着表达驱逐外敌之意。但局外人对局势的议论，已经不能详尽地显示实际局面的艰难，而要问如何才能自强呢？如何才能抵御外来欺侮呢？则茫然没有可以遵循的规划。自古以来，从来没有在不知己知彼的情况下战胜敌人的先例。如果我们在尚未了解敌方长处以及己方短处的情况下，即为逞意气而孤注一掷、与外敌作战，那岂不是把事关国家的大事当儿戏吗？本人虽然愚钝，但在军中服务十余年间，从来不敢畏缩，也从不愿给皇上留下忧患。只是办理洋务已有较长时间了，比以前增加了些见识，所以对于敌我长短处的对比，了解得较清楚。而全面观察当今的情势，我们的财力和人才，确实还没有达到我们期盼的标准；又有现行法规的约束，内部众多不同意见的掣肘。如此情形之下，即使我们想奋发图强，也无从施展。《周易》有言："遇阻不顺，就要改变，改变后，就会通畅。"如果内部的壅蔽不能打通，谈何进攻防守，就是对外媾和也难以长久。

　　现在根据总理衙门的原仪，逐条详细地筹措、拟定切实可行的办法，同时亦附上我本人的看法，并略作引申。…… 总之，在目前的情况下，我们要整顿海防，除了变法以及启用有才之人，再也没有其他办法了。我恳切地希望皇上，能念及国家、人民的福祉，考虑时局的极度艰危，心中常怀喜悦但不自足的心态；在节省不必要的开支、增强军队的实力、造就人才等方面，完全不必拘泥于以往的惯例；而特别要以培养人才为重中之重，以使国内有志之士都通晓西洋各国状况和如何处理对外事务。这样，或许练兵的水平，以及制造机器、舰船等的能力，就有可能逐渐提高。我们特别需要在一段较长的时间内，集聚诚意、专注于行动，这样才能对形势有利。目前一定要力保和平的局面，就是将来我们的装备精良了、防守牢固了，也不应冲动、引发争端。洋人或许对我们十分无礼，在不得已的情况下，我们应对一下即可。

……

　　…… 如果外国原本就是敌国，彼此只能以军力强弱而较量胜负，而对方的军器比我们强、军事技能也比我们好，那我们即使有可能取得暂时的胜利，最终也会失败。敌人如从海路进犯我内地，我们就必须尽快训练水师。只是各外洋敌国都是岛国，以水为家，长久以来，他们船坚炮利、士兵训练有素；我国的水师，在短时间内，还无法达到他们的水平。我国陆地多于水路，仍然以陆军为立国的基础。如果陆军训练有素，那么在敌军登陆后，我们还可以与他们激战。如果我们的炮台布局得法，敌船接近时，我们还可以拒守。但如果我们让使用箭、刀、矛以及拿鸟枪的旗、绿营的士兵抗击外敌，绝对不可能有效地阻止洋人入侵，而且也不能有效地消灭国内的土寇。即使像直隶的军队那样，士兵都经过多次挑选、整顿，而且最近又开始同时练习使用洋枪、小炸炮，也只能对付国内的土寇；我们实在不敢相信，他们可以抗御外敌的入侵。各省抽调出来训练的士兵大致如此，他们中使用洋枪的已经很少了，而使用后门炮以及炸炮的就更少了。在这种情况下，我们只能加强练兵，而不能削弱训练，只能添加外国造的武器并加强使用外来武器的训练，这样才有可能战胜外来入侵。在现在这样的情势下，我们不能为了要节省费用，而用旧规则束缚自己。

……

…… 西方国家水陆攻、守所用的精良武器，主要是枪、炮、水、电。炮分前后门、及生铁、熟铁、纯钢制造等不同的种类；枪则有前后门、滑膛、来福之分；水雷有碰触、摩擦以及电气等不同的引爆装置。……外国每造枪炮、机器，如果成套购买，价格都高达几十万金；另外从西方国家购运钢铁等材料，也非常昂贵。必须等我们能使用西方国家的科技方法自己开采煤、铁等矿后，再购买高炉、汽锤、压水机等机器，那时我们就可以仿造西方的枪炮、机器了。水雷是炸船破敌最有效的武器……现在上海、天津的工厂，只能仿造一些粗制的水雷；而电机、铜丝、铁绳、橡皮等，还要从外国进口。我们必须寻访、招募外国制造水雷的工程人员，到华来对我们的人员进行培训，或许可使后者在制造技术上不断精进。火器要尽量采用洋式；枪弹，小炮弹以及火药也是急需的。各省江防、海防所用洋枪、洋炮的子药，我们都应在内地设厂仿造；否则什么都从外国商人处购买，使我们根本无法应对紧急情况。而且福建、上海、天津等地的军工机器制造厂，都设在离海口很近地方；这当然是为了方便从海外进口材料，但倘若有突发事变，就必须先用重兵守护。所以这种工厂布局，实在不是很稳妥的。以后，各省筹措增设新工厂时，一定要将工厂建在内地水路交通方便的地方。这样，如果海防口岸发生战事，我们也可以为我们的士兵，源源不断地提供我们储存的自制军器。

……

…… 人们都知道，最近我们的资金严重短缺。如果我们要振兴国家，就必须统一规划全国的局势，并在全国范围内，进行统一的筹措，然后制订计划。……此外，命令沿江沿海各省，整顿对货物以及盐所征收的厘金。每省每年都要限定拨出数万两，以协助海防。以上所谈的几个方面，都是有关开辟财源的事情。如果我们能够削减艇船，以维持轮船的运作；裁减边防驻守军队，以维持海防士兵所需；停止供应官府所要的非急用物品及削减地方上不切实际且过度的花费，以补助军事运作，从而实现我们长远的计划；那么，我们也可以在节省开支方面，取得重大进展。如果不能上下一心、内外一心、局中局外一心，我们就只能半途而废了。

（4）筹议海防折[1][2]（节选）

李鸿章[2]

······

······ 洋人入中国已三十余年，驻京已十余年，以兵胁我，殆无虚岁；而求练达兵略精通洋法者恒不数观，由於不学之过，下不学由於上不教也。……似应於考试功令稍加变通，另开洋务进取一格，以资造就。现在京师既设同文馆[3]，江省[4]亦选幼童出洋学习，似已阐西学门径……拟请嗣后凡有海防省分，均宜设立洋学局，择通晓时务大员主持其事。分为格致[5]、测算、舆图[6]、火轮、机器、兵法、炮法、化学、电气学数门，此皆有切於民生日用军器制作之原。外国以之黜陟[7]人才，故心思日出而不穷。华人聪明才力本无不逮西人之处，但未得其法，未入其门，盖无以鼓励作新之耳。如有志趣思议，於各种略通一二者，选收入局，延西人之博学而精者为之师友，按照所学浅深，酌给薪水，俾[8]得研究精明，再试以事，或分派船厂炮局，或充补防营员弁。如有成效，分别文武，照军务保举章程，奏奖升阶，授以滨海沿江实缺，与正途出身无异；若始勤终怠，立予罢革。其京城同文馆、上海广方言馆[9]习算学生，及出洋子弟学成回国，皆可分调入局教习，并酌量派往各机器局、各兵船差遣。如此多方诱掖，劝惩兼施，就所学以课所事，即使十人中得一成就，已多一人之用，百人中得十成就，已多十人之用，二十年后制器、驶船自强之功效见矣。

……

……窃以古无久而不敝之法，惟在办事之人同心协力，后先相继，日益求精，不独保境息民，兼可推悟新意，裕财足用。如泰西[10]各国，皆起於弹丸之地，创造各样利器，未及百年而成就如此之精，规画如此之远，拓地如此之广，岂非其举国上下积虑殚精[11]，人思自奋之效乎？中国在五大洲中，自古称最强大，今乃为小邦所轻视。练兵、制器、购船诸事，师彼之长，去我之短，及今为之，而已迟矣。若再因循不办，或旋作旋辍，后患殆不忍言。若不稍变成法，於洋务开用人之途，使人人皆能通晓，将来即有防海万全之策，数十年后主持乏人，亦必名存实亡，渐归颓废。惟有中外一心，坚持必办，力排浮议[12]，以成格[13]为万不可泥，以风气为万不可不开，勿急近功，勿惜重费，精心果力，历久不懈，百折不回，庶几[14]军实渐强，人才渐进，制造渐精，由能守而能战，转贫弱而为富强，或有其时乎？是天下臣民所祷祀求之者也。

注释：

1. 见本章［1］（节选）注释1。

2. 见本章［1］（节选）注释2。

3. 京师同文馆于1862年8月24日成立于北京，是清末洋务运动期间中国政府官办、以教授西方语言为主的教育机构，也是中国近代最早成立的新式教育机构。该馆最初只设英文、法文、俄文三班，后陆续增加德文、日文及天文、算学、化学、万国公法、医学生理、物理、外国史地等班。光绪二十七年（1902）并入京师大学堂。

4. 江南省，于清顺治二年（1645）设置，省府位于江宁府（今江苏南京）。那时江南省的范围，大致相当于今天的江苏省、上海市和安徽省。清顺治十八年（1661），江南省被分为江苏（包括上海）和安徽两省。

5. 格致是中国古代认识论的一个命题，指穷究事物的道理而求得知识。清朝末年讲西学的人，用格致做物理、化学等自然科学的总称。

6. 疆土：土地；也指地图。

7. 指人才的进退，官吏的升降。

8. 使得；使之。

9. 上海广方言馆成立于1863年，是上海建立的第一所外国语专科学校。"广方言"，意指推广方言（当时清政府把外国语也视为"方言"）。上海广方言馆除英文、法文、算学外，亦有教授地矿、金属、机械、船炮等工科知识。同治六年（1867），江南制造总局设立翻译馆，同治八年（1869）广方言馆并入制造局，但仍保留广方言馆的名称。光绪三十一年（1905），上海广方言馆改制为工业学校，脱离江南制造总局。

10. 旧时泛指西方国家，一般指欧美各国。

11. 竭尽智谋与精力。

12. 没有根据的议论。

13. 常规、成例、固定的格式。

14. 或许可以，表示希望或推测。

译文：

筹议海防折 [2]（节选）

李鸿章

······

······ 洋人进入中国已有三十多年了，而且在北京也已经驻扎了十多年了，其对我进行的军事威胁，连年不断；而我们熟悉用兵谋略、精通外国法制的人，却十分缺乏。这些都是起因于我们不注重学习西学。而下边的人不学，则是由于上边、国家不提倡造成的。······我们似应对国家考试的法规，稍微进行一些变更，加设有关海外各国事务的考试晋升途径以选拔精通海外事务的人才。现在北京已经开办了外国语专门学校（同文馆），江省也选拔了幼童去西方留学；这些似乎已经开通了学习西学的途径，······今后，我打算请各海防省份，都设立学习西学的学校，选择了解现时情势的高级官员，负责管理。学校应设自然科学、测算、地图、汽轮、机器、兵法、炮法、化学、电气学等学科。所有这些学科，都与民众的日常生活以及军器制造的基本原理有关。外国以对这些学科的精通程度，决定人才的升迁、任用；所以外国的人才，每日都会有新的想法。华人的聪明才智，原本并没有不如西人的地方，但由于不知道正确的方法、没能进入正确的途径，所以他们的创新意愿，就没能得到激发。如有愿意思考、创新，又略通上述学科的人，我们应该选入西学学校，并邀学问博且精的西人，为他们的师友。对于这些选入西学学校的人士，也要按其对所学学科精通的程度，发给薪酬，使之能够在研究中取得成果；之后再尝试任用，或将他们分派到制造船、炮的工厂工作，或分至防御军营中任初级军官。如果他们工作有成效，则量其材质以归类其文、武职别，并按照军务保举章程，给予奖励、提升其官阶，并让他们到有官员空缺的沿海或靠近江河的地区任职。他们所得到的待遇，应等同于那些已通过国家正式考试的官员。但这些人如在以后的工作中表现懒散，则应立即罢免。那些在北京外国语专门学校（同文馆）、上海外国语专科学校（上海广方言馆）学习的学生，以及从西方国家留学归来的人士，都可以到西学学校任教，并也可考虑将他们派往各军工制造企业、各兵船制造厂工作。这样经过多方引导扶持、奖惩并用，这些人士就可用其所学的知识，检验其所从事的工作。如此，即使每十个人中，只有一位取得了成就，我们也可说多了一名有用之人，如果每百人中，我们可以得到十名有用之人，那么我们就多了十名人才。这样二十年后，我们推动的造军器、驶战船等自强运动的功效，就可以显现出来了。

⋯⋯

⋯⋯ 我以为，自古以来，没有哪种法制，长久实施后，仍无弊端；只有办事的人同心协力、前后相继、日益求精，且不仅要保护国家疆界、以使人民得以安宁，同时还能不断创新，这样国家才能富足。如欧美各国，都是从弹丸之地发展起来的。这些国家创造了各种先进的机器，在不到百年的时间内，就取得了如此精湛的成果、有了如此远大的规划、并拓展了如此广大的国土，难道这不是其举国上下久积思虑、竭尽其智谋与精力、且人人思虑自强奋斗的结果吗？自古以来，中国在五大洲中，一直就是最强大的国家；但如今却被小国轻视。练兵、制造机器、购买先进船只，学习西方国家的长处、去掉我们自己的短处，所有这些事宜，我们今日才开始做，已经晚了。如果再因守旧而不做，或者即做即停，那么后患，即会达到几乎无法说出口的程度了。如果不对现行法制稍作修改，不在办理西洋事务中开启用人的途径，使得人人都能通晓洋务；那么，将来就是有了防卫海疆的万全之策，数十年后，此万全之策也会因人才缺乏，而名存实亡，逐渐失效。我们只有中外一心，坚持必办，努力排除那些不切实际的想法，不拘泥于既有的章法、规矩，大力提倡新的风尚习俗，不急于追求近功，不计较花费重金，长期坚持不懈，百折不回，或许我们的军力会逐渐强大起来，人才会逐渐多起来，制造技术也会逐渐进步、发展起来；如此，我们的军力即可从仅能防守，发展到能够应战，我们的国家也会由贫弱转为富强。或许我们会有这一天？而这一天的到来，正是天下臣民所祈祷拜求的。

五、维新运动

(一) 维新运动概论

The Reform Movement:

Kang Youwei (1858 – 1927), Tan Sitong (1865 – 1898) and Liang Qichao (1873 – 1929).

Scholars in the wealthier east-coast provinces of China born between the late 1850s and the early 1870s grew up in a world shaped by the suppression of anti-Qing rebellions and by the Qing self-strengthening project. The orthodox Confucianism that the suppression of the revolt had established as the basis for moral regeneration of the empire was combined with the increasing spread of ideas, techniques and institutions adopted from abroad. The ideology of self-strengthening was articulated by Zeng Guofan, Li Hong Zhang and Zhang Zhidong in this era to encompass the twin aspects of the policies which the post-rebellion restoration group had sought to implement. This self-strengthening ideology was subject to two types of opposition: one from people who thought that the changes it brought were undermining the power of the Qing state, and the other from people who thought that reform of the system was not proceeding rapidly enough. O-verall, however, the institutions and ideologies of dynastic monarchy remained intact through this period.

Enormous attention has been given to those who by the late 19th century had begun to argue that reforms needed to be deepened and intensified. The three most famous figures associated with this late 19th-century call for reform were Kang Youwei, Tan Sitong and Liang Qichao, whose work is discussed here. The lives of these three scholars prior to their ascent to the court in 1898 to initiate a programme of structural reforms (which were ultimately rejected by opponents after the reformers had been in power for only a year) were dominated by three interacting elements: an intensified level of radical critique of established Confucianism arising from within the Confucian tradition, an intensified concern with new forms of knowledge, particularly those associated with the natural sciences and industrial technology, and a sense of a pressing international situation which endangered not simply the Qing state but the survival of the wider Chinese civilisational ethos.

A critical change in the period between the initiation of the self-strengthening movement and the attempted reform of the Qing order by Kang, Liang and Tan was the transformation of Japan, which established itself as an industrial monarchical state similar to those in Western Europe between the 1860s and the 1890s. A war between the Qing Dynasty and Japan which broke out in 1894 ended in defeat for the former, and Li Hongzhang's involvement in negotiating the peace settlement for this war, which was unfavourable to the Qing, resulted in his fall from power. This defeat stirred a new sense of urgency amongst scholars who felt that the defence of the realm required profound modifications.

The project of reform in the 1890s resembled the more idealistic strand of the self-strengthening movement in that it was based on a fusion of moral renewal with technical and institutional enhancement. What distinguished it from its predecessor, however, was not only the nature, extent and speed of the reforms proposed (which would move the Qing state closer to the structures of a constitutional monarchy) but also the utopian vision of a society of greater human harmony that would be initiated through the proper implementation of an alternative reading of the contents of the Confucian classics to that advocated by the proponents of self-strengthening. Monarchy, in this system, was to be not simply a form of ruling power constrained by other constituencies, but part of the fulfilment of a project to bring about a wider redemption of humankind through a form of Confucianism imbued with insights from other traditions; rather than there being conflict between Confucianism and Western thought, the two traditions belonged together in a great global unity.

Tan, like Wei Yuan and Zeng Guofan, was from Hunan. Kang and Liang (who was Kang's student) were from Guangdong, and were thus strongly affected by the new world of industrial maritime culture that emerged after the Opium War. All three scholars were also proponents of the form of scholarship that questioned Song-dynasty readings of the Confucian classics which Wei Yuan represented, although the approach to this tradition that Kang Tan and Liang promoted was far more utopian than that of Wei, in that he presented Confucius as a prophetic figure rather than a teacher.

The experiments in institutional transformation that these reformers undertook with the encouragement of the young Guangxu emperor were snuffed out quite quickly, ending after only 100 days in 1898. Tan Sitong was martyred, and he gone down in history as one of modern China's great scholar-patriots, admired as much for his proficiency in the martial arts as for his learning and moral uprightness. Kang and Liang both fled abroad; while in exile, Kang organized an oppositional movement of constitutional monarchists, which Liang initially supported but eventually rejected after the republican revolution of 1911.

The utopian universalism of Kang Youwei makes him attractive enough to advocates of republicanism interested in the radical transformation of the hierarchical power structures of the dynastic state for his loyalty to the Qing Dynasty and his lack of interest in the cause of anti-Manchu nationalism to be overlooked. His universalistic utopianism, expressed in the absence of hostility to imported science and technology, is also appealing to those republicans who suspect that the native intellectual tradition is too mired in the traditions of dynastic monarchy to serve the liberatory agendas of republican revolution. On the other hand, republicans who are worried that internationalist ideology will expose the country to foreign control can take heart from the intensity of Kang's commitment to the value of Confucian ideas. This commitment can be constructed as a core feature of national culture and not a manifestation of utopian universalism. We might also observe that 20th-century republican patriotism in China has possessed a utopian and universalistic tone that results from the successful assimilation of the ideologies of these late-Qing monarchists.

Sources and Further Reading

Good biographical information on Tan Sitong can be found on pp. 702 – 705 of Arthur W. Hummel (ed.), *Eminent Chinese of the Ch'ing Period*,

Taipei: Ch'eng-Wen Publishing Company, 1967. Biographies of Kang Youwei and Liang Qichao can be found on pp. 228 – 233 and pp. 346 – 351 of Howard L. Boorman *Biographical Dictionary of Republican China*, Vol. 2 New York: Columbia University Press, 1968.

How these three writers fit within the broader intellectual history of China in the Qing can be found in Liang Ch'i-ch'ao, *Intellectual Trends in the Ch'ing Period* (trans. Immanuel C. Y. Hsu), Cambridge, Massachussetts: Harvard University Press, 1959; this is an account produced by one of the individuals involved in and supportive of the critical view of Song and Ming Confucianism (including himself) . Liang Qichao, *Zhongguo Jin sanbainian Xueshu Shi* (A history of Chinese scholarship in the last 300 years), Vol. 2, Taipei: The Commercial Press of Taiwan, 1968, presents the events from the point of view of a supporter of the Song and Ming Confucian tradition, and therefore critical of Kang Youwei. Hou Wailu, *Jindai Zhongguo Sixiang Xueshuoshi* (A history of doctrines and thought in Modern China), Vol. 2, Shanghai: Life Publishing, 1947, presents late Qing thought from a broadly Marxist perspective. Li Zehou, *Zhongguo Jindai Sixiang Shilun* (An essay on the history of modern Chinese thought), Beijing: People's Publishing, 1979, and Wang Hui, *Xiandai Zhongguo Sixiang de Xingqi* (The rise of modern Chinese thought), Beijing: SDX Joint Publishing Company, 2004, examine intellectual developments in the late Qing from a late 20th and early 21st-century perspective.

All of the general histories of the late Qing discuss the reform period. See William T. Rowe, *China's Last Empire: The Great Qing*, Cambridge, Massachussetts, Belknap Press, 2009; Jonathan Spence, *The Search for Modern China*, (2nd ed.), New York: W. W. Norton, 1999, and Immanuel C. Y. Hsü, *The Rise of Modern China*, (fifth edition), New York:

Oxford University Press, 1995. Perhaps the most readable evocation of the individuals involved is Jonathan D. Spence, *The Gate of Heavenly Peace: The Chinese and their Revolution*, 1895 – 1980, Harmondsworth: Penguin, 1980. Peter Zarrow, in his *China in War and Revolution*, 1895 – 1945, London: Routledge, 2005, offers an important recent conceptualization of the period within the larger history of the emergence of republican ideology. An account of the origins of the 1898 reform by one of the major intellectual historians writing in English on this topic is Hao Chang, "Intellectual change and the reform movement, 1890 – 1898" in John K. Fairbank and Kwang-Ching Liu (ed.), *The Cambridge History of China*, Volume 11, Part 2, *Late Ch'ing*, Cambridge: Cambridge University Press, 1980; the same author's *Chinese Intellectuals in Crisis: Search for Order and Meaning* (1890 – 1911), Berkeley: University of California Press, 1987, is one of the most admired studies of this period in English. A fascinating placement of Kang Youwei within the evolution from monarchy to republic can be found in John Fitzgerald, *Awakening China: Politics, Culture, and Class in the Nationalist Revolution*, Stanford: Stanford University Press, 1996. Joseph R. Levenson's *Confucian China and Its Modern Fate: A Trilogy*, Berkeley: University of California Press, 1968, has been hugely influential on post-war Anglophone scholarship on the reform and on the transformation of Confucianism in the modern era.

For a study and translation of the thought of Tan Sitong, see Chan Sin-wai, *An Exposition of Benevolence: The "Jen-hsüeh" of T'an Ssu-t'ung*, Hong Kong: Chinese University Press, 1984. The image of Liang Qichao in the English-speaking world was profoundly shaped by Joseph R. Levenson's *Liang Ch'i-ch'ao and the Mind of Modern China*, Berkeley: University of California Press, 1967. Hao Chang's *Liang Ch'i-ch'ao and Intellectual Transition in China*, 1890 – 1907, Cambridge, Massachusetts:

Harvard University Press, 1971, sees Liang's life less in terms of a conflict between traditions than as part of a process of transition. Xiaobing Tang, *Global space and the nationalist discourse of modernity: the historical thinking of Liang Qichao* Stanford: Stanford University Press, 1996, positions Liang within a larger globalised cultural framework. There are numerous studies of Kang Youwei, although there have been no recent monographs in English. Older works include Kung-chuan Hsiao, *A Modern China and a New World: K'ang Yu-wei, Reformer and Utopian*, 1858 – 1927, Seattle: University of Washington Press, 1975.

（二）维新运动文献

（1）上清帝第一书[1]（节选）

康有为[2]

······

······窃见方今外夷交迫······教民会党遍江楚[3]河陇[4]间，将乱于内。臣到京师来，见兵弱财穷，节颓俗败，纪纲散乱固，人情偷惰，上兴土木之工，下习宴游之乐，晏安欢娱，若贺太平。

······

窃维国事蹙[5]迫，在危急存亡之间，未有若今日之可忧也。方今中外晏然，上下熙熙，臣独以为忧危必以为非狂则愚也。夫人有大疬恶疾不足为患，惟视若无病，而百脉俱败，病中骨髓，此扁鹊[6]、秦缓[7] 所望而大惧也。自古为国患者，内则权臣女谒[8]，外则强藩大盗而已。今皇太后皇上端拱在上，政体清明，内无权臣女谒阉寺[9] 之弄柄，外无强藩大盗之发难，宫府一体，中外安肃，宋、明承平时所无也。臣独汲汲私忧者何哉？诚以自古立国，未有四邻皆强敌，不自强政治而能晏然保全者也。

近者洋人智学之兴，器艺之奇，地利之辟，日新月异。今海外略地已竟，合而伺我，真非常之变局也。日本虽小，然其君臣自改纪后，日夜谋我，内治兵饷，外购铁舰，大小已三十艘，将蓻朝鲜而窥我边。俄筑铁路，前岁十月已到浩罕[10]，今三路分筑，二三年内可至珲春[11]，从其彼德罗堡[12] 都城运兵炮来，九日可至，则我盛京[13] 国本，祸不旋踵[14]。英之得缅甸，一日而举之，与我滇为界矣，滇五金之矿，垂涎久矣，其窥藏卫[15] 也，在道光十九年，已阴图其地，至今乃作衅焉。

法既得越南，开铁路以通商，设教堂以诱众，渐得越南之人心，又多使神父煽诱我民，今遍滇、粤间，皆从天主教者，其地百里，无一蒙学[16]，识字者寡，决事以巫，有司[17] 既不教民，法人因而诱之。又滇、越、暹罗[18] 间，有老挝、万象[19] 诸小国，及猓[20] 苗诸种，法人日煽之，比闻诸夷合尊法神父为总统焉。法与英仇，畏英属地之多也，近亦遍觅外府，攻马达加斯加[21] 而不得，取埃及而不能，乃专力越南以窥中国，数年之后，经营稍定，以诸夷数十万与我从教之民，内外并起，分两路以寇滇、粤，别以舟师扰我海疆，入我长江，江楚教民从焉，不审何以御之？

······

窃观内外人情，皆酣嬉偷惰，苟安旦夕，上下拱手，游宴从容，事无大小，无一能举，有心者叹息而无所为计，无耻者嗜利而借以营私，大厦将倾而处堂为安，积火将然而寝薪为乐，所谓安其危而利其灾者，譬彼病痿，卧不能起，身手麻木，举动不属。非徒痿也，又感风痰[22]，百窍迷塞，内溃外入，朝不保夕，此臣所谓百脉败溃，病中骨髓，却望而大忧者也。今兵则水陆不练，财则公私匮竭，官不择才而上且鬻官，学不教士而下患无学，此数者，人皆忧之痛恨焉，而未以为大忧者也[23]。

······

今论治者，皆知其弊，然以为祖宗之法，莫之敢言变，岂不诚恭顺哉？然未深思国家治败之故也。今之法例，虽云承列圣之旧，实皆六朝、唐、宋、元、明之弊政也。我先帝抚有天下，不用满洲之法典，而采前明之遗制，不过因其俗而已，然则世祖章皇帝[24]已变太祖[25]、太宗[26]之法矣。夫治国之有法，犹治病之有方也，病变则方亦变。若病既变而仍用旧方，可以增疾。时既变而仍用旧法，可以危国。董子[27]曰："为政不和，解而更张之，乃可以理。"吕览[28]曰："治国无法则乱，守而弗变则悖。"《易》曰："穷则变，变则通。"设今世祖章皇帝既定燕京，仍用八贝勒旧法[29]，分领天下，则我朝岂能一统久安至今日乎？故当今世而主守旧法者，不独不通古今之治法，亦失列圣治世之意也。

······

······皇太后皇上知旧法之害，即知变法之利，于是酌古今之宜，求事理之实，变通尽利，裁制厥中[30]，如欲采闻之，则农夫耕而君子食焉[31]，臣愚愿尽言于后也。尤望妙选仁贤，及深通治术之士，与论治道，讲求变法之宜而次第[32]行之，精神一变，岁月之间，纪纲已振，十年之内，富强可致，至二十年，久道化成，以恢属地而雪仇耻不难矣。

日本崎岖小岛，近者君臣变法兴治，十余年间，百废具举，南灭琉球[33]，北辟虾夷[34]，欧洲大国，睨而莫敢伺，况以中国地方之大，物产之盛，人民之众，二帝三王[35]所传，礼治之美，列圣所缔构，人心之固，加以皇太后皇上仁明之德，何弱不振哉？臣谓变法则治可立待也。

注释：

1.《上清帝第一书》通称《第一上书》，为康有为所撰，写于 1888 年 12 月 10 日（光绪十四年十一月初八日）。康有为鉴于中法战争后，帝国主义侵略势力伸入中国西南边陲，以及"洋务变动"开始破产，上书请求变法，提出"变成法"、"通下情"、"慎左右"三条纲领，这是资产阶级改良派第一次向清政府提出的建议。《上清帝第一书》手迹：见《南海先生遗稿》。有正书局印本，刊印较早的是《救时刍言》和光绪二十二年上海时务报馆印的《南海先生四上书记》。此外，《皇朝经世文新编》、《康南海书牍》等也都登载。本文选自刘琅主编《精读康有为》，鹭江出版社，2007年版。

2. 康有为（1858—1927），中国近代政治家、思想家；又名祖诒，字广厦，号长素，广东南海人，人称"康南海"；光绪年间进士，官授工部主事。康有为自幼学习儒家思想，1879年开始接触西方文化，后又通过阅读西方书籍，吸取了西方的进化论和政治观点，并初步形成了其维新变法的思想体系。他曾多次上书光绪帝，批判因循守旧，要求变法维新。1895年，得知《马关条约》签订，康有为联合各省一千三百多名举人上了万言书，即"公车上书"。康有为在《大同书》一书中，集中阐述了他的理想和政治主张。1898年，他与梁启超组织保国会，同年并得光绪皇帝支持推动变法事宜，史称戊戌变法。变法失败后，康有为逃往日本，并组织保皇会，鼓吹开明专制，反对革命。康有为1913年回国后，继续宣扬尊孔复辟，晚年亦始终宣称忠于清朝。1927年，康有为病逝青岛。近年学界对于康有为的历史地位，有着较大争议；对于其政治思想的研究结果，更是百家争鸣。

3. 江楚：江：扬子江；楚：战国时期楚国的地方。江楚所指的地方，大致就是现在的江浙，湖广和江西。

4. 河陇：古代指河西与陇右；相当于今甘肃省西部地区。

5. 紧迫。

6. 春秋战国时期名医。因其医术高超，所以人们用了上古神医"扁鹊"之名称呼他。另有说，扁鹊是一个传说中的人物。

7. 春秋时秦国良医。

8. 指通过宫中嬖宠的女子干求请托；也可泛指通过有权势的妇女干求请托。

9. 指宦官。

10. 古代中亚一国家，定都浩罕城。十九世纪三十年代国势最为强盛，1876年遭俄罗斯帝国吞并。

11. 珲春市现是隶属于延边朝鲜族自治州的县级市，位于吉林省东南部的图们江下游地区，地处中、朝、俄三国交界地带。珲春东南与俄罗斯海滨边疆区接壤。

12. 即俄罗斯城市圣彼得堡。该城始建于1703年，因是俄罗斯皇帝彼得大帝所建，故称圣彼得堡。1712年，圣彼得堡成为俄罗斯帝国的首都。

13. 后金（清）都城，即今辽宁省沈阳市。1621 年，清太祖努尔哈赤攻占了沈阳，并于 1625 年从辽阳迁都于此。1634 年，清太宗皇太极改称沈阳为"盛京"。1644 年清朝迁都北京后，沈阳为陪都。

14. 掉转脚跟，比喻时间极短。

15. 以拉萨为中心向西辐射的高原，大部叫做藏卫，又称卫藏。藏卫又可分为三部分：拉萨、山南地区称为"前藏"，日喀则地区则称为"后藏"，整个藏北高原称为"阿里"。藏卫是藏区的政治、宗教、经济及文化中心。

16. 即蒙馆，旧时对儿童进行启蒙教育的地方，相当于现在的幼儿园或小学；也可指在蒙馆学习的教材和内容。

17. 指官吏。古代设官分职，各有专司，故称"有司"。

18. 现东南亚国家泰国的古称。暹罗于 1949 年更名为"泰国"，意为"自由之国"。

19. 万象是一座历史悠久的城市，始建于公元前 4 世纪。长久以来，万象一直是老挝的首都和经济中心。

20. 古书上指一种长尾猿。文中所用，是对西南地区某些少数民族的蔑称。

21. 马达加斯加（Madagascar），非洲岛国，位于印度洋西部。

22. 病证名，痰扰肝经的病证。

23. 《救时刍言》作"而臣末以为大忧也"；《南海先生四上书记》作："而臣则末以为大忧也"。

24. 清世祖章皇帝，爱新觉罗·福临（1638—1661），即顺治帝，清朝入关后的第一位皇帝。

25. 爱新觉罗·努尔哈赤（1559—1626），后金政权的建立者，为后金首位可汗。其子爱新觉罗·皇太极称清帝后，追尊其为太祖高皇帝。

26. 爱新觉罗·皇太极（1592—1643），1626 年，继位后金可汗，改年号为天聪，史称"天聪汗"。1636 年，皇太极于盛京即皇帝位，改国号为"大清"，改元崇德。

27. 董仲舒（公元前 179—公元前 104），西汉一位与时俱进的思想家，哲学家。

28. 又称《吕氏春秋》，是战国末年的一部杂家著作，共 160 篇。该书为秦代丞相吕不韦及其门人集体编纂而成，其内容涉及甚广，以道家黄老思想为主，兼收儒、名、法、墨、农和阴阳各先秦诸子百家言论，是杂家的代表作。

29. 即"八和硕贝勒共治国政"，又称八王共治制，是后金（清）的创立者努尔哈赤为抑制八旗（八王）的分权倾向，制定并部分实施的一个国政管理制度。八王共治制的出台与部分实施表明，努尔哈赤本人对后金实行专权统治，但其为后金继承人设定的，却是八王共治的分权统治。

30. 中正之道。

31. 该句要说明的是，社会是有分工的。君子虽不耕而食，但他们会在治国方面，做出自己的贡献，所以君子并不是不劳而食的人。参见《孟子·尽心上》："君子居是国也，其君用之，则安富尊荣；其子弟从之，则孝悌忠信。'不素餐兮'，孰大于是？"

32. 依一定顺序。

33. 琉球群岛，琉球群岛历史上曾有琉球国等国家。明治维新之后，日本强制"册封"琉球国王为藩王，后日军武力占领了琉球群岛。1872 年，日本宣布琉球群岛是日本的领土，并设置琉球藩，封琉球国王尚泰为藩王。1879 年，琉球藩被废除，编入鹿儿岛县，同年设置冲绳县。同年，日本正式宣布兼并琉球群岛，琉球被分别划入冲绳县和鹿儿岛县。

34. 虾夷为日本北海道的古称，而虾夷人则是古代日本的族群之一。

35. 二帝：唐尧、虞舜；三王：夏禹、商汤、周文王（或周武王）。

译文

上清帝第一书（节选）

康有为

......

...... 我看到，如今我们正面临着外国的侵扰......而信教及结党的民众，也正活跃于江浙、湖广、江西及甘肃省西部地区；这即意味着将发生内乱。来到京城我看到的，是军队不强、财政竭蹶、礼仪风俗败坏、法制不振、民情懒散；官方大兴土木工程，民众则大肆吃喝游乐；社会上一片安闲欢庆之象，好似在庆贺太平盛世。

......

我觉得，现在国家正面临危急，处于生死存亡的关头；而且我们从来也没有遇到过，像现在这样令人担忧的境况。如今国内外安定平静，国家上下一片兴盛景象。唯独我认为国家处于危机境况，人们一定以为，我不是发狂了，就是愚钝。人患大病，并十分可怕，可怕的是，人在患重病时，还以为没事。这样就会导致百脉全坏、病入骨髓。病至如此，就算把扁鹊和秦缓请来诊断，也只能是表示震惊和忧虑而已。自古以来，国家遭遇的危机，内部源于权臣及有权势的女宠；外部则来自于列强的侵略。如今，皇太后及皇上主持朝政，政府管理体制清明，内部没有女宠、宦官玩弄权术、干扰朝政，外部也没有列强挑衅侵扰，皇上与朝廷间没有隔阂、分歧，国家内外都无大乱，这一情景是宋、明两朝太平盛世时都没有的。但我为什么会这样急切地为国家担忧呢？因为我确实认为，自古以来，没有哪个国家在被四周强敌围困之下，能在不加强治理的情况下，仍然可平安无事的。

近年洋人在创办新学、开发制造技术、开拓和霸占更为广阔的疆土上，都有日新月异的发展。如今，各列强在海外已经抢完地盘，现正联合起来窥伺我国；现在的形势，真是在大动荡之际。日本虽然是小国，但在其国君及朝廷进行政治改革后，无时无刻不在策划侵犯我国。该国在国内筹集军费，并从国外购买铁制舰船，如今已购买了大小舰船三十艘。日本将会侵占朝鲜，从而进一步窥伺我国边境地区。俄国人一直在修铁路，并已于前年将铁路修到了浩罕。如今，俄国人正分别修建三条铁路，且两三年内，即可将铁路修到珲春。届时，俄国人只需九天，即可将军队及大炮，从彼德罗堡城运来；如此，我国大本营盛京，不久也会面临祸端。英国一日之内，即侵占了缅甸，这样其势力就延伸至我国的云南边界了。云南有丰富的矿藏，长久以来，英国一直想将其占为己有；除此之外，英国还窥伺我国西藏的大部分地区。道光十九年（1839），英国即已策划占据这些地区，现在开始进行挑衅。

法国已经侵占了越南，并在那里为通商而修建了铁路，同时为了诱惑当地民众，还设立了教堂；不仅如此，法国还多次指使神父，诱惑我国民众。如今，在云南至广东的广大区域内，民众皆信奉天主教；在方圆百里间，没有人学习蒙学，识字的人也不多，民众有事都询问巫师。既然官府不教导民众，那么法国人就可以借机诱惑我国民众了。另外，在云南、越南、泰国之间还有老挝、万象等小国以及苗等不同的少数民族。我听说，法国人在这些地区，每日煽动；如今这些地方的民众，已经把法国神父视为总统了。法国与英国有仇，且惧怕英国占据的属地太多，所以近年来，也在到处寻找属地；但由于对马达加斯加发动的攻击行动失败了，同时也没能占领埃及，所以法国只能全力攻占越南，以窥伺中国。而数年之后，当其在这些地区的统治稍微稳定后，法国就会动用这一地区内的几十万人以及我国境内信教的民众，从我国境内、境外两路发起进攻，以图侵占云南及广东；另外，还会用其舰船侵扰我国的海疆，甚至进入长江；届时江浙、湖广和江西一带的信教民众，也会响应并追随法国的入侵。如果我们不了解这些情况，那我们怎么能够防御这些侵扰呢？

......

我观察到，现在人们都沉湎于嬉游，而且苟且怠惰，只顾眼前的安闲。他们只知拱手行礼，吃喝游玩；但论起做事，无论大事还是小事，他们都不能做。为此忧心的人，也只能叹息，因为他们也想不出什么好办法来。而那些贪利的无耻之人，则利用这一机会，为自己谋取私利。现在我们面临的形势，就如同一座大厦即将倒塌，但里面的人还觉得平安无事；又如同一场大火即将燃起，但人们还睡在干柴上享受。这种处于危机时，仍只知安闲度日；在面临灾难时，仍只知为自己谋取私利的人，就如同一个人患了病，身体机能丧失了，所以卧床不起，身体、四肢麻木，自己不能控制自己的身体活动；加之又感患风寒，百脉堵塞，体内腐烂，外部病毒侵入；此时，这个人随时都会有生命危险。这就是我所说的，百脉腐烂，且已病入骨髓，看上去就足以引起人们极大的忧患意识。如今我们的士兵，既不在陆地训练，也不在水上演练；在财政方面，无论是政府还是个人，都处于财源枯竭的状态；官员的选拔，不是根据人的才能，而是贩卖官位；学校不培养读书人，导致将来人才缺乏。但这种种情况，虽引起人们的忧虑及痛恨，我却并不认为是值得引起极忧虑的。

......

如今，统治者们都知道这些弊端，然而他们却认为，制度、法规是祖宗传下来的；如果有谁敢谈论变革，那不就是对祖宗的不诚及不恭顺吗？然而统治者这样想的原因，实际上是因为他们没能深入思考，如何才能使国家摆脱困境。虽然我们说，现行的法制是列祖传下来的，但实际上那都是六朝、唐、宋、元、明所实施的弊政。我们的先帝并没有用满洲的法典，而是用明朝遗留下来的法规，安抚天下。这样做的目的，只不过是为了延续旧制而已。然而世祖章皇帝已对太祖、太宗的施政之法，进行了改革。治理国家需要法规，这就如同治病要有药方一样，病症变化了，药方就要随之调整。如病症已起了变化，但仍用旧药方，病症就会恶化。所以说，如果在时代已变的情况下，我们仍沿用旧法治国，那就会给国家造成危害。董仲舒说："如果国家治理不协调，就应弃旧法创新规，这样才能把国家治理好。"《吕氏春秋》中记载："治理国家必须要有法，否则国家会乱；但如只知守旧法，而不知根据情况变化对法规进行革新，则是错误的。"《周易》里说，"遇阻不顺，就要改变；改变后，就会通畅。"假设当今世祖皇帝在定都燕京后，仍用八贝勒旧法分统天下，那我清朝怎么可能到今日还能维持国家的统一和安定呢？所以说，在今天的形势下，那些仍然坚持遵循旧法的人，不仅不理解古今的治国之法，而且其做法也违背了我朝各先祖的治国思想。

……

…… 皇太后和皇上知道旧法的害处，这即是说，皇太后和皇上也知道变革的益处；既如此，就应该认真参考古今治国的原理，寻求事情的真实道理，实施变革以求不断发展、获取最大利益，开创中正之道。如果能够这样做，那么农民耕种，君子食用（注：这里强调的是社会分工，君子并不是白吃，他们会在治国方面做出贡献；参见孟子答学生公孙丑所问），我也愿意随后尽我所能，提出治国建议。我尤其希望能够采用好的办法，选拔德才兼备及有治国方略的人士，参与探讨治国的办法，修习研究变革的道理并依次实施。这样人们的精神就会有变化，经过一段时间，法度就会振兴，十年之内即可富强；二十年后，我们长期倡导的变革，就会取得成功。这样我们就不难做到收复失地、报仇雪耻了。

日本只是一个小岛，但近年来由于其君臣一起推动改革，振兴法制，至今十几年，就做到了百废俱兴，不仅灭到了南边的琉球，而且还占领了北边的虾夷（今日本北海道地区）。欧洲大国看到了，也不敢对日本有所图谋。而中国地大物博，人口众多，得尧、舜二帝，夏、商、周三朝圣明君主传下来的完美礼仪、法制，有历史上众多圣贤所建造的坚定、牢固的人心，再加上皇太后和皇上仁爱、明理的美德，我们怎么不能由弱变强呢？所以我认为，如实施变革，不久即可达到振兴的目的。

（2）仁学[1]（节选）

谭嗣同[2]

······

三十四

······ 夫其祸为前朝所有之祸，则前代之人既已顺受，今之人或可不较；无如外患深矣，海军熸[3]矣，要害扼矣，堂奥[4]入矣，利权夺矣，财源竭矣，分割兆矣，民倒悬矣，国与教兴种将偕亡矣。唯变法可以救之，而卒坚持不变。岂不以方将愚民，变法则民智；方将贫民，变法则民富；力将弱民，变法则民强；方将死民，变法则民生；方将私其智其富其强其生于一己，而以愚贫弱死归诸民，变法则与己争智争富争强争生，故坚持不变也。

······

三十五

······ 故东西各国之压制中国，天实使之，所以曲用其仁爱，至于极致也。中国不知感，乃欲以挟忿寻仇为务，多见其不量，而自窒其生矣。又令如策者之意见，竟驱彼于海外，绝不往来。前此本未尝相通，仍守中国之旧政。伈伈俔俔[5]，为大盗乡愿吞剥愚弄，绵延长夜，丰薶[6] 万劫，不闻一新理，不睹一新法，则二千年由三代[7] 之文化降而今日之土番野蛮者，再二千年，将由今日之土番野蛮降而猿狖，而犬豕，而蛙蚌，而生理殄绝，惟余荒荒大陆，若未始生人生物之沙漠而已。夫焉得不感天之仁爱，阴使中外和会，救黄人将亡之种，以脱独夫民贼之鞅轭乎？

……

三十九

西人悯中国之愚于三纲[8] 也，亟劝中国称天而治，以天纲人，世法平等，则人人不失自主之权，可扫除三纲畸轻畸重之弊矣。

……

四十四

……中国士民之不欲变法，良以繁重之习，渐渍于骨髓；不变其至切近之衣冠，终无由耸其听闻，决其志虑，而咸与新也。日本之强，则自变衣冠始，可谓知所先务矣。乃若中国，尤有不可不亟变者，剃发而垂发辫是也。姑无论其出于北狄[9] 鄙俗之制，为生人之大不便；吾试举古今中外所以处发之道，听人之自择焉。处发之道凡四：曰"全发"，中国之古制是也。发受于天，必有所以用之，盖保护脑气筋者也，全而不偏，此其所以长也；而其病则有重腘之累。曰"全剃"，僧制是也。清洁无累，此其所以长也；而其病则无以护恼。曰"半剪"，西制是也。既足以护脑，而又轻其累，是得两利。曰"半剃"，蒙古、鞑靼[10] 之制是也。剃处适当大脑，既无以蔽护于前，而长发垂辫，又适足以重累于后，是得两害。孰得孰失，奚舍奚从，明者自能辨之，无俟烦言而解矣。

······

注释：

1. 《仁学》是中国近代思想家谭嗣同的重要哲学著作，于 1897 年 1 月 17 日完成，全书 5 万多字，文 50 篇，分为两卷。书写出后，谭嗣同曾抄录副本分别寄给梁启超和唐才常。谭氏牺牲后，1899 年梁、唐分别在日本出版的《清议报》和上海出版的《亚东时报》上连载发表，以后出版过多种单行本。目前以中华书局 1981 年出版，由蔡尚思、方行编集的《谭嗣同全集（增订本）》所收《仁学》校勘最完善。周振甫著《谭嗣同文选注》所收《仁学》有详细注释。基督教思想对于谭嗣同《仁学》一书的建构，有着特别重要的作用。《仁学》的核心思想"仁—通—平等"最后一个立脚点是"平等"。《仁学》反封建的激进思想，对资产阶级革命民主派产生过积极的影响。本文选自加润国选注《仁学——谭嗣同集》，辽宁人民出版社，1994 年版。

2. 谭嗣同（1865—1898），汉族，湖南浏阳人，字复生，号壮飞，又号华相众生、东海褰冥氏、廖天一阁主等。谭嗣同曾钻研儒家典籍，广泛涉猎文史百科，同时又致力于探讨自然科学。他曾奉父命，入赀为江苏候补知府，供职南京；后亦曾被征入京，光绪帝授其四品卿衔军机章京。谭嗣同是中国近代政治家、思想家，著名维新派人物。他公开提出废科举、兴学校、开矿藏、修铁路、办工厂、改官制等变法维新的主张。1898 年，谭嗣同参加戊戌变法，变法失败后被清政府杀害，就义时年仅 33 岁，为世称"戊戌六君子"之一。谭嗣同的代表作有《仁学》、《寥天一阁文》、《莽苍苍斋诗》、《远遗堂集外文》等；后人并将其著作合编为《谭嗣同全集》。

3. 溃败。

4. 腹地。

5. 伈伈：小心恐惧的样子。俔俔：眼睛不敢睁大的样子。小心害怕或低声下气的样子。

6. 遮蔽。

7. 夏、商、周三个朝代。

8. 旧时礼教所提倡的三种人伦从属关系。三纲：父为子纲、君为臣纲、夫为妻纲。

9. 古代北方少数民族的统称。

10. 古代对北方游牧民族的称呼。

译文：

仁学（节选）

谭嗣同

······

三十四

······前朝的所有灾祸，前朝的人们已经承受了，现在的人们对那些灾祸，或许已经不再关注了。但是今天我们面临的来自外部的祸患，也已十分严峻，我们的海军已全军溃败，我们的战略要地已被别人控制，内地已遭外侵，权利也已经丧失，我们的财源已经枯竭，我们的国家也有被瓜分的危险。如今我们的民众犹如被倒吊了起来，我们的国家、我们的学说、我们的种族，都面临着消亡的危险。在这种情况下，只有变革，才能使我们免于消亡，但现在我们还是在坚守现行的法规。难道这是因为变法将开启民智，使愚民政策难以实施；变法后民众将会致富，现时所行让民众处于贫困状态的政策，就会失效；变法会使民众的力量变得强大，而试图削弱民众力量的统治方略，就会终结；变法将使民众获得新生，而置民于死地的统治也将无法继续？统治者只想独占知识、财富，只想让自己强大，自己的生命得到保障，而将无知、贫困、弱小、生命不保，推给民众。因为统治者担心变法后，民众会要求打破统治者对知识、财富的独占，会变得强大，会为自己争取生存权，所以统治者一直拒不推动变法。

······

三十五

······东、西方国家对中国的压制，是上天的意愿；是上天仁爱之心的最深刻体现。中国不知道其中的道理，才会一心要报仇雪耻。这就意味着，中国其实并不知道自己的弱点，从而会断送自己发展的机会。更有甚者，中国还采用了驱逐外国人，并与之断绝往来的意见。结果，中国未能与外部世界交流；而在国家治理方面，则仍旧遵循旧法。中国民众仍生活在恐惧中，他们被那些大强盗及地方上的伪君子，疯狂得剥削、愚弄。在漫长的黑暗生活中，有无数的灾难被掩盖了。他们没有听说过新的道理，也没有见过新的法制。所以，两千年来，我们已经从三代时期的文明，堕落到今日的野蛮时代；如这样下去，再过两千年，我们将会从今日的野蛮时代，回到猿猴时代，并进一步降到狗猪、蛙蚌时代。再下一步，生物就会灭绝，唯一留下来的，只能是茫茫荒野，就如同人类及各种生物都无法生存的沙漠一样。如果这样，我们现在为什么不感激上天将仁爱带给我们，并努力使我们和外国建立联系，以从危亡中挽救中国人民，并使其摆脱残暴统治者的控制呢？

……

三十九

西方人怜悯中国人被三纲所迷惑，所以急切地奉劝中国遵循上天的治理。因为只有遵循上天的治理，世间才会平等、且人人才不会失去自主权。这样，中国就可以消除三纲带给人们的不平等的弊端。

……

四十四

……中国官民不想变革的原因，是因为他们有着根深蒂固的追求繁重礼俗的传统。除非要求他们更换服装式样，否则没有任何其他方法可以唤醒他们，以及告诉他们下决心，将所有事情更新。日本的强大，就是从改变服饰开始的。他们知道，什么是首先应该改变的。对于中国而言，当务之急，是要改变剃发、留辫子的规定。姑且不论这一规定是出于北狄蛮族的陋俗，以及这一规定给人们生活造成的不便，我这里试着列举出古今中外头发修饰的方法，看后，人们可以自己做出判断。头发修饰的方法，大概有四种。一种叫"全发"；这是中国古代流传下来的头发修饰方法。人们的头发是上天赐予的，所以必有它的用处，那就是要保护脑神经。"全发"方法的益处，就是能够保留全部头发。但这种方式也有弊端，那就是人的身体，要承载头发的重量。另一种方式是"全剃"，即将头发全部剃光。这是僧人采用的方式。清洁、方便，是这种方式的长处；但其弊端，是无法保护脑部。"剪去一半头发"，是西方人的头发修饰方法。这种方式的长处，是既可保护脑部，又可减轻头发的重量。"剃光一半头"是蒙古人、鞑靼人采用的头发修饰方式。由于剃光的部位正好在头的前半部大脑之上，所以这种方式存在双重弊端：即，非但不能保护头前部的大脑，而且又因长发编成的辫子垂在身后而加重了身体的负担。上述各种头发的修饰方式，哪种好、那种不好；应采用哪种方式，聪明人自然能够知道，所以已经无需再作进一步的说明了。

……

（3）变法通议¹ [1]（节选）

梁启超²

自序

法何以必变？凡在天地之间者，莫不变。……故夫变者，古今之公理也。……上下千岁，无时不变，无事不变。公理有固然，非夫人之为也。……言治旧国必用新法也。其事甚顺，其义至明，有可为之机，有可取之法，有不得不行之势，有不容少缓之故。为不变之说者，犹曰守古守古，坐视其因循³ 废弛⁴，而漠然无所动于中。呜呼，可不谓大惑不解者乎？《易》曰："穷则变，变则通，通则久。"伊尹⁵ 曰："用其新，去其陈，病乃不存。夜不炳烛则昧，冬不御裘⁶ 则寒，渡河而乘陆车者危，易证而尝旧方者死。"

……

论不变法之害

…… 外而交邻，始用闭关绝市之法，一变而通商者十数国，再变而命使者十数国矣。此又以本朝变本朝之法者也。吾闻圣者虑时而动，使圣祖[7]世宗[8] 生于今日，吾知其变法之锐，必不在大彼得[9]（俄皇名），威廉第一[10]（德皇名），睦仁[11]（日皇名），之下也。

……

难者曰：法固因时而易，亦因地而行。今子所谓新法者，西人习而安之，故能有功，苟迁其地则弗良矣。

释之曰：泰西[12]治国之道，富强之原，非振古如兹[13]也，盖自百年以来焉耳。举官新制，起于嘉庆十七年 …… 民兵之制，起于嘉庆十七年。工艺会所，起于道光四年。农学会，起于道光二十八年。国家拨款以兴学校，起于道光十三年。报纸免税之议，起于道光十六年。邮政售票，起于道光十七年。轻减刑律，起于嘉庆二十五年。汽机之制，起于乾隆三十四年。行海轮船，起于嘉庆十二年。铁路，起于道光十年。电线，起于道光十七年。自余一切保国之经，利民之策，相因而至，大率皆在中朝嘉、道之间。盖自法皇拿破仑[14]倡祸以后，欧洲忽生动力，因以更新。至其前此之旧俗，则视今日之中国无以远过 ……惟其幡然[15]而变，不百年间，乃浡然而兴矣。然则吾所谓新法者，皆非西人所故有，而实为西人所改造。改而施之西方，与改而施之东方，其情形不殊，盖无疑矣。况蒸蒸然起于东土者，尚明有因变致强之日本乎？

……

　　难者曰……然中国当败衄之后，穷蹙[16]之日，虑无余力克任此举。强敌交逼，眈眈思启，亦未必能吾待也。

　　释之曰：日本败于三国，受迫通商，反以成维新之功。法败于普，为城下之盟，偿五千兆福兰格[17]，割奥斯[18]、鹿林[19]两省，此其痛创过于中国今日也。然不及十年，法之盛强，转逾畴昔[20]。然则败衄非国之大患，患不能自强耳。

……

注释：

1. 《变法通议》是梁启超担任上海《时务报》主笔时发表的早期政论文章的结集，发表的起止日期为 1896 年至 1899 年，共有 14 篇，其中 12 篇刊于 1896 年至 1898 年的《时务报》，另外两篇刊于 1898 年底至 1899 年初的《清议报》。《变法通议》收入《饮冰室合集·文集》第一册的第一卷、入选时，编次略有更动。《变法通议》全篇都是在谈论变法，倡言维新。由于梁启超和其他维新派人士一样，是教育救国论者，因此，在《变法通议》中，教育救国思想非常明显，其中，教育思想比较集中的篇目为《学校总论》、《论科举》、《论师范》、《论女学》和《论幼学》等。本文选自何光宇评注梁启超著《变法通议》，华夏出版社，2002 年版。

2. 梁启超（1873—1929），汉族，广东新会人，字卓如，号任公，又号饮冰室主人，光绪年间举人；中国近代政治活动家、启蒙思想家、教育家、学者。梁启超自幼在家中接受传统教育，后又阅读西书。1898 年 7 月，梁启超曾受光绪帝召见，并奉命进呈所著《变法通议》。他与老师康有为一起领导了戊戌变法；变法失败后，逃亡日本。在日期间，梁启超宣传改良，反对革命，同时也大量介绍了西方社会政治学说。民国初年，梁启超曾支持袁世凯，但之后他反对袁氏称帝，并与蔡锷策划武力反袁。梁启超曾出任段祺瑞北洋政府的财政总长。之后梁启超退出政坛，并于 1922 年起在清华学校兼课，1925 年应聘任清华国学研究院导师，1927 年，离开清华研究院。1929 年一月十九日，梁启超于北京协和医院病逝。在学术研究方面，梁启超亦涉猎广泛，其著作后被合编为《饮冰室合集》。

3. 沿袭按老办法做事；守旧而不改变。

4. 荒废懈怠，败坏；朝纲废弛。

5. 商初大臣，名伊，一说名挚，相传生于伊水，生卒年不详。尹为官名。伊尹曾辅佐商汤王灭夏，又帮助商汤制定了各种典章制度。伊尹还被视为中国烹饪界的鼻祖，也是中药史上伟大的药剂学家。

6. 皮衣，即皮毛服装。

7. 清圣祖，爱新觉罗·玄烨（1654—1722），为清入关后第二代君主，在位六十一年，年号康熙，又称康熙帝。

8. 清世宗，爱新觉罗·胤禛（1678—1735），康熙帝第四子，年号雍正，又称雍正帝。

9. 彼得一世，阿列克谢耶维奇·罗曼诺夫（Пётр Алексе́евич Рома́нов）（1672—1725），人称彼得大帝，为俄罗斯帝国罗曼诺夫王朝沙皇（1682—1725），及俄国皇帝（1721—1725）。在位期间力行改革，他制定的西方化政策，是使俄国变成一个强国的主要因素。

10. 威廉一世（Wilhelm I, 1797—1888），全名威廉·腓特烈·路德维希（Wilhelm Friedrich Ludwig），普鲁士国王（1861—1888），1871 年 1 月 18 日就任德意志帝国第一任皇帝。

11. 明治天皇（1852—1912），第一百二十二代日本天皇（1867—1912 在位）。1860 年被定为储君，并赐名睦仁。

12. 旧时泛指西方国家，一般指欧美各国。

13. 振古：自古；兹：这样。意为：历来如此；自古以来就是这样。

14. 拿破仑·波拿巴（Napoléon Bonaparte, 1769—1821），法国近代军事家、政治家；法兰西第一共和国第一执政（1799—1804），法兰西第一帝国及百日王朝皇帝（1804—1814，1815）；在其统治下，法国曾经占领过西欧和中欧的广大领土。

15. 迅速而彻底地。

16. 窘迫；困厄。

17. 50 亿法郎。

18. 即阿尔萨斯（Région Alsace），法国东北部的一个地区。普法战争（1870—1871）后被割让给普鲁士。一战结束后属法国领土，二战初期再度归德国。1944 年，法国重新获得了阿尔萨斯的控制权。

19. 即洛林（Lorraine），法国东北部的一个地区。普法战争（1870—1871）后，洛林东部和阿尔萨斯被割让给德国；1919 年依据《凡尔赛和约》，归还给法国；1940 至 1945 年间，再度被德国占领；1945 年，法国重新获得了洛林的主权。

20. 往昔；日前；以前。

译文：

变法通议 [1]（节选）

梁启超

自序

为什么一定要变法呢？凡是存在于天地之间的事物，没有不变的。……所以变革是古今世间的真理。……上下千年，变化无时无刻不在进行着，事物不分何种何类，也都在进行着变化。这是自然规律，不是人为可以改变的。……治理古老的国家，必须要用新的法制；这样事情就会非常顺利，道义就会非常明确，就会有可以做事的机会，有值得遵循的法规，有不得不行的时机，有不容怠慢的办法。可那些不想变革的人仍然在说，遵守古训、遵守古训；他们看到了因为遵循旧制而造成的衰败，但却坐视不管，无动于衷。唉，难道这不让人感到非常迷惑、无法理解吗？《周易》里说，"遇阻不顺，就要改变，改变后，就会通畅。"伊尹说，"用新生的东西、屏除陈腐的东西，疾病就会痊愈。夜间不点蜡烛，会很暗；冬天不穿皮衣，会很冷；使用旱路交通工具渡河，会有危险；病症出现了变化，但仍用旧药方医治，病人就会有生命的危险。"

……

论不变法之害

……在对外交流方面，我们开始时封闭关口，不与外国通商；而变革后，开始与十几个国家通商；进一步变革后，我们使者出使的国家，已经达到了几十个；而这些又是本朝人对本朝法规进行的变革。我听说，圣人会分析时局的变化，进而采取相应的治理措施。假如圣祖世宗生于今日，我知道，其推动变法的急切的心情与坚决的态度，绝不在俄皇大彼得、德皇威廉一世、日皇睦仁之下。

……

守旧者说，法制应因时代改变，而有所改变；但也应该因地区不同，而有所不同。现在人们所说的新法，西方国家实施后，国家得以安定，所以新法对西方国家来说，是有益的。但如果将这些新法拿到其他国家实施，则是不好的。

主张变法的人认为，欧美国家的治国之道，是其富强的原因；但这些国家并不是自古以来都是如此，其所以富强，只是大约百年来实施了新法。其新的选官制度，在嘉庆十七年开始实施……民兵制度也始于嘉庆十七年；工艺会所的建立，始于道光二十八年；国家拨款振兴学校，始于道光三十年；有关报纸免税的主张，起于道光十六年；邮政售票始于道光十七年；减轻刑律，起于嘉庆二十五年；汽轮机的制造，始于乾隆三十四年；轮船航海，始于嘉庆十二年；铁路始于道光十年；电线的使用，始于道光十七年。自那以后，西方国家一切保国利民的政策，大都在嘉庆至道光年间（1796—1850），相承制定出来。大概在法皇拿破仑带头发起争端后，欧洲很快孕生出发展的动力，并因此而发生了变革。而欧洲此前所实施的旧俗，甚至还劣于今日中国的旧法。但由于欧洲实施了迅速而彻底的变革，所以不到百年，就兴盛起来了。既然这样，我们所说的新法，绝不是本来就属于西人的，西人只是对其进行了改造。将法制改造后在西方实施与将其改造后在东方实施，没有什么不同，这点大概是不会有疑问的。何况还有在东方因变法而强盛起来的国家——日本。

……

守旧者说……中国由于在战事中受损，现正处于窘迫情形中，我们担心此时的中国，并没有额外的能力，进行变法革新；加之现在强敌逼近，且正虎视眈眈地注视着我们，无时无刻不在图谋侵犯我国，所以我们也未必有时间推动变革。

主张变法的人认为，日本在与三个国家进行的战事中都失败了，并被迫与外国通商。但这一切反而促成了日本的变法维新。法国败于普鲁士，并被迫签订了城下之盟，不但赔偿了五千兆福兰格，而且还割让了奥斯、鹿林两省；法国因此遭受的损失，其程度超过了今日中国受创的程度。但在不到十年的时间内，法国不但振兴强盛起来了，而且其强盛程度还超过了以往的法国。由此可见，战败并不是一个国家所面临的大患，对于一个国家来说，真正的灾难，是其不能自强。

……

（4）变法通议[1] [2]（节选）

梁启超[2]

……

论不变法之害

天下之为说者，动曰"一劳永逸"，此误人家国之言也。今夫人一日三食，苟有持说者曰"一食永饱"，虽愚者犹知其不能也。以饱之后历数时而必饥，饥而必更求食也。今夫立法以治天下，则亦若是矣。法行十年，或数十年，或百年而必敝，敝而必更求变，天之道也。故一食而求永饱者必死，一劳而求永逸者必亡。今之为不变之说者，实则非真有见于新法之为民害也。

……

论变法不知本原之害

难者曰：中国之法，非不变也，中兴以后，讲求洋务，三十余年，创行新政，不一而足。然屡见败衄，莫克振救，若是乎新法之果无益于人国也。

释之曰：前此之言变者，非真能变也，即吾向者所谓补苴罅漏[3]，弥缝[4]蚁穴[5]，漂摇一至，同归死亡；而于去陈用新，改弦更张之道，未始有合也。……日人之游欧洲者，讨论学业，讲求官制，归而行之；中人之游欧洲者，询某厂船炮之利，某厂价值之廉，购而用之。强弱之原，其在此乎！呜呼！今虽不幸而言中矣，惩前毖后，亡羊补牢，有天下之责者，尚可以知所从也。

今之言变法者，其荦荦大端[6]，必曰练兵也，开矿也，通商也。斯固然矣。然将率[7]不由学校，能知兵乎？选兵不用医生，任意招募，半属流丐，体之羸壮所不知，识字与否所不计，能用命乎？将俸极薄，兵饷极微，伤废无养其终身之文，死亡无恤其家之典，能洁己效死乎？图学不兴，厄塞不知，能制胜乎？船械不能自造，仰息他人，能如志乎？海军不游弋他国，将卒不习风波，一旦临敌，能有功乎？如是则练兵如不练。矿务学堂不兴，矿师乏绝，重金延聘西人，尚不可信，能尽利乎？机器不备，化分不精，能无弃材乎？道路不通，从矿地运至海口，其运费视原价或至数倍，能有利乎？如是，则开矿如不开。商务学堂不立，罕明贸易之理，能保富乎？工艺不兴，制造不讲，土货销场，寥寥无几，能争利乎？道路梗塞，运费笨重，能广销乎？厘卡[8]满地，抑勒逗留，朘膏削脂，有如虎狼，能劝商乎？领事不报外国商务，国家不护侨寓商民，能自立乎？如是，则通商如不通。其稍进者曰：欲求新政，必兴学校。可谓知本矣。然师学不讲，教习乏人，能育才乎？科举不改，聪明之士，皆务习帖括[9]，以取富贵，趋舍异路，能俯就[10]乎？官制不改，学成而无所用，投闲置散，如前者出洋学生故事，奇才异能，能自安乎？既欲省、府、州、县，皆设学校，然立学诸务，责在有司[11]，今之守令，能奉行尽善乎？如是，则兴学如不兴。自余[12]庶政[13]，若铁路，若轮船，若银行，若邮政，若农务，若制造，莫不类是。盖事事皆有相因而至之端，而万事皆同出于一本原之地，不掣其领而握其枢，犹治丝而棼之[14]，故百举而无一效也。

今之言变法者，其蔽有二。其一，欲以震古铄今[15]之事，责成于肉食官吏之手；其二，则以为黄种之人，无一可语，委心异族，有终焉之志。夫当急则治标之时，吾固非谓西人之必不当用，虽然，则乌可以久也！中国之行新政也，用西人者，其事多成；不用西人者，其事多败。询其故，则曰西人明达，华人固陋；西人奉法，华人营私也。吾闻之日本变法之始，客卿[16]之多，过于中国也。十年以后，按年裁减，至今一切省署，皆日人自任其事，欧洲之人，百不一存矣。今中国之言变法，亦既数十年，而犹然借材异地，乃能图成，其可耻孰甚也！夫以西人而任中国之事，其爱中国与爱其国也孰愈？夫人而知之矣，况吾所用之西人，又未必为彼中之贤者乎！

······

吾今为一言以蔽之曰：变法之本，在育人才；人才之兴，在开学校；学校之立，在变科举；而一切要其大成，在变官制。难者曰：子之论探本穷原，靡[17]有遗矣。然兹事体大，非天下才，惧弗克任······释之曰：不然。夫渡江者泛乎中流，暴风忽至，握舵击楫，虽极疲顿，无敢云者。以偷安一息，而死亡在其后也！······虽曰难也，将焉[18]避之！抑岂不闻东海之滨，区区三岛，外受劫盟，内逼藩镇，崎岖多难，濒于灭亡，而转圜之间，化弱为强，岂不由斯道[19]矣乎！则又乌知乎今之必不可行也。有非常之才，则足以济非常之变······

······

注释：

1. 见本章［1］（节选）注释1。

2. 见本章［1］（节选）注释2。

3. 补苴：补缀；罅漏：缝隙。补好裂缝，堵住漏洞；比喻弥补事物的缺陷。

4. 弥补缝合缺陷。

5. 蚂蚁的巢穴；也可用来比喻可以酿成大祸的小漏洞。

6. 荦荦：清楚、分明的样子；大端：事情的重要方面。指主要的项目，明显的要点。

7. 同"将帅"。

8. 旧时征收厘金的机构。一般于通商要道设置正卡，下设分卡、巡卡等。

9. 泛指科举应试文章，明清时亦用指八股文。

10. 屈尊而就职。

11. 指官吏。古代设官分职，各有专司，故称"有司"。

12. 以外；此外。

13. 各种政务。

14. 指理丝不找头绪，就会越理越乱。比喻解决问题的方法不正确，使问题更加复杂。 棼：纷乱。

15. 震动古人，显耀当世，形容事业或功绩伟大。

16. 指在本国做官的外国人。

17. 这里指"无"。

18. 怎么。

19. 这条道路。

译文：

变法通议 [2]（节选）

梁启超

论不变法之害

世上著书立说的人常常说，一劳永逸。但这一说法，是一个误人误国的说法。现在人们都是一日三餐；但如果有人说，吃一顿饭就永远不会饿，那么就是愚昧无知的人也知道，这是不可能的。吃饱后，过几个时辰就又会感到饿，进而还要再吃。如今我们立法治国也是一样。一种法制实施了十年或几十年、上百年后，一定会有不合时宜的弊端；而弊端出现后，就必须变更法制，这是天理。所以吃一顿饭就想永远不饿的人，定会饿死；想一次把事情做好以后就不用再做的人，也一定会失败。如今为守旧辩解的人，实际上并没有见到任何由于实施新法而给民众造成的伤害。

......

论变法不知本原之害

守旧者说，中国的法制，并不是没有变。中兴以后，我们推动了洋务运动；三十多年来，我们创立并实施了新政，这里无法一一列举。但在这期间，我们却屡遭挫败，而且还无法从挫败中振兴。如此，新法果然是对国人无益了。

主张变法的人认为，前面守旧者所说的变革，并不是真正的变革，而只是我以前所说的对一些事物缺陷的弥补，而当动荡来时，大家还会同归于尽。而真正去旧施新的改革、变更措施，我们还从未真正实施过。……日本人去欧洲，会与西人讨论学业，修习研究西方国家的官制，回来后即效仿实施；中国人去欧洲，会去询问哪些兵工厂生产的舰船、火炮威力大，哪些工厂的产品便宜，然后买回去用。导致一个国家强与弱的根本原因，是不是就在这一区别上呢？唉，虽然不幸，但今天还是让我说中了。但那些懂得惩前毖后、亡羊补牢的道理，且对国家有责任感的人，仍然可以从中得到今后应该如何做的启示。

如今主张变法的人，其所强调的重要方面，一定是练兵、开矿、通商；这是当然的。但是将帅不经过学校培养，怎能知道兵法？不经体检就任意招募士兵，其结果会是，半数所招的士兵，都是流浪乞讨的人，我们不知道他们体质的强弱；且不论这些士兵识字与否，但他们能不能听从命令呢？对于这一点，我们也不清楚。军人的薪俸都很低，如果在战场上受伤，他们没有钱供养自己的余生，如战死在战场上，我们也没有为其家属提供抚恤金的规章制度。在这样的情况下，我们的军人能遵守行为规范、为国效命吗？如果不发展地图学，我们就不知哪里是险阻要塞，这样我们能够取胜吗？自己不能制造船械，而必须依赖从外国购买，这样能够实现我们的意愿吗？如果我们的海军不能到他国遊弋，军官、士兵不能适应海上的风浪，这样一旦敌人来犯，我们能打败敌人吗？真如上述所言，那练兵就如同不练一样。

不办矿务学校，即会缺乏矿务专业人员；虽可用高薪聘请西人，但我们仍然无法完全信任西人；在这样的情况下，我们能够获得最大的利益吗？机器不完备，分类不精细，能不生产废品吗？道路不通，将矿产从产地运至海港的运费就会高出数倍，这样能有利润吗？如果真是如此，开矿就如同不开矿一样。不办商务学校，就不会有什么人懂得商贸理论；这样我们能保护我们的财富吗？技术不进步，不注重制造业，而且销售本地产品的市场，寥寥无几；这样我们能为自己争取利益吗？道路阻塞，运费昂贵，这样我们能够大量销售产品吗？到处都设征收厘金的机构，勒索、克扣，延误商机，如同虎狼般搜刮民财，这样能勉励人们从商吗？领事不报告外国商务的情况，国家不能保护侨居外国的商民，这样国家能够自立吗？果真如此，通商就如同没有通商。稍有些变革思想的人认为，要推动新政，就必须兴办学校。这些人可说是看到了问题的本质。但不重视学校，缺乏教师，这样能培养人才吗？科举制度不改，聪明人士都要学习八股文、埋头科举，以获取荣华富贵，选择这样不同的道路，能屈尊任官吗？官制不改，就是学成也无用武之地，只能被安排在闲散职位上，不能被重用。如前述出洋留学的学生，虽有奇才异能，但如不能被重用，他们会心甘情愿吗？既然省、府、州、县都要办学校，那么办学的各种事务，责任就都在官员身上，但现时的地方官能遵循规章、将办学事务做得十分完善吗？此外各种政务，如铁路、轮船、银行、邮政、农业、制造业，无不如此。大概事务都有相因而至的原因，但所有的事务，都出于同一本源。不抓住事务的重点，掌握其起决定性作用的部分，就如同整理丝线时，不先找出头绪，这样就会越理越乱，做百件事，也不会有一件有成效。

如今主张变法的人士，有两个毛病：一是要把震古铄今的宏伟大业，交由享有厚禄的官员负责；一是认为黄种人，没有一人是值得理睬的；他们倾心西人，有让其在中国安身终老的想法。目前中国的当务之急是治标，而不是要从根本上彻底根治存在的问题。我原本并不是说，西人一定不能用，虽是如此，但怎么可以长时间地任用他们呢！中国推行的新政，在任用西人的时候，很多事情都可以办好；不用西人，则很多事情都办不好。这是因为，西人明达，中国人见识浅薄；西人遵守法令，中国人只谋求私利。我听说，日本开始变法的时候，任用的外国官员比我们还多。但十年之后，即按年裁减，至今日本的所有中央官署，都已由日本人自己管理，欧洲人已经见不到了。如今中国谈论变法，也已经几十年了，但我们仍然要任用外国人，才能促使事情办成；如此，我们和日本，谁更应该感到羞愧。任用西人为中国做事，我们是更爱中国，还是更爱外国，人们都是很清楚的。何况我们所任用的西人，也未必就是西人中有德、有才的人士。

......

总而言之，变法最重要的一个方面，就是要培育人才；而培育人才，就要开办学校；能否办好学校，则要看我们能不能改变科举制度。而所有这些，又都取决于我们能否改革官制。守旧者认为：上述说法，说到了变法的根本，没有遗漏。但此事重大，除非是世间才子，否则是不敢轻易承担此重任的。主张变法的人认为：不对。如果渡江的人，渡到江中时，忽然刮起了大风，那他们就一定要掌好舵、划好浆，而且虽已极度疲劳，也没有人敢于放弃；因为如果只顾当时的疲劳，而稍事休息，那么渡江的人就会有生命危险。......虽说很难，但将怎么逃避呢！难道没有听说过东海之滨的三个小岛，既受到来自外部的劫盟，又遭遇到向内进逼的藩镇，其发展过程崎岖多难，甚至曾一度濒于灭亡。但其在调整、变革、挽回危局的时期，即能够转弱为强；如此看，难道不应该走变革的路吗？而我们又怎么知道，这条路今日一定走不通呢？只要有优秀的人才，就足以推动意义重大的变革。

六、共和思想

（一） 共和思想概论

The Republican Movement:

Zou Rong (1885 – 1905), Chen Tianhua (1875 – 1905) and Sun Yat-sen (1866 – 1924).

Sun Yat-sen (who is known as Sun Zhongshan in the Mandarin romanization of his name) is honoured as the father of the Chinese republic and the most famous of the revolutionaries who sought from the end of the 19th century to bring both Manchu domination and monarchical rule to an end. He was born a year after Tan Sitong. Like Kang Youwei and Liang Qichao, he came from Guangdong Province and was influenced by the wider maritime world whose structures Wei Yuan had sought to chronicle and Lin Zexu had sought to manage. Like Chen Tianhua (another of the two other revolutionary republicans whose writing is surveyed here), who was two years younger than Liang, he was a product of the broad atmosphere of dynastic restoration engineered by Zeng Guofan, Li Hongzhang and the other self strengtheners. However, Sun Yatsen was only superficially

learned in the Chinese classics; he certainly did not grasp the complexities
of the scholarly debates that framed the writings of Gu Yanwu, Huang
Zongxi, Wei Yuan, Lin Zexu, Zeng Guofan, Li Hongzhang, Zhang Zhidong or Kang, Tan and Liang. He received a crucial part of his education in
two places under monarchical rule where English was commonly used in
daily life: the Hawaiian Kingdom and the British colony in Hong Kong.
His commitment to the cause of revolutionary republicanism was sharpened
by Japan's defeat of the Qing in the war of 1894 - 1895 and then by the o-
verturning of the reforms advocated by Kang, Tan and Liang; his ideology
fused opposition to dynastic monarchy with a broad globalism, opposition
to Manchu rule, and commitment to a rendering of Chinese thought traditions as a national culture which was broadly defined (in a not dissimilar
way to that of its American counterpart) as having a message for human-
kind as a whole.

Foreign education differentiated Sun Yat-sen from the scholars raised
in the Qing academies that had spawned such people as Kang Youwei and
Tan Sitong. Some might argue that this lessened his commitment to the institutions of monarchy, or that residence in countries where Chinese people
existed as a community defined by outsiders' perception of their common
ethnicity, and not their relationship to monarchy, helped to create his sense
of a Chinese nation that might be defined separately from the institutions of
monarchy. Sun's foreign education was privately paid for. In this regard he
was different from the other two revolutionaries whose writings are studied
in this section of the book. Chen Tianhua and Zou Rong studied in Japan as
part of the general movement to encourage Chinese students to go abroad
that was promoted by the Self-Strengtheners, and in particular by Zhang
Zhidong. During their stay in Japan, the forms of scholar-student activism
on behalf of the state which Kang Youwei, Tan Sitong and Liang Qichao

represented became fused with those of a global culture of the radicalism of the educated that was attacking established regimes all around the world and would go on to influence the movements to establish revolutionary (or at least liberal) republics across the globe in the 20th century. For Zou Rong, the struggle to overthrow autocracy and the struggle to expel foreign rulers are linked projects. His most famous work, "Revolutionary Army", is an anti-Manchu tract full of traditional Chinese cultural imagery whose language is very largely classical Chinese; it fits within the broad global idiom of an anti-dynastic radicalism that urges independence from foreign rule that could be found throughout the world in the early 20th century. It seeks to mobilise a community of citizens who are not separated by the divisions of age, status or gender in a common cause of independence and liberation for the country, and to achieve a place of equality for China with the other strong countries of the world; it speaks simultaneously of revolutionary liberation and the acquisition of national strength. The project of state-strengthening which had been the animating concern of Zeng Guofan and Li Hongzhang was connected by Zou not with the defence of monarchical institutions but with their overthrow, a situation that perhaps equates with other cases where the ideologies of a monarchical state supplied the material from which a republican programme could be fashioned.

In the writings of Chen Tianhua, the question of China's place within the world is framed by the question of how individuals are treated: China, like other nations, is conceived as a person, and it should not be bullied. If countries are people, then the history of those countries appears much like the history of the forebears of a person. This helps to lay the foundation for creating a history for the republic that avoids the difficult problem of how the culture that defines its differences from other states is a product of the institutions of dynastic monarchy.

Sun Yat-sen, Zou Rong and Chen Tianhua developed their republican ideologies through contact with written and spoken languages that differed from the various forms of Chinese used within Qing territory, indeed the languages of the countries that most seemed to threaten China: English and Japanese. In the 20th century, the question of how to develop a language that would be shared by the citizens of the republic, and would also differentiate it from both its dynastic predecessor and other countries in this world, would become acute. The texts of Chen Tianhua and Sun Yat-sen that are excerpted here are written not in the Classical Chinese used by the writers in the earlier chapters of this book, but in written vernacular Chinese, the language that would become the standard form of written communication in the republic.

Chen and Zou both died in 1905. Their visions of republican liberation had perhaps assumed that the expulsion of the Manchus and the end of monarchy would solve the core problems facing the Chinese state and its people. Sun Yat-sen came to preside over the new republic that was established after revolutionaries brought down the Qing in 1911, though internal problems meant that he was never able to wield authority over the whole of the territory claimed by the republic. For Sun, as for many others in the early years of the republic, the key question became that of how to develop an ethos amongst the citizenry that would be commensurate with the ideals that animated the revolution. Without a monarch, the burden was placed upon the citizenry to take full responsibilities for the moral health of the nation, both as individuals and as a collectivity. Where the old dynastic morality had conceived of political morality in terms of the dyadic relationship between paired individuals (ruler and minister, father and son and so on), the republic had to generate moral frameworks that were based on the equality of individuals. Its critics saw the republic as failing to overcome the legacies of the monarchical social order, or as having lost the morality of the traditional structure. This perceived predicament has frequently been presented as a consequence of either abandoning (or failing to abandon) modernity or of abandoning (or failing to abandon) Chinese values. It might also be argued that the problems in the conduct of the Chinese citizenry which Sun Yat-sen detected were symptoms of the typical problems found in republican political cultures where the ongoing attack on monarchical culture was combined with the ongoing campaign to resist foreign domination, and where an alliance between the constituencies committed to these two different agendas needed to be maintained.

Sources and Further Reading

Good biographical information on Zou Rong can be found on p. 769 of Arthur W. Hummel (ed.), *Eminent Chinese of the Ch'ing Period*, Taipei: Ch'eng-Wen Publishing Company, 1967. A biographical account of Sun Yat-sen appears on pp. 170—189, Howard L. Boorman, *Biographical Dictionary of Republican China*, (Vol. 3), New York: Columbia University Press, 1970.

The revolution is described in all major works on modern Chinese history. See, for example, Immanuel C. Y. Hsü, *The Rise of Modern China*, (fifth edition), New York: Oxford University Press, 1995. A highly readable evocation of the individuals involved—especially Zou Rong—is Jonathan D. Spence, *The Gate of Heavenly Peace: The Chinese and their Revolution*, 1895 - 1980, Harmondsworth: Penguin, 1980. Peter Zarrow, *China in War and Revolution*, 1895 - 1945, London: Routledge, 2005, is an excellent account of the period. A good single-chapter survey can be found in Michael Gasster's "The Republican Revolutionary Movement" in

John K. Fairbank and Kwang-Ching Liu（eds），*The Cambridge History of China*，Vol. 11，Part 2，*Late Ch'ing*，Cambridge：Cambridge University Press，1980。Perhaps the best English-language description of Sun Yat-sen's life and thought is to be found in Marie-Claire Bergère，*Sun Yat-sen*，Stanford：Stanford University Press，1998。

（二）共和思想文献

（1）革命军[1]（节选）

邹容[2]

第一章 绪论

扫除数千年种种之专制政体，脱去数千年种种之奴隶性质，诛绝五百万有奇被毛戴角之满洲种，洗尽二百六十年残惨虐酷之大耻辱，使中国大陆成干净土，黄帝 子孙皆华盛顿，则有起死回生，还命反魄，出十八层地狱，升三十三天堂，郁郁勃勃，莽莽苍苍，至尊极高，独一无二，伟大绝伦之一目的，曰"革命"。巍巍哉！革命也！皇皇哉！革命也！

吾于是沿万里长城，登昆仑，游扬子江上下，溯黄河，竖独立之旗，撞自由之钟，呼天吁地，破颡[3]裂喉，以鸣于我同胞前曰：呜呼！我中国今日不可不革命，我中国今日欲脱满洲人之羁缚，不可不革命；我中国欲独立，不可不革命；我中国欲与世界列强并雄，不可不革命；我中国欲长存于二十世纪新世界上，不可不革命；我中国欲为地球上名国、地球上主人翁，不可不革命。革命哉！革命哉！我同胞中，老年、中年、壮年、少年、幼年、无量男女，其有言革命而实行革命者乎？我同胞其欲相存相养相生活于革命也。吾今大声疾呼，以宣布革命之旨于天下。

·······

第三章　革命之教育

野蛮之革命，有文明之革命。

·······

文明之革命。有破坏，有建设。为建设而破坏，为国民购自由平等独立自主之一切权利；为国民增幸福。

革命者，国民之天职也；其根底源于国民，因于国民，而非一二人所得而私有也。今试问吾侪[4]何为而革命？必有障碍吾国民天赋权利之恶魔焉，吾侪得而扫除之，以复我天赋之权利。是则革命者、除祸害而求幸福者也。为除祸害而求幸福，此吾同胞所当顶礼膜拜者。为除祸害而求幸福，则是为文明之革命，此更吾同胞所当顶礼膜拜者也。

欲大建设，必先破坏，欲大破坏，必先建设，此千古不易之定论。吾侪今日所行之革命，为建设而破坏之革命也。虽然，欲行破坏，必先有以建设之。

·······

今日之中国，实无教育之中国也，吾不忍执社会上种种可丑、可贱、可厌嫌之状态，以出于笔下。吾但谥之曰："五官不具，四肢不全，人格不完。"吾闻法国未革命以前，其教育与邻邦等，美国未革命以前，其教育与英人等，此兴国之往迹，为中国所未梦见也。吾闻印度之亡也，其无教育与中国等，犹太之灭也，其无教育与中国等，此亡国之往迹，我国擅其有也。不宁惟是：十三洲之独立，德意志之联邦，意大利之统一，试读其革命时代之历史，所以鼓舞民气，宣战君主，推倒母国，诛杀贵族，倡言自由，力尊自治，内修战事，外抗强邻。上自议院宪法，下至地方制度，往往于兵连祸结之时，举国糜烂之日，建立宏猷，体国经野，以为人极。一时所谓革命之健儿，建国之豪杰，流血之巨子，其道德，其智识，其学术，均具有振衣昆仑顶，濯足太平洋之慨焉。吾崇拜之，吾倾慕亡，吾究其所以致此之 原因。要不外乎教育耳。若华盛顿，若拿破仑，此地球人种所推尊为大豪杰者也，然一华盛顿、一拿破仑倡之，而无百千万亿兆华盛顿、拿破仑和之，一华盛顿何 如？一拿破仑何如？其有愈于华、拿二人之才之识之学者又何如？有有名之英雄，有无名之英雄，华、拿者，不过其时抛头颅溅热血无名无量之华、拿之代表耳！今日之中国，固非一华盛顿、一拿破仑所克有济也，然必须制造无量无名之华盛顿、拿破仑，其庶乎有济。吾见有爱国忧时之志士，平居深念，自尊为华、拿者，若而人其才识之愈于华。拿与否，吾不敢知之、吾但以有名之英雄尊之。而此无量无名之英雄，则归诸冥冥之中、甲以尊诸乙，乙又以尊诸丙，呜呼，不能得其主名者也。今专标斯义，相约数事，以与我同胞共勉之。

......

一、人人当知平等自由之大义。有生之初，无人不自由，即无人不平等，初无所谓君也。所谓臣也。若尧、舜，若禹、稷，其能尽义务于同胞，开莫大之利益，以孝敬于同胞，故吾同胞视之为代表，尊之为君，实不过一团体之头领耳。而平等自由也自若。后世之人，不知此意，一任无数之民贼、独夫、大冠、巨盗，举众人 所有而独有之，以为一家一姓之私产，而自尊曰君，曰皇帝，使天下之人无一平等，无一自由，甚至使成吉思仟[5]、觉罗福临[6] 等，以游牧贱族，入主我中国，以羞我始祖黄帝于九原，故我同胞今日之革命. 当共逐君临我之异种，专制我之君主，以复我天赋之人权，以立于性天智日之下，以与我同胞熙熙攘攘，游幸于平等自由城郭之中。

二、当有政治法律之观念。政治者，一国办事之总机关也，非一二人所得有之事也。譬如机器，各机之能运动，要在一总枢纽，倘使余机有损，则枢纽不灵。人民之于政治，亦犹是也。然人民无政治上之观念，则灭亡随之；鉴于印度，鉴于波兰，鉴于已亡之国罔不然。法律者，所以范围我同胞，使之无过失耳。昔有曰："野蛮人无自由。"野蛮人何以无自由？无法律之谓耳。我能杀人，人亦能杀我，是两不自由也。条顿人之自治力，驾于他种人者何？有法律亡观念故耳。由斯三义，更生四种：

一曰养成上天下地，惟我独尊，独立不羁之精神。

一曰养成冒险进取，赴汤蹈火，乐死不辟之气慨。

一曰养成相亲相爱。爱群敬己，尽瘁义务之公德。

一曰养成个人自治，团体自治，以进人格之人群。

第五章　革命必先去奴隶之根性。

曰国民，曰奴隶，国民强，奴隶亡。国民独立，奴隶服从。中国黄龙旗之下，有一种若国民，非国民，若奴隶，非奴隶，杂糅不一，以组织成一大种。谓其为国民乎？吾敢谓群四万万人而居者，即具有完全之奴颜妾面。国民乎何有！尊之以国民，其污秽此优美之名词也孰甚！若然，则以奴隶界之、吾敢拍手叫绝曰："奴隶 者，为中国人不雷同，不普通，独一无二之徽号。"

······

奴隶者，与国民相对待，而不耻于人类之贱称也。国民者，有自治之才力，有独立之性质，有参政之公权，有自由之幸福，无论所执何业，而皆得为完全无缺之人。曰奴隶也，则既无自治之力，亦无独立之心，举凡饮食、男女、衣服、居处，莫不待命于主人，而天赋之人权，应享之幸福，亦莫不奉之主人之手。衣主人之 衣，食主人之食，言主人之言，事主人之事，倚赖之外无思想，服从之外无性质，谄媚之外无笑语，奔走之外无事业，伺候之外无精神，呼之不敢不来，麾之不敢不 去，命之生不敢不生，命之死不敢不死。得主人之一盼，博主人之一笑，如获异宝，登天堂，夸耀于侪辈以为荣；及樱主人之怒，则俯首屈膝，气下股栗，至极其鞭扑践踏，不敢有分毫抵忤[7]之色，不敢生分毫愤奋之心，他人视为大耻辱，不能一刻忍受，而彼无怒色，无忤容，怡然安其本分，乃几不复自知为人。而其人亦为国人所贱耻，别为异类，视为贱种，妻耻以为夫，父耻以为子，弟耻以为兄，严而逐之于平民之外，此固天下奴隶之公同性质，而天下之视奴隶者，即无不同此贱视者也。我中国人固擅奴隶之所长，父以教子，兄以勉弟，妻以谏夫，日日演其惯为奴隶之手段。呜呼！人何幸而为奴隶哉！亦何不幸而为奴隶哉！

......

吾先以一言叫起我同胞曰：国民，吾愿我同胞，万众一心，肢体努力，以砥以砺，拔去奴隶之根性，以进为中国之国民。法人革命前之奴隶，卒收革命之成功。美洲独立前之奴隶，卒脱英人之制缚。此无他，能自认为国民耳。吾故曰：革命必先去奴隶之根性。

......

第六章　革命独立之大义

与贵族重大之权利，害人民营业之生活，擅加租赋，胁征公债，重抽航税，此英国议院所以不服查理王而倡革命之原因也。滥用名器，致贵贱贫富之格。大相悬殊，既失保民之道，而又赋敛无度，此法国志士仁人所以不辞暴举逆乱之名，而出于革命之原因也。重征茶课，横加印税，不待立法院之承允，而驻兵民间，此美人所以抗论于英人之前。遂以亚美利加之义旗，飘扬于般岌剌山，而大倡革命至成独立之原因也。吾不惜再三重申详言曰："内为满洲人之奴隶，受满洲人之暴虐，外受列国人之刺击，为数重之奴隶，将有亡种殄种之难者，此吾黄帝神明之汉种，今日倡革命独立之原因也。"

自格致学日明，而天予神授为皇帝之邪说可灭。自世界文明日开，而专制政体一人奄有天下之制可倒。自人智日聪明，而人人皆得有天赋之权利可享。今日，今日，我皇汉人民，永脱满洲之羁绊，尽复所失之权利，而介于地球强国之间，盖欲全我天赋平等自由之位置，不得不革命而保我独立之权。嗟予小子无学，顽陋不足 以言革命独立之大义。兢兢业业，谨模拟美国革命独立之义，约为数事，再拜顿首，献于我最敬最亲爱之皇汉人种四万万同胞前，以备采行焉如下：

中国为中国人之中国。我同胞皆须自认自己的汉种中国人之中国。

不许异种人沾染我中国丝毫权利。

所有服从满洲人之义务一律取消。

先推倒满洲人所立之北京野蛮政府。

驱逐住居中国中之满洲人，或杀以报仇。

诛杀满洲人所立之皇帝，以做万世不复有专制之君主。

对敌干预我中国革命独立之外国及本国人。

建立中国政府，为全国办事之总机关。

区分省分，于各省中投票公举一总议员，由各省总议员中投票公举一人为暂行大总统，为全国之代表人，又举一人为副总统，各府州县，又举议员若干。

全国无论男女，皆为国民。

全国男子有军国民之义务。

人人有承担国税之义务。

全国当致忠于此所新建国家之义务。

凡为国人，男女一律平等，无上下贵贱之分。

各人不可夺之权利，皆由天授。

生命，自由，及一切利益之事，皆属天赋之权利。

不得侵人自由，如言论。思想、出版等事。

各人权利必要保护。须经人民公许，建设政府，而各假以权，专掌保护人民权利之事。

无论何时，政府所为，有干犯人民权利之事，人民即可革命，推倒旧日政府，而求遂其安全康乐之心。迨其既得安全康乐之后，经承公认，整顿权利，更立新政府，亦为人民应有之权利。

若建立政府之后，少有不洽众望，即欲群起革命，朝更夕改，如奕棋之不定，因非新建国家之道。天下事不能无弊，要能以平和为贵，使其弊不致大害人民，则与其颠覆昔日之政府，而求伸其权利，毋宁平和之为愈。然政府之中，日持其弊端暴政相继放行，举一国人民，悉措诸专制政体之下，则人民起而颠覆之，更立新政，以求遂其保全权利之心，岂非人民至大之权利，且为人民自重之义务哉？我中国人之忍苦受困，已至是而极矣。今既革命独立，而犹为专制政体所苦，则万万不得甘心者矣，此所以不得不变昔日之政体也。

定名中华共和国（清为一朝名号，支那为外人呼我之词）。

中华共和国，为自由独立之国。

自由独立国中，所有宣战、议和、订盟、通商，及独立国一切应为之事，俱有十分权利与各大国平等。

立宪法，悉照美国宪法，参照中国性质立定。

自治之法律，悉照美国自治法律。

凡关全体个人之事，及交涉之事，及设官分职，国家上之事，悉准美国办理。皇天后土，实共鉴之。

注释：

1.《革命军》是中国清末资产阶级革命家宣传家演说家邹容的代表作。1903 年 5 月由上海大同书局出版。以"革命军中马前卒"署名写成的《革命军》一书，旗帜鲜明、通俗易懂地回答了中国民主革命的基本问题，特别是提出了"中华共和国"二十五政纲，系统地阐发了孙中山"建立民国"的设想。中国资产阶级革命理论经历了孙中山提出—邹容发展—同盟会政纲确立的发展轨迹，这是邹容对资产阶级革命的历史重大贡献。在这本书中，邹容开宗明义的提出，要用革命的手段推翻清朝的皇权，建立资产阶级民主国家，并为这个国家定名"中华共和国"。《革命军》为两千多年的封建专制制度敲响了丧钟，为资产阶级民主革命吹响了号角，成为一篇名符其实的反帝、反封建的战斗檄文。在这部书的结尾，邹容高喊："中华共和国万岁！""中华共和国 4 万万同胞的自由万岁！"这部书被誉为中国近代的《人权宣言》。孙中山赞誉它为"为排满最激烈之言论"，"能大动人心，他日必收好果"的作品。当时《苏报》主笔章士钊著文说：《革命军》"诚今日国民教育之一教科书也"。可见其宣传鼓动力量之巨大。这部书对当时日益高涨的资产阶级革命思潮起了极大的推波助澜的作用，实属中国第一部系统地、旗帜鲜明地鼓吹资产阶级民主革命、宣传资产阶级共和国的不朽之作。《革命军》一书在政治上与写作上都有鲜明的特点。它深刻揭露清朝的民族压迫和二千年来的封建专制制度的罪恶，指出中国当时面临着争取民族解放与民主自由的双重任务，提出了建立资产阶级民主共和国的目标和纲领；同时又分析了铲除奴隶精神，进行革命教育，培养国民，缔造资产阶级革命大军的必要，堪称当时最激进的资产阶级民主革命纲领。《革命军》的语言犀利泼辣，嬉笑怒骂，淋漓尽致。作者的思想观点与爱憎情感不求含蓄蕴藉，而是务求鲜明，具有强烈的抒情色彩。不少地方，反映出作者呼天吁地，破颡裂喉，为革命而呐喊的英武形象。邹容自言"辞多恣肆，无所回避"，章太炎称其"叫咷恣言"（章太炎《革命军序》），都指明了它的特点。本文选自邹容《革命军》，中华书局，1958 年版。

2. 邹容（1885—1905），四川省巴县（今重庆渝中区）人。原名绍陶，又名桂文，字蔚丹（威丹），留学日本时改名为邹容。1901 年夏，到成都参加官费留学日本的考试，被录取。临行前，当局以其平时思想激进，取消了他官费留学日本的资格。1902 年春，他冲破重重阻力，自费东渡日本，进入东京同文书院补习日语，大量接触西方资产阶级民主思想与文化，接受西方资产阶级革命时代的"天赋人权"、"自由平等"的学说，积极参加留日学生的爱国活动。他刚毅勇为，常争先讲演，陈述己见，切齿于清朝统治的暗弱腐败，向往中华民族的新生崛起。其辞犀利悲壮，鲜与伦比，为公认的革命分子。1903 年 4 月回上海，加入爱国学社，组建中国学生同盟会，写成《革命军》一书，号召推翻清廷，创建中华共和国，颂扬革命为世界之公理，自称为"革命军中马前卒"，为清廷所忌恨，与章太炎一同被捕入狱。1905 年 4 月 3 日死于狱中，年仅 21 岁。其遗体由《中外日报》馆收殓后葬于华泾。辛亥革命胜利后，孙中山就任临时大总统，追授邹容为陆军大将军衔。

3. 颡：音 sang，意为额头，脑门。

4. 侪：音 chai，意为同类同辈，吾侪即我们，我辈。

5. 成吉思忏：指元太祖成吉思汗。

6. 觉罗福临：指清世祖爱新觉罗福临顺治皇帝。

7. 忤：音 wu，意为逆反，不顺从。

（2）警世钟[1]（节选）

陈天华[2]

耻！耻！耻！你看堂堂中国，岂不是自古到今，四夷[3] 小国所称为天朝大国吗？为什么到于今，由头等国降为第四等国呀？外洋人不骂为东方病夫，就骂为野蛮贱种，中国人到了外洋，连牛马也比不上。……各国的人也是一个人，中国的人也是一个人，为何中国人要受各国人这样欺侮呢？若说各国的人聪明些，中国的人愚蠢些，现在中国的留学生在各国留学的，他们本国人要十余年学得成的，中国学生三四年就够了，各国的学者莫不拜服中国留学生的能干。若说各国的人多些，中国的人少些，各国的人极多的不过中国三分之一，少的没有中国十分之一。若说各国的地方大些，中国的地方小些，除了俄罗斯以外，大的不过如中国的二三省，小的不过如中国一省。若说各国富些，中国穷些，各国地面地内的物件，差不多就要用尽了，中国的五金各矿，不计其数，大半没开，并且地方很肥，出产很多。这样讲来，就应该中国居上，各国居下，只有各国怕中国的，断没有中国怕各国的。哪知把中国比各国，倒相差百余级，做了他们的奴隶还不算，还要做他们的牛马；做了他们的牛马还不算，还要灭种，连牛马都做不着。世间可耻可羞的事，哪有比这个还重些的吗？我们于这等事还不知耻，也就无可耻的事了。唉！伤心呀！

杀呀！杀呀！杀呀！于今的人，都说中国此时贫弱极了，枪炮也少得很，怎么能和外国开战呢？这话我也晓得，但是各国不来瓜分我中国，断不能无故自己挑衅，学那义和团的举动。至今各国不由我分说，硬要瓜分我了，横也是瓜分，竖也是瓜分，与其不知不觉地被他瓜分了，不如杀他几个，就是瓜分了也值得些儿。俗语说的："赶狗逼到墙，总要回转头来咬他几口。"难道四万万人，连狗都不如吗？洋兵不来便罢，洋兵若来，奉劝各人把胆子放大，全不要怕他。读书的放了笔，耕田的放了犁耙，做生意的放了职事，做手艺的放了器具，齐把刀子磨快，子药上足，同饮一杯血酒，呼的呼，喊的喊，万众直前，杀那洋鬼子，杀投降那洋鬼子的二毛子[4]。满人若是帮助洋人杀我们，便先把满人杀尽；那些贼官若是帮助洋人杀我们，便先把贼官杀尽。"手执钢刀九十九，杀尽仇人方罢手！"我所最亲爱的同胞，我所最亲爱的同胞，向前去，杀！向前去，杀！向前去，杀！杀！杀！杀我累世的国仇，杀我新来的大敌，杀我媚外的汉奸。杀！杀！杀！

注释：

1. 1903 年秋，陈天华蘸着革命激情挥笔写下《警世钟》时，鉴于当时的形势，他未签署真名，在题目之上标有"最新新闻白话演说"八个字，署"神州痛哭人著"。《警世钟》。陈天华所著《警世钟》以通俗的语言，强烈的爱国精神和勇气，宣传革命思想，以血泪之声，深刻揭露帝国主义列强侵略中国欺侮国人的行径和清廷卖国投降的种种罪行，力主拿起武器，号召"手执钢刀九十九，杀尽仇人方罢手"，高呼"万众直前，杀那洋鬼子，杀那投降洋鬼子的二毛子"。本文有理有据，感情真挚强烈，具有极大的鼓动性和感染力。本文选自杨忠，《学生阅读经典·名家演讲：激情的震撼》，人民日报出版社，2004 年版。

2. 陈天华（1875—1905），湖南省新化县人。原名显宿，字星台，亦字过庭，别号思黄。陈天华少年时因家境贫寒，曾辍学在乡间做小贩。后经族人周济入资江书院学习。光绪二十四年（1898），考入在新化的新学"求实学堂"。入该学堂后，受到维新思想的影响，倡办不缠足会，成为变法运动的拥护者。1900 年春考入省城的岳麓书院求学。1903 年初，入省城师范馆，同年春，以官费生被送日本留学，入东京弘文学院师范科。同年 4 月，写血书抗议俄国侵占中国东北三省，并参加留日中国学生组织的拒俄义勇队、军国民教育会。1904 年回国。同黄兴、宋教仁在长沙创立华兴会，准备在湖南发动武装起义，事泄逃亡日本。1905 年在日本东京与宋教仁等创办《二十世纪之支那》杂志，8 月参加组建中国同盟会，被举为会章起草员，并参与《革命方略》的拟定工作。同盟会机关报《民报》创刊，任撰述员。同年 11 月日本政府文部省颁布《取缔清国留日学生规则》，陈天华奋起反对，欲以死激励国人觉醒，留下《绝命书》《绝命辞》，勉励人们"坚韧奉公，力学爱国，去绝非行，共讲爱国"，1905 年 12 月 8 日在东京大森海湾蹈海自杀，时年 30 岁。在辛亥革命准备时期，陈天华写下了大量的宣传革命的作品，其中尤以《警世钟》、《猛回头》、《狮子吼》最为著名，其生平遗著收入《陈天华集》。

3. 四夷：在中国中心主义的天下观中，中国古代华夏民族用来区分华夏和所谓不开化民族夷蛮的名词和称呼。在地位上，华夏位居中央，番夷依方位分为"四夷"，即东夷、南蛮、北狄、西戎并称四夷。

4. 二毛子：中国民间对投靠洋人的汉奸的俗称之一，也称"二鬼子"。在清朝末年，义和团称外国人为"大毛子"。中国人如信奉天主教、基督教，常被称为"二毛子"。

（3）三民主义—民权主义[1]第一讲（节选）

孙中山[2]

诸君：

今天开始来讲民权主义，什么叫做民权民义呢？现在要把民权来定一个解释，便先要知道什么是民。大凡有团体组织的众人，就叫做民。什么是权呢？权就是力量，就是威势，那些力量大到同国家一样，就叫做权。力量最大的那些国家，中国话说"列强"，外国话便说"列权"。又机器的力量，中国话说"马力"，外国话说是"马权"。所以权和力实在是相同，有行使命令的力量，有制服群伦的力量，就叫做权，把民同权合拢起来说，民权就是人民的政治力量。什么叫做政治力量呢？我们要明白这个道理，便先要明白什么是政治。许多人以为政治是很奥妙、很艰深的东西，是通常人不容易明白的。所以中国的军人常常说，我们是军人，不懂得政治。为什么不懂得政治呢？就是因为他们把政治看作是很奥妙、很艰深的，殊不知道政治是很浅白、很明了的。如果军人说不干涉政治，还可以讲得通，但是说不懂得政治，便讲不通了。因为政治原动力便在军人，所以军人当然要懂得正当，要明白什么是正当。政治两字的意思，浅而言之，政是众人的事，治就是管理，管理众人的事便是政治。有管理众人之事的力量，便是政权，今以人民管理政事，便叫做民权。

……

世界潮流的趋势，好比长江、黄河的流水一样，水流的方向或都有许多，曲折，向北流或向南流的，但是流到最后一定是向东的，无论是怎么样都阻止不住的。所以世界的潮流，由神权流到君权，由君权流到民权；现在流到了民权，便没有方法可以反抗。如果反抗潮流，就是有很大的力量象袁世凯，很蛮悍的军队象张勋，都是终归失败。

......

我现在讲民权主义，便要大家明白民权是什么意思。如果不明白这个意思，想做皇帝的心理便永远不能消灭。大家若是有了想做皇帝的心理，一来同志就要打同志，二来本国人更要打本国人。全国长年相争相打，人民的祸害便没有止境。我从前因为要免去这种祸害，所以发起革命的时候便主张民权，决心建立一个共和国。共和国成立以后，是用谁来皇帝呢？是用人民来做皇帝，用四万万人来做皇帝。照这样办法，便免得大家相争，便可以减少中国的战祸，就中国历史讲，每换一个朝代，都有战争。比方秦始皇专制，人民都反对他，后来陈涉、吴广起义，各省都响应，那本是民权的风潮；到了刘邦、项羽 出来，便发生楚汉相争。刘邦、皇帝的。中国历史常是一治一乱，当乱的时候，总是争皇帝。外国尝有因宗教而战、自由而战的，但中国几吉年以来所战的都是皇帝一个问题。我们革命党为将来战争起见，所以当初发起的时候，便主张共和，不要皇帝。现在共和成立了，但是还有想做皇帝的，象现立的陈炯明[3] 是想做皇帝呢？此外还更有不知多少人，都是想做皇帝的，北方的曹锟[4] 也是想做皇帝的，广西的陆荣廷[5] 是不是想做皇帝呢？此外还更有不知多少人，都是想要做皇帝的。中国历代改朝换姓的时候，兵权大的就争皇帝，兵权小的就争王争侯，现在一般军人已不敢"王者王，小者侯"，这也是历史上竞争的一个进步了。

注释：

1. 《三民主义》中"民权主义"部分是孙中山晚年的主要著述之一。1924 年 1 月国民党第一次全国代表大会期间，及会后的 3—4 月和 8 月间，孙中山几乎每个星期的休息日都要从珠江南岸的广东士敏土厂大元帅府出发，前去珠江北岸的广州文明路广东高师礼堂（今广东省博物馆）演讲"三民主义"。他所讲的"民族主义" 6 讲、"民权主义" 6 讲及"民生主义" 4 讲，都是由秘书黄昌谷负责主要记录、并由高师校长邹鲁负责读校的。孙中山曾要求邹鲁在读校时，"除将笔记之文字校正外，如有意见不妨尽量参加进来。"邹受命后，每次孙演讲都到场聆听。孙中山每讲完一讲，即要黄昌谷将记录整理抄正稿，送给邹鲁读校。邹在读校时，先将记录稿阅读一遍，看所记之内容与孙讲的内容是否相符合，若发现有不符之处，则用另纸记下，就这样或改正、或删节、或增补，统将签注纸条贴在错漏处；然后，他再逐字逐句诵读，进行文理和词句上的润色，直至自认为全篇文意不差和文理无瑕时，才送交孙中山亲自审阅。孙将演讲词审视修订后，再次发交邹读校。如是者经往还约 3 次，直到孙中山反复修订到认为全篇完全满意时，他才交给负责宣传事务的戴季陶拿去正式出版发行。本文选自中国社科院近代史所，《孙中山全集》第九卷，中华书局，1981年版。

2. 孙中山（1866—1925），汉族，中国广东省香山翠亨村（今中山市）人，幼名帝象，学名孙文，字载之（又一说字德明），号日新，后改号逸仙，1897 年在日本化名中山樵，其后"孙中山"之称谓最广为人知。孙中山早年受基督教教会教育，先后求学于檀香山、广州、香港，行医于澳门、广州。1894 年 5 月，他曾上书李鸿章，主张变法自强，遭冷遇，遂赴檀香山创建中国第一个资产阶级革命团体兴中会。孙中山是最早提倡以革命推翻清朝统治的政治家和发起者之一，主张"起共和而终帝制"。他被视为中国近代民主主义革命的先行者，中华民国和中国国民党创始人。1905 年 8 月他在日本东京领导成立中国同盟会，被推为总理，制订"驱除鞑虏，恢复中华，建立民国，平均地权"的革命纲领；创办《民报》，提出"民族、民权、民生"三民主义。1911 年 12 月 25 日被十七省代表会议推选为中华民国临时大总统。1912 年 1 月 1 日在南京誓就职，建立中华民国临时政府，组成临时参议院，颁布《中华民国临时约法》。1919 年创办《星期评论》和《建设》杂志，发表《实业计划》，并将中华革命党改组为中国国民党，任总理。1921 年就任中华民国非常大总统。1924 年 1 月在广州召开了中国国民党第一次全国代表大会，通过党纲、党章，重新解释了三民主义；同时创办黄埔军官学校。同年 10 月他扶病为商国事北上北京，因积劳病剧，1925 年 3 月 12 日在北京逝世，1929 年 6 月 1 日，根据其生前遗愿，将陵墓永久迁葬于南京紫金山中山陵。1940 年，国民政府通令全国，尊称其为"中华民国国父"。遗著辑为《中山全书》、《总理全集》、《国父全集》、《孙中山全集》等。

3. 陈炯明（1878—1933），字竞存，广东海丰人，中华民国时期广东军政领袖。

4. 曹锟（1862—1938），字仲珊，天津人。是中华民国初年直系军阀的首领。

5. 陆荣廷（1856—1927），字干卿，广西省思恩府武缘县（今广西壮族自治区南宁市武鸣县）人，是中国清朝末年及民国初年的政治人物及旧桂系首领。

（4）三民主义—民权主义[1] 第六讲（节选）

孙中山[2]

　　我在前一次讲过了，欧美对于民权问题的研究，还没有彻底。因为不彻底，所以人民和政府日日相冲突。因为民权是新力量，政府是旧机器，我们现在要解决民权问题，便要另造一架新机器，造成这种新机器的原理，是要分开权和能。人民是要有权的，机器是要有能的。现在有大能的新机器用人去管理，要开动就开动，要停止就停止。这是由于欧美对于机器有完全的发明，但是他们对于政治还是没有很完全的发明，我们现在要有很完全的革命，无从学起，便要自己想出一个新办法。要我们自己想出一个新办法，可不可以做得对呢？中国人从经过民义和团之后，完全失掉了自信力，一般人的心理总是信仰外国，不敢信仰自己，无论什么事，以为要自己去做成、单独来发明是不可能的，一定要步欧美的后尘，要仿效欧美的办法，至于在义和团之前，我们的自信力是很丰富的。一般人的心理，都以为中国固有的文明、中国人的思想才力是超过欧美，我们自己要做到什么新发明是可能的事，到了现在，便以为是不可能的事，殊不知欧美的文明，只在物质的一方面，不在其他的政治各方面，专就物质文明科学说，欧美近来本是很发达的。一个人对于一种学问固然是特长，但是对于其余的各科学问未必都是很精通的，还是许多都是盲然的。他们的物质科学，一百多年以来发明到了极点，许多新发明真是巧夺天工，是我们梦想不到的。如果说政治学问，他们从前没有想到的我们现在也想不到，那便是没有理由，欧美的机器近来本有很完全的进步，但是不能说他们的机器是进步，政治也是进步。因为近两百多年以来，欧美的特长只有科学，大科学家对于本行的学问固然是有专长，对于其余的学问象政治哲学等，未必就有兼长。

……

　　我在第一讲中，已经把政治这个名词下一个定义，说：政是众人之事，治是管理众人之事。现在分开权与能，所造成的政治机器就是象物质的机器一样。其中有机器本体的力量，有管理机器的力量。现在用新发明来造新国家，就要把这两种力量分别清楚。要怎么样才可以分别清楚呢？根本上还是要再从政治的意义来研究。政是众人之事，集合众人之事的大力量，便叫做政权；政权就可以说是民权。治是管理众人之事，集合管理众人之事的大力量，便叫做治权；政权就可以说是民权。治权就可以说是政府权。所以政治之中，包含有两个力量：一个是政权，一个是治权。两个力量，一个是管理政府的力量，一个是政府自身的力量。

……

　　关于民权一方面的方法，世界上有了一些什么最新式的发明呢？第一个是选举权，现在世界上所谓先进的民权国家，普通的只实行这一个民权。专行这全个民权，在政治之是是不是够用呢？专行这一个民权，好比是最初的旧机器，只有把机器推到前进的力，没有拉回来的力，现在新式的方法除了选举权之外，第二个就是罢免权。人民有了这个权，便有拉回来的力。这两个权是管理官吏的，人民有了这个权，对于政府之中的一切官吏，一面可以放出去，又一面可以调回来，来去都可以从人民的自由。这好比是新式的机器，一推一拉，都可以由机器的自动。国家除了官吏之外，还有什么重要东西呢？其次的就是法律，所谓有了治人，还要有治法。人民要有什么权，才可以管理法律呢？如果大家看到了一种法律，以为是很有利于人民的，便要有一种权，自己决定以来，交到政府去执行。关于这种权，叫做创制权，这就是第三个民权。若是大家看到了从前的旧法律，以为是很不利于人民的，便要有一种权，自己去修改，修改好了之后，便要政府执行修改的新法律，废止从前的旧法律，关于这种权，叫做复决权；能够实行这四个权，才算是充分的民权；能够实行这四个权。人民有了这四个权；才算是充分的民权；能够实行这四个权，才算上彻底的直接民权。从前没有充分民权的时候，人民选举了官吏、议员之后便不能够再问，这种民权，是间接民权。间接民权就是代议政体，用代议士去管理政府，人民不能直接去管理政府。要人民能够直接管理政府，便要人民能够实行这四个权。人民能够实行四个民权，才叫做全民政治。全民政治是什么意思呢？就是从前讲过了的，用四万万人来做皇帝。四万万人要怎么样才可以做皇帝呢？就是要有这四个民权来管理国家的大事。所以这四个民权，就是四个放水制[3]，或者是四个接电钮。我们有了放水制，便可以直接管理自来水；有了接电钮，便可以直接管理电灯；有了四个民权，便可以直接管理国家的政治。这四个民权，又叫做政权，就是管理政府的权。

......

人民有了这四个大权管理政府，要政府去做工夫，在政府之中用什么方法呢？要政府有完全的机关，去做很好的工夫，便要用五权宪法。用五权宪法所组织的政府，才是完全政府，才是完全的政府机关，有了这种政府机关去替人民做工夫，才可以做很好完全的工夫。从前说美国有一位学者，对于政治学理上的最新发明，是说在一国之内，最怕的是有了一个万能政府，人民不能管理；最希望的是要一个万能政府，为人民使用，以谋人民的幸福。有了这种政府，民治才算是最发达。我们现在分开与能，说人民是工程师，政府是机器。在一方面要政府的机器是万能，无论什么事都可以做；又在他一方面要人民的工程师也有大力量，可以管理万能的机器。那么，在人民一政府的两方面彼此要有一些什么的大权，才可以彼此平衡呢？在人民一方面的大权刚才已经讲过了，是要有四个权，这四个权是选举权、罢免权、制创权、复决权。在政府一方面的，是要有五个权，这五个权是行政权、立法权、司法权、考试权、监察权。用人民的四个政权来管理政府的五个治权，那才算是一个完全的民权政治机关。有了这样的政治机关，人民和政府的力量才可以彼此平衡。……人民要怎么样管理政府，就是实行选举权、罢免权、创制权和复决权；政府要怎么样替人民做工夫，就是实行行政权、立法权、司法权、考试权和监察权。有了这九个权，彼此保持平衡，民权问题才算上真解决，政治才算是轨道。

······

不过，外国从前只有三权分立，我们现在为什么要五权分立呢？其余两个权是从什么地方来的呢？这两个权是中国固有的东西。中国古时举行考试和监察的独立制度，也有很好的成绩。象满清的御史[4]，唐朝的谏议大夫[5]，都是很好的监察制度。举行这种制度的大权，就是监察权。监察权就是弹劾权。外国现在也有这种权，不过把他放在立法机关之中，不能够独立成一种治权罢了。至于历代举行考试，拔取真才，更是中国几千年的特色，外国学者近来考察中国的制度，便极赞美中国考试的独立制度，也有仿效中国的考试制度去拔取真才，象英国近来举行文官考试，便是说从中国仿效过去的。不过英国的考试制度，只考试普通文官，还没有达到中国考试之独立的真精神。所以就中国政府权的情形讲，只有司法、立法、行政三个权是由皇帝拿在掌握之中，其余监察权和考试还是独立的。就是中国的专制政府，和外国从前的专制政府便大不相同，从前外国在专制政府的时候，无论是什么权都是由皇帝一个人垄断。中国在专制政府的时候，关于考试和监察权，皇帝还没有垄断。所以分开政府的大权，便可以说外国是三权分立，中国也是三权分立。中国从前实行君权、考试权和监察权的分立，有了几千年，外国实行立法权，司法权和行政权的分立，有了一百多年。不过外国近来实行这种三权分立，还是大不完全。中国从前实行那种三权分立，更是有很大的流弊。我们现在要集合中外的精华，防止一切的流弊，便要采用外国的行政权、立法权、司法权，加入中国的考试权和监察权，连成一个很好的完璧，造成一个五权分立的政府。象这样的政府，才是世界是最完全、最良善的政府。国家有了这样的纯良有政府，才可以做到民有、民治、民享的国家。

注释：

1. 参上篇注释 1。

2. 参上篇注释 2。

3. 放水制：指放水开关，水龙头。

4. 满清的御史：御史，是中国古代一种官名。自秦朝开始，御史专门为监察性质的官职，一直延续到清朝，在清朝为三品。

5. 唐朝的谏议大夫：谏议大夫，中国古代一种官名，秦代始。唐代的谏官有权力驳回明显不合理的诏书。

七、新文化运动

(一) 新文化运动概论

The New Culture Movement:

Chen Duxiu (1879 – 1942), Qian Xuantong, (1887 – 1939), Li Dazhao (1889 – 1927) and Qu Qiubai (1899 – 1935).

The fall of the Qing propelled, and was propelled by, a wave of global radicalism that sought not only republican government but also a more profound transformation of cultural, social and political relations. Anarchists, socialists and feminists were all part of this movement. In the decade or so after the establishment of the Chinese republic, the question for such radicals was how to ensure that the republic did not collapse into a mere copy of the old dynastic order even though the emperor was gone. The Bolshevik revolution in Russia in 1917 was a powerful source of inspiration for these republican activists. Similarly, the failure of the government of the Chinese republic to negotiate the return to China of Germany's colonies in its territory convinced people that the republic had not lived up to the radical republican dream of creating a progressive new order.

The republic, this new generation of republicans felt, needed a new culture, one that was an alternative to that of dynastic monarchy and to the culture of the industrial imperial powers (be they monarchies like Japan and Britain or republics like France and the United States). The Soviet Union looked like one source of inspiration for the forging of this new model of republican culture, in part because it officially opposed the ideologies of colonialism and the theories of race hierarchy that had been used to justify imperial expansion and ethnic hierarchies. While anti-dynastic revolution was six years younger in the Soviet Union than it was in China (Lenin had praised the 1911 revolution as an inspiration to revolutionaries worldwide), Chinese intellectuals felt that the Russian case could serve as an example for the radicalism they sought to use to reinvigorate their own movement.

Chen Duxiu, Li Dazhao and Qu Qiubai were all important figures in the early history of the Chinese Communist Party. They were attracted to communist ideas largely because of their disillusionment with the republic's failure to eradicate the problems of the unequal social structures that they believed derived from imperial times and—a view held by other leftists worldwide in this period—from the inequities of capitalism. A thoroughgoing transformation of culture was called for, a transformation that would enable the realization of the utopian project envisaged by Kang Youwei but which would be grounded in science and technical modernization, albeit not on the capitalist platform which the Self-Strengtheners and many non-socialist republicans had supported.

The risk for these republicans—as for their peers in other historical situations where radical republicanism is associated with the critique of a domestic social and cultural order that is held to be not yet fully liberated from the legacies of dynastic monarchy—was that they would be seen as too favourable to an imported culture that was linked to foreign powers. The association of the overthrow of monarchy with foreign forces—the fact that anti-Qing revolutionaries like Zou Rong, Chen Tianhua and Sun Yat-sen had worked from outside China and had received significant parts of their educations abroad—meant that an authentically local republican culture needed to be forged. Language became a particularly critical question in this regard. The form of written vernacular Chinese in which Chen Tianhua had written was taken up by the advocates of this new culture, in part out of resistance to conservative power-holders at the time who were continuing to advocate the use of Classical Chinese—the same individuals who were thought of as responsible for the failure of the Republic to secure China's interests at the Versailles treaty negotiations, the event that has generally been seen as the catalyst fot the New Culture Movement).

The promoters of this new vernacular were, in many cases, people who were themselves learned in the classics. Chen Duxiu and Qian Xuantong, for example, were both as preoccupied with the texts and contents of the Chinese classical tradition as with language reform. Their conviction that a new written language was needed came in part from the view that culture—both local and foreign—should be communicated to Chinese people in a form that all people in the republic could understand. An interpretation of this cultural reform project from the long-term perspective of projects of renewal of moral community at popular level (advocated by many of the thinkers in this book) might consider it to be not so much something iconoclastic as the fulfilment of a longstanding commitment to the creation of a state unified around a common moral vision based on education. At the same time, this new vision of vernacular education was linked to the global structures of republican culture.

How republics should relate to the heritage of classical learning was a problem that had been under discussion since the revolutions in the Americas. Should the new republics be seen as fulfilments of classical models that had been corrupted by monarchical dynasticism, as some North and South American revolutionaries thought? Or should they be founded in the culture of the present, or the future, and in particular the culture of the global cosmopolitan present and future? Or should they be founded in a local vernacular culture that celebrated its differences not only from classical culture and contemporary internationalism (especially that linked to other continents) but also from neighbouring countries with closely related cultural traditions?

The forging of a socialist culture in modern China has often been seen as an attempt to negotiate the divide between Chinese culture (which, although it is often conceived as "traditional", is also seen as an authentic, local popular culture and equally as a high culture whose technical and intellectual achievements can be admired if only they can be uncoupled from the structures of social inequality) and the culture of the West (not simply in its capitalist and industrial forms, but also the legacies of Marxism). Thinkers like Qu Qiubai, educated in French and Russian, represent the internationalist wing of this movement: strongly committed to a shared project of socialist republicanism with many allies abroad, especially in France and Russia, who had taken the path of anti-monarchical and anti ruling-class revolution. Some of their critics, however, may be seen as having continued to operate in terms of the division that Zhang Zhidong had created, in which the Chinese element in revolution was the core and the Western element (which might include Marxism) was the means or the instrument. Yet we may also argue that these questions were also part foundational issues faced in all revolutionary republics where the battle against the structures of dynastic monarchy needed to be combined with a battle against foreign domination. Chinese socialist culture has both embraced and condemned elements of monarchical culture and has embraced and condemned elements of foreign culture. This can be read as part of a global republican history just as it can be read as a story that follows a distinctive local dynamic.

Sources and Further Reading

Good biographical accounts of Chen Duxiu, Qian Xuantong and Qu Qiubai appear on pp. 240 – 248, pp. 367 – 368 and pp. 475 – 479 of Howard L. Boorman, *Biographical Dictionary of Republican China*, (Vol. 1), New York: Columbia University Press, 1967. Li Dazhao appears on pp. 329 – 333 of Howard L. Boorman, *Biographical Dictionary of Republican China*, (Vol. 2), New York: Columbia University Press, 1968.

The major works on modern Chinese history all discuss the New Culture movement. Among them are Immanuel C. Y. Hsü, *The Rise of Modern China*, (fifth edition), New York: Oxford University Press, 1995, and Jonathan Spence, *The Search for Modern China*, (second edition), New York: W. W. Norton, 1999. Jonathan Spence's, *The Gate of Heavenly Peace: The Chinese and Their Revolution*, 1895 – 1980, Harmondsworth: Penguin, 1980, is evocative and is particularly good on Qu Qiubai. Peter Zarrow, *China in War and* Revolution, 1895 – 1945, London: Routledge, 2005, gives an excellent sense of the issues. A fine study of the agendas of the period can be found in Benjamin I. Schwartz "Themes in intellectual history: May Fourth and after" in John K. Fairbank *The Cambridge History of China*, Volume 12, *Republican China*, 1912 – 1949,

Part 1, Cambridge: Cambridge University Press, 1983; and one of the best-regarded studies of the last three decades is Vera Schwarcz, *The Chinese Enlightenment: Intellectuals and the Legacy of the May Fourth Movement of* 1919, Berkeley: University of California Press, 1986. The lives, ideas and politics of key figures in the Communist movement are described in Maurice Meisner, *Li Ta-chao and the Origins of Chinese Marxism*, Cambridge: Harvard University Press, 1967, and also in Lee Feigon, *Chen Duxiu, founder of the Chinese Communist Party*, Princeton: Princeton University Press, 1983. The work of Qu Qiubai is discussed in Jamie Greenbaum (trans. and ed.), *Superfluous Words: A Translation of Qu Quibai's Prison Memoirs*, Canberra: Pandanus Books, 2005. An excellent account of the politics of language in this period, which includes discussion of Qian Xuantong and Chen Duxiu, is Elisabeth Kaske, *The Politics of Language in Chinese Education*, 1895 - 1919, Leiden: Brill, 2008.

（二）新文化运动文献

（1）敬告青年[1]（节选）

陈独秀[2]

窃[3] 以[4] 少年老成[5]，中国称人之语也；年长而勿衰（Keep young while growing old），英美人相勖[6] 之辞也；此亦东西民族涉想[7] 不同观象趋异之一端欤[8]？青年如初春，如朝日，如百卉之萌动，如利刃之新发于硎[9]，人生最可宝贵之时期也。青年之于社会，犹新鲜活泼细胞之在人身。新陈代谢，陈腐朽败者无时不在天然淘汰之途，与新鲜活泼者以空间之位置及时间之生命。人身遵新陈代谢之道则健康，陈腐朽败之细胞充塞人身则人身死；社会遵新陈代谢之道则隆盛，陈腐朽败之分子充塞社会则社会亡。

......

循[10]斯[11]现象，于人身则必死，于社会则必亡。欲救此病，非太息[12]咨[13]嗟[14]之所能济，是在一二敏于自觉勇于奋斗之青年，发挥人间固有之智能，抉择人间种种之思想。——孰为新鲜活泼而适于今世之争存，孰为陈腐朽败而不容留置于脑里——利刃断铁，快刀理麻，决不作牵就依违[15]之想，自度度人，社会庶几[16]其有清宁之日也。青年乎！其有以此自任者乎？若夫明其是非，以供抉择，谨陈[17]六义[18]，幸[19]平心[20]察之：

......

（六）科学的而非想象的

科学者何？吾人对于事物之概念，综合客观之现象，诉之主观之理性而不矛盾之谓也。想象者何？既超脱客观之现象，复抛弃主观之理性，凭空构造，有假定而无实证，不可以人间已有之智灵，明其理由，道其法则者也。在昔蒙昧之世，当今浅化之民，有想象而无科学。宗教美文，皆想象时代之产物。近代欧洲之所以优越他族者，科学之兴，其功不在人权说下，若舟车之有两轮焉。今且日新月异，举凡一事之兴，一物之细，罔[21]不诉之科学法则，以定其得失从违；其效将使人间之思想云[22]为，一遵理性，而迷信斩焉，而无知妄作之风息焉。

国人而欲脱蒙昧时代，羞为浅化之民也，则急起直追，当以科学与人权并重。士[23]不知科学，故袭[24]阴阳家符瑞五行之说，惑世诬民；地气风水之谈，乞灵[25]枯骨。农不知科学，故无择种去虫之术。工不知科学，故货弃于地，战斗生事之所需，一一仰给[26]于异国。商不知科学，故惟识罔取近利，未来之胜算，无容心焉。医不知科学，既不解人身之构造，复不事药性之分析，菌毒传染，更无闻焉；惟知附会五行生克寒热阴阳之说，袭古方以投药饵，其术殆[27]与矢人同科；其想象之最神奇者，莫如"气"之一说；其说且通于力士羽流之术；试遍索宇宙间，诚不知此"气"之果为何物也！凡此无常识之思惟，无理由之信仰，欲根治之，厥[28]维[29]科学。夫以科学说明真理，事事求诸证实，较之想象武断之所为，其步度诚缓；然其步步皆踏实地，不若幻想突飞者之终无寸进也。宇宙间之事理无穷，科学领土内之膏腴[30]待辟者，正自广阔。青年勉乎哉！

……

答皆平（广东——科学思想）[31]

皆平先生：

广东在政治上有责任的人都注重教育，至少也不反对教育，社会上空气稍差一点，然尚未到绝望的地步。说到科学思想，实在是一件悲观的事，我们中国人底[32]脑子被几千年底文学、哲学闹得发昏，此时简直可以说没有科学的头脑和兴趣了。平常人不用说，就是习科学的人只是书架上放了几本科学书，书房里书桌上很少陈设着化学药品或机械工具。无论什么学校里都是国文、外国语、历史、地理底功课占了最大部分，出版界更是不用说了。更进一步说，不但中国，合全世界说，现在只应该专门研究科学，已经不是空谈哲学的时代了。西洋自苏格拉底[33]以至杜威[34]、罗素[35]，印度自邬婆尼沙陀[36]大师以至达哥尔[37]，中国自老聃[38]、孔丘[39]以至康有为[40]、章炳麟[41]都是胡说乱讲，都是过去的梦话，今后我们对于学术思想的责任，只应该把人事物质一样一样地分析出不可动摇的事实来，我以为这就是科学，也可以说是哲学。若离开人事物质底分析而空谈什么形而上的哲学，想用这种玄[42]杳[43]的速成法来解决什么宇宙人生问题，简直是过去的迷梦，我们快醒了！试问人事物质而外，还有什么宇宙人生？听说朱谦之也颇力学，可惜头脑里为中国、印度的昏乱思想占领了，不知道用科学的方法研究人事物质底分析。他此时虽然出了家，而我敢说他出家不会长久。出家也好，在家也好，不用科学的方法从客观上潜心研究人事物质底分析，天天用冥想的方法从主观上来解决宇宙人生问题，亦终于造谣言说梦话而已。中国、印度古来诸大冥想家，谣言造了几千年，梦话说了几千年，他们告诉我们的宇宙人生底知识，比起近百余年的科学家来真是九牛之一毛，我们快醒了。此间编译局若成立，当然要注重科学书，但这还不是提倡科学的好法子，不但科学风尚未成，出书无人购阅，而书籍上的科学，还是文、哲学式的科学，去真科学还差一点。我以为造成科学底风尚，有四件事最要紧：一是在出版界鼓吹科学思想；二是在普通学校里强迫矫正重文史、轻理科底习惯；三是在高级学校里设立较高深的研究科学底机关；四是设立贩卖极普通的科学药品及工具，使人人得有研究科学之机会。这四件都是我们在广东正在要做的事。匆匆不及详答，乞恕。

独秀一九二一，六，一。

注释：

1. 本文刊载于《青年杂志》（后改名《新青年》）第一卷第一号。《敬告青年》一文提出"民主"和"科学"的口号，他说："我们现在认定只有两位先生，可以救治中国政治上、道德上、学术上、思想上一切的黑暗。"陈独秀针对封建思想文化的束缚，提出六方面要求：①自主的而非奴隶的；②进步的而非保守的；③进取的而非退隐的；④世界的而非锁国的；⑤实利的而非虚文的；⑥科学的而非想象的。陈独秀提倡的科学内容包括了科学和民主。从文中我们可以看到陈独秀对当时青年表现出的殷切期望，在现在仍有其积极的意义。如今读来，仍有醍醐灌顶、振聋发聩之感。区区两千多字，却将中国青年之于中国社会的不可推卸的责任说得至情至理、淋漓尽致。《新青年》杂志，1915 年由陈独秀在上海创办，掀起了一场批判封建礼教、提倡科学民主的新文化运动。他把民主称为"德先生"，把科学叫做"赛先生"，认定只有科学和民主才能救中国，在中国成了第一个举起科学民主大旗的人。讲"事实"、拿"证据"，这就是"科学"；否则就是"虚妄"。《新青年》主编的脑子全然被"唯物"的观念所征服。自 1915 年 9 月《新青年》创刊号的《社告》和《敬告青年》宣布办刊宗旨，到新文化运动高潮过后的《本志宣言》，再到 1923 年 6 月 15 日《新青年》杂志成为一年四期的季刊之后发表《新青年之新宣言》，杂志虽然历经磨难，但追求"科学"和"民主"的精神可谓矢志不改。

2. 陈独秀（1879—1942），原名庆同，官名乾生，字仲甫，号实庵字仲甫，安徽怀宁

（今属安庆市）人。新文化运动的发起人和旗帜，中国文化启蒙运动的先驱，五四运动的总司令，中国共产党的创始人及首任总书记，中共一大至五大期间党的最高领袖。1915 年 9 月，在上海创办并主编《青年》杂志（1 年后改名《新青年》）。1917 年初受聘为北京大学文科学长。1918 年 12 月与李大钊等创办《每周评论》。这期间，他以《新青年》、《每周评论》和北京大学为主要阵地，积极提倡民主与科学，提倡文学革命，反对封建的旧思想、旧文化、旧礼教，成为新文化运动的倡导者和主要领导人之一。科学与民主，是他一生追求的两大目标。1932 年 10 月，在上海被国民党政府逮捕，判刑后囚禁于南京。抗战爆发后，他于 1937 年 8 月出狱，先后住在武汉、重庆，最后长期居住在四川江津。1942 年 5 月在贫病交加中逝世。

3. 窃：私下；私自。多用作谦辞。

4. 以：认为；以为。

5. 少年老成：年轻而稳重，有如阅历多的年长者。

6. 勖（xù）：勉励。

7. 涉想：念及；想象。

8. 欤（yú）：语气词，表示疑问语气。

9. 硎（xíng）：磨刀石。

10. 循：遵守；遵从；遵循。

11. 斯：指示代词。这；此；这个；这里。

12. 太息：大声长叹，深深地叹息。

13. 咨：征询；商议。

14. 磋：商量讨论。

15. 依违：依从或违背。指模棱或迟疑。

16. 庶几：或许，也许。

17. 谨陈：陈述；述说。

18. 六义：意义；道理。

19. 幸：希望；期望。

20. 平心：指心情平和；态度冷静。

21. 罔：无，没有。

22. 云：说。

23. 士：智者、贤者。后泛指读书人，知识阶层。

24. 袭：继承；沿袭。

25. 乞灵：乞求福佑。

26. 仰给：依赖。

27. 殆：几乎。

28. 厥：助词。无义。

29. 维：连接。

30. 膏腴：（土地）肥沃。

31. 该信是 1921 年 6 月 1 日，当广东读者皆平来信讨论"科学思想"时，陈独秀给读者的回信，在回信中对空泛的旧文学、哲学提出了质疑，而且表示要以纯粹"事实"论证的态度痛改前非。刊载于 1921 年 6 月 1 日《新青年》第九卷第二号。

32. 底：的。

33. 苏格拉底：希腊文：Σωκράτης，拉丁文：Socrates，469 B. C. —399 B. C.。他被后人广泛认为是西方哲学的奠基者。

34. 杜威：约翰·杜威（John Dewey，1859—1952）是美国哲学家和教育家，与皮尔士、詹姆士一起被认为是美国实用主义哲学的重要代表人物。

35. 罗素：伯特兰·罗素（1872—1970），英国哲学家、数学家和逻辑学家，1950 年获得诺贝尔文学奖。

36. 邬婆尼沙陀：Upanishads。

37. 哒哥尔：罗宾德拉纳特·泰戈尔（1861—1941）是一位印度诗人、哲学家和反现代民族主义者，1913 年获得诺贝尔文学奖，是第一位获得诺贝尔文学奖的亚洲人。

38. 老聃：老子（约前 571—前 471）姓李名耳，字伯阳，有人说又称老聃。中国春秋时代思想家，老子著有《道德经》，是道家学派的始祖，他的学说后被庄周发展。

39. 孔丘：孔子（约前 551—前 479）春秋末期思想家、政治家、教育家、儒家的创始者。

40. 康有为（1858—1927），近代著名政治家、思想家、社会改革家、书法家和学者，他信奉孔子的儒家学说，并致力于将儒家学说改造为可以适应现代社会的国教，曾担任孔教会会长。

41. 张炳麟：章太炎（1869—1936），原名学乘，字枚叔，以纪念汉代辞赋家枚乘。后易名为炳麟。中国浙江余杭人，清末民初思想家，史学家，朴学大师，民族主义革命者。

42. 玄：深奥；玄妙。

43. 杳：深远；高远。

（2）随感录[1]（节选）

钱玄同[2]

（三十）[3]

适用于现在世界的一切科学、哲学、文学、政治、道德，都是西洋人发明的。我们该虚心去学他，才是正办。若说科学是墨老爹[4]发明的，哲学是我国固有的，无待外求；我国的文学，既有《文选》[5]，又有"八家"[6]，为世界之冠；周公作《周礼》[7]是极好的政治；中国道德，又是天下第一：那便是发昏做梦。请问如此好法，何以会有什么"甲午一败于东邻，庚子再创于八国"的把戏出现？何以还要讲什么"中学为体，西学为用"的说话？何以还要造船制械，用"以夷制夷"的办法？

（五十）[8]

王闿运[9]说，耶教的十字架，是墨家[10]"钜子"的变相。钜子就是"矩子"，姑勿论矩的形状和十字架的形状是否一样，就算是一样，请问有什么凭据，知道从中国传出去的呢？就算查到了传出去的凭据，请问又有什么大道理在里头？近来中国人常说："大同[11]是孔夫子[12]发明的，民权议院是孟夫子[13]发明的，共和是二千七百六十年前周公和召公发明的，立宪是管仲发明的，阳历是沈括发明的，大礼帽和燕尾服又是孔夫子发明的。"（这是康有为说的。）此外如电报，飞行机之类，都是"古已有之"。这种瞎七搭八的附会不但可笑，并且无耻。请问：就算上列种种新道理、新事物，的确是中国传到西洋去的。然而人家学了去，一天一天的改良进步，到了现在的样子；我们自己不但不会改良进步，连老样子都守不住，还有脸来讲这种话吗？这好比一家人家，祖上略有积蓄，子孙不善守成，被隔壁人家盘了去；隔壁人家善于经理，数十年之后，变成了大富翁；这家人家的子弟已经流为乞丐，隔壁人家看了不善，给他钱用，给他饭吃，他还要翘其大拇指以告人曰："这隔壁人家的钱，是用了我们祖宗的本钱去孳生的，我们祖宗原是大富翁哩！"你们听了这话，可要不要骂他无耻？——何况隔壁人家的本钱是自己的，并不是盘了这位乞丐的祖宗的钱呢？

（五一）[14]

同有一位中国派的医生说："外国医生动辄讲微生虫。其实那里有什么微生虫呢？就算有微生虫也不要紧。这微生虫我们既看不见，想必比虾子鱼子还要校我们天天吃虾子鱼子还吃不死，难道吃了比他小的什么微生虫，倒会死吗？"我想这位医生的话讲得还不好。我代他再来说一句："那么大的牛，吃了还不会死，难道这么小的微生虫吃了倒还死吗？"——闲话少讲。那位医生自己爱拿微生虫当虾子鱼子吃，我们原可不必去管他。独是中国这样的医生，恐怕着实不少。病人受了他的教训，去放量吃那些小的虾子鱼子，吃死的人大概也就不少。我想中国人给"青天[15]老爷"和"丘八[16]太爷"弄死了还不够，还有这班"功同良相"的"大夫"来帮忙，也未免太可怜了。但是"大夫"医死了人，人家不但死而无怨，还要敬送"仁心仁术"，"三折[17]之良"，"卢扁再世"的招牌给他，也未免太奇怪了。

注释：

1. "随感录"是五四新文化运动的主要阵地《新青年》所首创的报刊专栏，作者陈独秀，唐俟（鲁迅）、周作人、钱玄同、陶孟和、刘半农、张赤、孟真八人共发表 67 篇随感录，按顺序从 1 编到 67，每篇文末署作者名。其中钱玄同发表 14 篇。"随感录"以其独特的言说方式在它的周围聚集了一批"五四运动"的主将，成为他们抨击封建思想文化和不良时政的一种理想方式。他的开创者陈独秀不仅首创了"随感录"这种讲究时效性、新闻性的杂感类专栏，启发了当时的许多报刊纷纷仿效并开辟了"随感录"以及类似的专栏，为当时知识分子开拓了一种新的批评空间；同时"随感录"也成为一个文体概念，陈独秀首创的这一文体成为中国现代杂文的雏形，并为日后以鲁迅为代表的杂文的成熟奠定了基础。

2. 钱玄同（1887—1939），原名钱夏，字德潜，号疑古，浙江吴兴（现浙江湖州市）

人。现代文字学家，是新文化运动的先驱者之一。早年赴日本留学，入早稻田大学。回国后，1913 年到北京，任国立北京高等师范学校及附属中学国文、经学教员。后又长期在国立北京大学兼课。1917 年加入中华民国国语研究会为会员，兼任教育部国语统一筹备会常驻干事，致力国语运动。他向陈独秀主办的《新青年》杂志投稿，倡导文学革命，成为"五四"新文化运动的揭幕人之一。1918 年至 1919 年的《新青年》杂志，钱玄同是轮流编辑之一。他所著的《文字学音篇》是中国高等学校最早的音韵学教科书。数十年来，影响颇大，迄今仍为音韵学家所称引。他早年积极宣传汉语改用拼音文字，曾采用国际音标制定汉语拼音字母。后来他和赵元任、黎锦熙等数人共同制定"国语罗马字拼音法式"。1935 年他抱病坚持起草了《第一批简体字表》，为共产党执政后推行"简化字"立下先例。

3. 原载《新青年》第 5 卷第 3 号。

4. 墨子（约前 468—前 376），春秋末战国初思想家、学者，墨家学派创始人。

5. 《文选》：又称《昭明文选》，是中国现存的最早一部诗文总集，由南朝梁武帝的长子萧统组织文人共同编选。

6. 八家：即"西泠八家"是指由丁敬、蒋仁、黄易、奚冈、陈豫钟、陈鸿寿、赵之琛、钱松等八人组成的篆刻家。

7. 《周礼》：是中国古代关于政治经济制度的一部著作，是古代儒家主要经典之一。西周时期的著名政治家、思想家、文学家、军事家周公旦所著。

8. 原载《新青年》第 6 卷第 2 号。

9. 王闿（kǎi）运（1833—1916），晚清经学家、文学家。

10. 墨家：战国时期的学派。创始人墨子。主张功利，否定天命。对中国古代逻辑学作出过重要贡献。

11. 大同：指天下为公，人人平等自由的社会景象，是中国历史上某些思想家的一种理想。

12. 孔夫子：春秋末期思想家、政治家、教育家，儒家学派的创始人。

13. 孟夫子：战国时著名思想家、政治家、教育家。

14. 原载《新青年》第 6 卷第 2 号。

15. 喻指清官。

16. 丘八："兵"的隐语。

17. 三折：来自"三折肱成良医"。

（3）Pan...ism 之失败与 Democracy 之胜利[1]（节选）

李大钊[2]

　　一九一四年世界战祸之勃发，与夫吾国近来政局之翻复，虽原因多端，凑泊而成，未可以一概而论，然挈其要领，不外二大精神之冲突，即 Pan...ism 与 Democracy 之冲突。

　　Pan...ism 者，译云"大……主义"。持此主义者，但求逞一己之欲求，不恤以强压之势力，迫制他人，使之屈伏于其肘腋之下焉。是等关系，国家与国家间有之，地域与地域间有之，阀阅与阀阅间有之，党派与党派间有之。于是世界之中，有所谓大欧罗巴[3] 主义焉，大美利坚[4] 主义焉，大亚细亚[5] 主义焉，大……主义焉；欧洲之中，更有所谓大日尔曼[6] 主义焉，大斯拉夫[7] 主义焉，大……主义焉；亚洲之中，更有所谓大日本主义焉，大……主义焉。最近于吾一国之中，又有所谓大北方主义焉，大西南主义焉，大……主义焉；同一北方主义之下，亦有所谓大……主义焉，大……主义焉；同一西南主义之下，亦有所谓大……主义焉，大……主义焉。凡此者，其范围之广狭，区分之性质，虽各不同，而其本专制之精神，以侵犯他人之自由，扩张一己之势力于固有之范围以外则一。故"大……主义"者，乃专制之隐语也。

　　吾于此发见二种奇迹焉，即他人之"大……主义"，乃奋其全力以向外部发展；吾国之"大……主义"，乃互相侵陵，以自裂其本体。故他人之"大……主义"，为扩充之主义；吾国之"大……主义"，为缩小之主义。窃尝推原其故焉：人类有好争之性，每求所以为争之方向。强大优越之民族，所争多在外部之发展，其民族精神之缔结，国家位置之优胜，均足以助其争之本能，以高其固有之境遇，而一致以注泄于外竞。独至弱小之国，其民似皆能自觉其懦弱无能，对外言争，已决不敢作此梦想，所得以发泄其好争之性者，惟有对内以自相残杀焉耳。历史所告，凡外竞无力之民族，其内争必烈，卒至亡国而后已。斯诚伤心之景象也。复次吾国之持"大……主义"者，包涵于此"大"之范围，固不嫌其大，而统驭此

"大"之中心，则不嫌其小，且欲其愈趋愈小，至于一身而止焉。

······

宇宙间凡能承一命而为存在者，必皆有其自由之域，守之以与外界之体相调和、相对抗，以图与之并存而两立。倘有悍然自大而不恤侵及他人者，则彼之大即此之小，彼之张即此之屈，彼之强即此之弱，彼之长即此之消；一方蒙厥幸运，一方即被厥灾殃，一方引为福利，一方即指为祸患。彼大者、张者、强者、长者，蒙幸运而乐福利者，固自以为得矣；然而小者、屈者、弱者、消者，被灾殃而逢祸患者之无限烦冤，无限痛苦，遏郁日久，势且集合众力而谋所以报之，此等心理，将易成为中坚，而卒然迸发，至于不可抑止。且人之欲大，谁不如我，苟有第二之持"大……主义"者进而挟其力以与争其大焉，征之物莫两大之理，则争而败者，二者必居其一。然则持"大……主义"者，不败亡于众弱之反抗，即粉碎于两大之俱伤。此即观于欧战中之德国，吾国最近之南北关系、滇蜀关系、桂粤关系，均足为持"大……主义"者之棒喝。而其演成之公例，则为凡持"大……主义"以侵陵他人者，其结果必遭失败而无疑。

与"大……主义"适居反对者，则为 Democracy。是语也，或译为民主，或译为民治，实则欧美最近行用是语，乃以当"平权主义"之义。前者尚力，后者尚理；前者重专制，后者重自由；前者谋一力之独行，后者谋各个之并立，此其大较也。

世每谓欧战为专制与自由之争，而以德国代表专制，以联合国代表自由。综合世界而为大量之观察，诚[8] 有若[9] 斯之采色[10]。但即德、奥、土诸国中，亦何尝不有专制与自由之争者，例如德国社会党之在议院绝叫民主也，德皇不得已而允与修正宪法也，奥国之革命运动也，同盟罢工也，土国青年党之奋足也，在平时断无行之之希望者，均于大战中行之而无阻。反而观之英、俄诸国，俄则由极端之专制主义，依猛烈之革命，一跃而为社会民主矣；英则各殖民地对于本国之地位，将更进一步而成联邦之一员矣；本国内之工人与女子，其政治上社会上之地位亦日益加高，此足证

Democracy 之胜利。潮流所至，持"大……主义"者，莫不退避三舍，凡足为其进路之障者，莫不一扫而空之。为时代之精神，具神圣之权威，十九世纪生活上之一切见象，皆依 Democracy 而增饰彰采。美术也，文学也，习俗也，乃至衣服等等，罔不著其采色。近更藉机关炮、轮船、新闻、电报之力，自西徂东，拯我数千年横陈于专制坑内惰眠之亚洲，以竟其征服世界之全功。同一袁世凯[11]氏也，迎之则跻于总统之尊，背之则伏天诛之罪。同一段祺瑞[12]君也，忽而反抗洪宪，与 Democracy 为友，则首揆之位，群戴斯人；忽而纵容群督干宪，与 Democracy 为仇，则颠覆踣顿，复职免职，玩弄废置如弈棋。此其显者著者。其他居要位，享荣名者，举无不以对于 Democracy 之向背为准。由是观之，袁世凯氏之胜利，非袁氏之胜利，乃 Democracy 之胜利；其失败也，非 Democracy 之失败，乃袁氏之失败。段祺瑞君之胜利，非段君之胜利，乃 Democracy 之胜利；其失败也，亦非 Democracy 之失败，乃段君之失败。Democracy 于今日之世界，正犹罗马教于中世之欧洲；今人对于 Democracy 之信仰，正犹中世欧人对于宗教之信仰。吾目所见者，皆 Democracy 战胜之旗，耳所闻者，皆 Democracy 凯旋之声。顺 Democracy 者昌，逆 Democracy 者亡，事迹昭然，在人耳目。奈何今之人，犹纷纷树 'Pan...ism 之帜，或依于其下以与 Democracy 为难，其不自取覆亡者鲜矣！吾不暇为失败之 Pan...ism 哀，吾但愿为胜利之 Democracy 祝！

注释：

1. 李大钊所著，发表于《太平洋》杂志第一卷第十号，一九一八年七月十五日出版，署名守常。这篇论文，明确显示了十月革命后其"民主主义"观的特质。这里，李大钊把"Pan...ism（大……主义）"作为专制的隐语，并与"Democracy"对置来进行了如下的论述：前者（大……主义）尚力，后者（Democracy）尚理；前者重专制，后者重自由；前者谋一力之独行，后者谋各个之并立。全篇都贯穿着他对民主主义的赞歌。而他指的民主主义是与"大……主义"和"专制主义"相对而言的，对这种民主主义世界潮流的期望和关心，正是他从俄国十月革命中发现新世纪文明曙光的思想基础。

2. 李大钊（1889—1927），中国共产主义运动的先驱和最早的马克思主义者，中国共产党的主要创始人之一，字守常，河北省乐亭县人。1907 年夏至 1913 年夏，入天津北洋法政专门学校求学。1913 年底东渡日本留学。在日期间，曾参加反对袁世凯复辟、卖国的斗争。1916 年 5 月回国后任北京《晨钟报》主编。1917 年 1 月又任《甲寅》日刊编辑。在此期间，在《甲寅》、《新青年》等刊物上发表了不少宣传民主主义思想和社会进步的文章。1917 年底，入北京大学任图书馆主任，并参与编辑《新青年》，先后任北京大学评议会评议员，经济、历史等系教授。1920 年春，和陈独秀开始酝酿筹建中国共产党。同年 10 月，在北京创建共产党小组，11 月小组改称中国共产党北京支部，任书记。1926 年"三一八"惨案发生后，遭到段祺瑞政府的通缉，遂避入苏联驻北京大使馆兵营，继续坚持斗争。1927 年 4 月 6 日，奉系军阀张作霖派军警搜查苏联大使馆，李大钊等 60 余人被捕，28 日在北京英勇就义。

3. 欧罗巴：Europe。

4. 美利坚：America。

5. 亚细亚：Asia。

6. 日耳曼：German。

7. 斯拉夫：Slav。

8. 诚：实在；确实。

9. 若：如；像。

10. 采色：色彩。

11. 袁世凯（1859—1916）是中国近代史上最具争议的人物之一。传统上认为他的本质是反动、落后的，并且是图谋复辟的窃国大盗，也有人认为他是著名的政治家、军事家。他曾是北洋军阀的领导人，在辛亥革命后当选为中华民国第一任大总统，1916 年初他恢复帝制，名洪宪皇帝。但是此称帝举措并没有得到广泛支持，被迫于 1916 年 3 月 22 日宣布取消帝制，恢复"中华民国"年号。6 月 6 日在郁愤中病死。

12. 段祺瑞（1865—1936）民国时期政治家，"北洋三杰"之一。皖系军阀首领。他帮助袁世凯练北洋军，而后以此纵横政坛十五载，一手主导了袁世凯死后北洋政府的内政外交。

（4）新的现实[1]（节选）

瞿秋白[2]

中国一九一一年以来，万里长城为怒潮所冲破，依稀的晓梦"初"

回。满天飞舞的"新""生义""哲学""论"……无限，无限。

　　然而，中国二十世纪二十年代的一辈青年，刚处于社会思想史的"蜂腰时期"。有清一代对宋学的反动，汉学的今古文派，佛学派，到光绪末年——二十世纪之初，梁启超[3]、刘申叔[4]、章炳麟[5]诸人后，突然中绝。从此时起，西欧日本新学说如潮的"乱流"湍入。东西文化区别界限之大，骤然迎受不及，皮相的居多。中国此时一辈青年，所受社会思想的训育可想而知；旧的"汉学考证法"、"印度因明学"，不知道；新的、西欧的科学方法，浮光掠影得很。同时经济状况的发展，新资产阶级发生，自然而然，自由派的民治派的思想勃起，浮浮掠过。他们的确知道"要"了。可是他们只知道"要"……要自由，要平等……"怎么样？""是什么？"蒋梦麟[6]说"问题符号满天飞"，其实就因为问题符号只在飞，可见还不知道怎样设问，怎样摆这符号，何况答案！

　　再加以总原因：中国向来没有社会，因此也没有现代的社会科学。中国对社会现象向来是漠然的，现在突然间要他去解决"社会问题"，他从没有这一层经验习惯，一下手就慌乱了。从不知道科学方法，仅有热烈的主观的愿望，不会设问问及社会问题之人，置于社会现象之前，难怪他眼花缭乱。于是大多数所谓'群众的'青年思想，突然陷入于"孔子诛少正卯"的旋涡里，或者是'晒洋的'亚里士多德的论理监狱里。——"总解决与零解决"，"改良与革命"，"独裁主义与自由主义"，"放任主义与干涉主义"，"有政府主义与无政府主义"……"集权主义与分权主义"，群性主义与个性主义……彻底与妥协……如此无穷无尽，两相对待："咻们是反对分权主义的，那一定主张集权了"——"专制了"——不是这个，就一定是那个！头脑不妨如此简单，社会现象可不是如此简单！

　　我们假使除"要"之外，还有看"所要的"眼睛在，细细的戴上克罗克眼镜看看清楚，我们就可以知道上述的许多"外国字"，——西欧文字，对于中国人，实在难学难懂！——都是人造的抽象字，从社会生活里"抽出来的象"；不是有了集权主义"四个中国字"才有集权制度的！"抽象名词爱"的青年当再进一步看看现实，那时才知道实际生活，社会生活中每每是"非集权非分权"，"非彻底非妥协"，"亦总解决，亦零解决"……现实是活的，一切一切主义都是生活中流出的，不是先立一理想的"主义"，像中国写方块字似的一笔一笔描在白纸上去的。……"不是那个，就是这个"的"西洋"笨逻辑，东方人所笑的，现在自己学来了！

......

三月二十四日

注释：

1. 选自瞿秋白的《赤都心史》之"四十八新的现实"。一九二零年初，他以北京《晨报》记者的身份访苏俄期间，写下的一部游记体散文著作，记录了他在莫斯科的所见所闻、所思所感，真实地反映了那个时代一个先进的中国人在"赤者"的心路历程。正如作者说述，"《赤都心史》将记我个人心理上之经过，在此赤色的莫斯科里，所闻所见所思所感。……只有社会实际生活，参观游设，读书心得，冥想感会，是我心理记录的底稿。"《赤都心史》由陈独秀通过胡适推荐给商务出版社于 1924 年出版。

2. 瞿秋白（1899—1935），原名瞿双，后改名瞿霜、瞿爽。江苏常州人。早年曾到武昌外国语学校学英文，后到北京谋生。1917 年考入北洋政府外交部办的俄文专修馆读书。1919 年参加五四爱国运动，同年 11 月参与创办《新社会》旬刊。1920 年初，参加李大钊组织的马克思学说研究会。同年 10 月，以北京《晨报》记者身份赴苏俄采访，是最早有系统地向中国人民报道苏俄情况的新闻界先驱。1922 年加入中国共产党。1923 年任中共中央机关刊物《新青年》、《前锋》主编和《向导》编辑。是中共三大、四大、五大、六大中央委员，四大中央局成员，五大、六大中央政治局委员，五大中央政治局常委。1934 年 2 月到瑞金，任中华苏维埃共和国中央政府人民教育委员。还兼任苏维埃大学校长。同年 10 月中央红军主力长征后，留在南方，任中央分局宣传部长。1935 年 2 月 23 日在福建被捕，6 月 18 日英勇就义，年仅 36 岁。

3. 梁启超（1873—1929），中国近代维新派代表人物，近代中国的思想启蒙者，深度参与了中国从旧社会向现代社会变革的伟大社会活动家，民初清华大学国学院四大教授之一、著名新闻报刊活动家。

4. 刘师培（1884—1919），字申叔，号左盦。其主要著作由南桂馨、钱玄同等搜集整理，计 74 篇，称《刘申叔先生遗书》。

5. 章太炎（1869—1936），原名学乘，后易名为炳麟。中国浙江余杭人，清末民初思想家，史学家，朴学大师，民族主义革命者。

6. 蒋梦麟（1886—1964），教育家。浙江余姚人。在美国哥伦比亚大学获得教育学博士学位，导师为哲学家约翰·杜威。

后　记

　　《从帝制到共和：明末至民初中国思想的变迁》一书的体例，应是中国近代思想研究中一个新的尝试。作者希望，这一体例，能以更简捷的方式，为读者描述中国近代思想发展的概貌，及西方学界有关十七世纪以来中国社会思潮嬗变的论述。

　　在成书过程中，作者得到了澳大利亚墨尔本大学多方面的支持，本书最终得以顺利出版，也有赖于湖南师范大学出版社的大力协助、指导，我们在此一并表示感谢。

　　我们深知，本书难免有疏漏及论述欠妥之处，因此，我们竭诚欢迎专家学者以及广大读者的热心指正。

刘　一（Lewis Mayo，The University of Melbourne，Australia）

杜立平（Du Liping，The University of Melbourne，Australia）

姜德成（Jiang Decheng，The University of Melbourne，Australia）

郭珍谊（Guo Zhenyi，The University of Melbourne，Australia）

高保强（Gao Baoqiang，La Trobe University，Australia）

2011 年 10 月于澳大利亚墨尔本